The Media of Diaspora

Are the media of diasporas contributing to an alternative form of globalisation? Are transnational communities' global networks encouraging the growth of a world citizenship? Are diasporic media a threat to national governments and international security? Do diasporic media contribute to the fragmentation of national communities and international order?

The Media of Diaspora examines how diasporic communities have used communications media to maintain and develop community ties on a local and transnational level. This collection of essays explores how transnational communities' links and identities are maintained through film, television, videotape, Internet chatgroups and websites.

Contributors to this unique volume discuss critically the uses of media by transnational communities originating and residing in six continents. They address complex historical, social and cultural dynamics within Fiji Indian, Aboriginal, Arab, Armenian, Assyrian, Iranian, Jewish, Hispanic, Kurdish, Turkish, Macedonian, Vietnamese, Muslim, Chinese, Greek, Rhodesian, Tibetan and Ghanaian diaspora groups and their relationships with other groups. Readers interested in the areas of diaspora, ethnicity, community and transnational media, religious communication, globalisation and migration will find the discussions in this volume to be informative and thought-provoking.

Karim H. Karim is Associate Professor in the School of Journalism and Communication at Carleton University in Ottawa. He previously worked as a multiculturalism policy analyst. His book *Islamic Peril: Media and Global Violence* won the 2001 Robinson Prize. He has also written on diasporic communication, the social contexts of technology, new media policies, multiculturalism and social development in Muslim societies.

Transnationalism

Series Editor: Steven Vertovec

University of Oxford

'Transnationalism' broadly refers to multiple ties and interactions linking people or institutions across the borders of nation states. Today myriad systems of relationship, exchange and mobility function intensively and in real time while being spread across the world. New technologies, especially involving telecommunications, serve to connect such networks. Despite great distances and notwithstanding the presence of international borders (and all the laws, regulations and national narratives they represent), many forms of association have been globally intensified and now take place paradoxically in a planet-spanning yet common arena of activity. In some instances transnational forms and processes serve to speed up or exacerbate historical patterns of activity, in others they represent arguably new forms of human interaction. Transnational practices and their consequent configurations of power are shaping the world of the twenty-first century.

This book forms part of a series of volumes concerned with describing and analysing a range of phenomena surrounding this field. Serving to ground theory and research on 'globalisation', the Routledge book series on Transnationalism offers the latest empirical studies and ground-breaking theoretical works on contemporary socio-economic, political and cultural processes which span international boundaries. Contributions to the series are drawn from Sociology, Economics, Anthropology, Politics, Geography, International Relations, Business Studies and Cultural Studies.

The series is associated with the Transnational Communities Research Programme of the Economic and Social Research Council (see www.trans comm.ox.ac.uk).

The series consists of two strands:

Transnationalism aims to address the needs of students and teachers and these titles will be published in hardback and paperback. Titles include:

Culture and Politics in the Information Age

A new politics?

Edited by Frank Webster

Transnational Democracy

Political spaces and border crossings

Edited by James Anderson

Routledge Research in Transnationalism is a forum for innovative new research intended for a high-level specialist readership, and the titles will be available in hardback only. Titles include:

The Media of Diaspora

Edited by Karim H. Karim

Routledge
Taylor & Francis Group

LONDON AND NEW YORK

First published 2003 by Routledge
2 Park Square, Milton Park, Abingdon, Oxon, OX14 4RN

Simultaneously published in the USA and Canada by Routledge
270 Madison Ave, New York NY 10016

Routledge is an imprint of the Taylor & Francis Group

Transferred to Digital Printing 2006

Typeset in Baskerville by The Running Head Limited, Cambridge

British Library Cataloguing in Publication Data
A catalogue record for this book is available from the British Library

Library of Congress Cataloging-in-Publication Data
The media of Diaspora / edited by Karim H. Karim
p. cm
Includes graphical references and index
1. Mass media and minorities. 2. Transnationalism. 3. Mass
media – Technological innovations. 4. Communication – Data
processing
I. Karim, Karim H. (Karim Haiderali), *1956*-P94.5.M55 M44 2003
302.23'086'93 – dc21
2002012978

ISBN10: 0–415–27930–5 (hbk)
ISBN10: 0–415–40675–7 (pbk)

ISBN13: 978–0–415–27930–7 (hbk)
ISBN13: 978–0–415–40675–8 (pbk)

In memory of my grandfathers Essa Karim and Kanji Mohammed, diasporic communicators both

Contents

Contributors

William Ackah researches the politics and cultures of Africa and the African diaspora and is the author of *Pan-Africanism: Exploring the Contradictions, Politics, Identity and Development in Africa and the African Diaspora* (Aldershot). He is currently the Equality and Basic Skills Manager for the Gloucestershire Learning and Skills Council, a body who help fund post-16 education in England. He was formerly lecturer in Race Equality Studies at Edge Hill College of Higher Education UK, and has been lecturer in politics at the University of Liverpool.

Asu Aksoy has written extensively on Turkish media and society, in English and Turkish publications. She has been working with Kevin Robins on a research project within the UK Economic and Social Research Council's Transnational Communities Programme. The project – Negotiating Spaces: Media and Cultural Practices in the Turkish Diaspora in Britain, France and Germany – was concerned with media production and use among Turkish migrants in Europe. Asu Aksoy is based in London and Istanbul.

Valerie Alia is Reader in Media Ethics and Culture, University of Sunderland and Associate of the Scott Polar Research Institute, Cambridge University. She was the inaugural Distinguished Professor of Canadian Culture at Western Washington University, has a doctorate in Social and Political Thought from York University and is the author of *Un/Covering the North: News, Media, and Aboriginal People* and *Names, Numbers, and Northern Policy: Inuit, Project Surname, and the Politics of Identity* (University of British Columbia Press).

Stuart Cunningham is Professor and Director of the Creative Industries Research and Applications Centre (CIRAC), Queensland University of Technology. He is co-editor (with John Sinclair) of *Floating Lives: The Media and Asian Diasporas* (Rowman and Littlefield). Previous publications include (with John Sinclair and Elizabeth Jacka), *New Patterns in Global Television: Peripheral Vision* (Oxford University Press) and (with Graeme Turner) standard Australian media textbooks *The Australian TV Book* (Allen and Unwin) and *Media and Communications in Australia* (third edition, Allen and Unwin).

Heather De Santis has worked in the fields of international relations, policy development and international comparative research. Her interests include cultural policy, broadcasting, and international cultural relations. She has published studies on hate on the Internet, multiculturalism policies and cultural industries. She is a PhD candidate in the Mass Communication programme of Carleton University's School of Journalism and Communication in Ottawa.

Amir Hassanpour is Assistant Professor at the Department of Near and Middle Eastern Civilizations, University of Toronto, Canada, where he teaches courses on mass media, nationalism and social movements in the Middle East. He has taught communication studies at the University of Windsor and Concordia University in Montreal. He is author of *Nationalism and Language in Kurdistan, 1918–1985* (Mellen Research University Press). He has contributed articles to the *Encyclopedia of Television* and has written on satellite television and the Kurdish diaspora.

Karim H. Karim is Associate Professor in the School of Journalism and Communication at Carleton University in Ottawa. His book *Islamic Peril: Media and Global Violence* (Black Rose Books) won the 2001 Robinson Prize. He has also written on diasporic communication, the social contexts of technology, new media policies, multiculturalism and social development in Muslim societies. He previously worked as Senior Researcher in the Department of Canadian Heritage and as a journalist for Inter Press Service and Compass News Features.

Tony King wrote his DPhil dissertation at Oxford University on white Rhodesian identity and political discourse. He is currently Research Co-ordinator for the Centre for Development and Enterprise, an NGO which advises the South African government and business community on social and political matters. He previously worked as a Research Fellow at Monash University's South Africa campus, and undertook joint research on public history in post-apartheid South Africa.

Dona Kolar-Panov is a Professor of Communication Studies and Head of the Department for Postgraduate Studies at Ss. Cyril and Methodius University, Institute for Sociological, Political and Juridical Research in Skopje, Macedonia. She has written and researched widely on broadcasting, media and cultural identities and on new information and communication technologies. Among other publications she is the author of *Video, War and the Diasporic Imagination* (Routledge) and the co-author of *Mediumite vo procesot na politicka i socijalna transformacija vo Republika Makedonija – Media and the Processes of Political and Social Transformation in the Republic of Macedonia* (ISPPI, Skopje).

Peter Mandaville is Assistant Professor of International Relations at George Mason University outside Washington DC. He formerly taught at the University of Kent at Canterbury in the UK. His most recent publications include a Routledge monograph *Transnational Muslim Politics: Reimagining the Umma* and a co-edited volume, *The Zen of International Relations: IR Theory from East to West* (Palgrave). Current research interests centre on globalisation and alternative conceptions of political community.

Hamid Naficy is Nina J. Cullinan Professor of Art and Art History/Film and Media Studies and Chair of Department of Art and Art History, Rice University, Houston. His English language books are *An Accented Cinema: Exilic and Diasporic Filmmaking* (Princeton), *The Making of Exile Cultures: Iranian Television in Los Angeles* (University of Minnesota Press) and *Iran Media Index* (Greenwood). He has also published extensively in Persian and his works have been translated into other languages including French, German and Italian.

James Newman is a Senior Lecturer in Media and Communication and Programme Leader for BA (Hons) NewMedia at Edge Hill College where he teaches digital media production and aesthetics. His recent publications include investigations of player–character relationships and representations in video games and interactive entertainment media.

Tina Nguyen is a tutor in the Creative Industries Faculty, Queensland University of Technology and a contributor to the Vietnamese print media in Australia. She holds a masters degree in international relations.

Hong Qiu is a Senior Technical Writer at Nortel Networks. His Master of Journalism thesis, written at the School of Journalism and Communication of Carleton University, Ottawa, addressed the use of new communication technologies by expatriate Chinese students.

Manas Ray is a Fellow at the Centre for Studies in Social Sciences, Calcutta. He conducted research on Indian diasporas in Australia as a Postdoctoral Fellow in the Australian Key Centre for Cultural and Media Policy of Queensland University of Technology in Brisbane from 1996 to 1998. He is currently working on a monograph on memory, history and local politics of post-partition Calcutta, and has previously written on Indian media and cultural theory and ethics.

Kevin Robins is Professor of Communications at Goldsmiths College, University of London. He is the author of *Into the Image* (Routledge, 1996), and co-editor (with David Morley) of *British Cultural Studies* (Oxford University Press, 2001). He has been working with Asu Aksoy on a research project within the UK Economic and Social Research Council's Transnational Communities Programme. The project – Negotiating Spaces: Media and Cultural Practices in the Turkish Diaspora in Britain, France and Germany – was concerned with media production and use among Turkish migrants in Europe.

Michael Santianni has an MA in Mass Communication from Carleton University in Ottawa, Canada. His most recent research has concerned globalisation and the construction of global protest events in news discourse.

Liza Tsaliki is a Marie Curie Post-Doctoral fellow at the Department of Communications at the University of Nijmegen. Her current research is on digital democracy, exploring the potential of the Internet to be the forum of a digital public sphere and problematising the construction of digital citizenship in the European Union. Prior to this, she was a Lecturer in Media and Cultural Studies (Senior Lecturer from June 1999) at the University of Sunderland. She has also taken an active role as an evaluator of the DG-XII of the European Commission in the Key Action: Improving the Human Potential and the Socio-Economic Base of the 5th Framework programme.

Preface

Interest in the area of diaspora and communication has been steadily increasing since the mid-1990s. The idea for this collection orginated at the 1998 conference of the International Association for Mass Communication Research held in Glasgow, Scotland. It received further impetus in the following year at the Nationalism, Identity and Minorities conference in Bristol, England. Locating prospective authors who could write authoritatively on diasporic media around the world proved to be easier than I had expected, confirming that this was an anthology whose time had arrived.

No collection of this kind can be inclusive of all transnational communities. However, it does manage to cover specific diasporas who either originate or reside in six continents. This work primarily seeks to address cross-border flows of media content rather than localised ethnic media. In terms of technology, the focus is on the diasporic uses of audio-visual and computer-based media. This is not to suggest that print diasporic media are non-existent or irrelevant. The decision to leave them out of this collection was determined by a combination of the research interests of authors, limitations of space and coherence of the anthology.

The publication hopes to make a timely contribution to the emergent body of literature on diasporic media. It brings together several of the established authors on the subject with young scholars who offer fresh insights into how transnational communities communicate. The various chapters read together like an extended conversation on the media of diasporas, agreeing or disagreeing with each other on conceptual approaches or particular issues. Diaspora studies are in a formative period, and even the definition of diaspora remains the subject of debate. The present collection participates actively in this discussion, apart from directly addressing the uses of media. It is expected that authors' observations on diasporic media will extend the theory in this nascent field of scholarly research.

I would like to acknowledge Steve Vertovec's encouragement for this project. Carleton University generously stepped in to bear copyright expenses and provide funding for editorial assistance. Dina Salha, Faiza Hirji and Imran Karim ably fulfilled the latter role. Thanks are also due to all the contributors to this anthology for their patience during the editing and production process.

Karim H. Karim
Associate Professor
School of Journalism and Communication
Carleton University
Ottawa
Canada

Acknowledgements

The authors and publishers would like to thank the following for granting permission to reproduce material in this work:

Duke University Press for allowing us to reprint 'Narrowcasting in Diaspora: Middle Eastern Television in Los Angeles' by Hamid Naficy, which originally appeared in *Living Color: Race and Television in the United States*, edited by Sasha Torres, 1998 (all rights reserved).

Sage Publications for allowing us to reprint 'Reimaging Islam in Diaspora: The Politics of Mediated Community' by Peter Mandaville, which originally appeared in *Gazette*, vol. 63, no. 2–3, May 2001.

1 Mapping diasporic mediascapes

Karim H. Karim

The attention of most commentators on globalisation is on powerful inter-governmental organisations and giant corporations; but the myriad economic and cultural activities of transnational groups that are neither government- nor corporate-based constitute a distinct 'globalisation-from-below' (Falk 1993; also see Brecher, Costello and Smith 2000). This form of globalisation is charac-terised by the complex formal and informal intercontinental networking of associations, many of which are loosely organised. The planetary connections produced by transnational migrations contribute significantly to globalisation-from-below.[1] This human activity is not a recent development; it has been occurring for many centuries and has led to the growth of diasporas linked by social characteristics like ethnicity, language, religion and culture. These groups have been developing intercontinental networks of communication that use a variety of media that include mail, telephone, fax, film, audiotape, videotape, satellite television and the Internet. The social implications of such diasporic 'mediascapes' (Appadurai 1996) are the subject of scholarly debate and are under discussion in this volume. Its authors analyse the uses of media by various transnational communities originating and residing in six continents.

The manifestations of diaspora

'Diaspora' is derived from the Greek *diaspeirein*, which suggests the scattering of seeds. The term has traditionally referred to the Jewish dispersal outside Israel but is now applied to a growing list of migratory groups. Research on diaspora is conducted from numerous academic perspectives including anthropology, sociology, human geography, migration, culture, race, multiculturalism, post-colonialism, political economy and communication. The multidisciplinary nature of the present anthology seeks to capture some of the complex manifes-tations and consequences of media use by various transnational groups. An ongoing debate about what 'diaspora' should denote has accompanied the increasing focus on this topic. Whereas some scholars have argued in favour of identifying a closed set of characteristics in order to develop social scientific parameters for the study of diasporas (e.g. Cohen 1997), others have acknowl-edged its use in an increasingly broader range of human dispersals (Tölöyan

1996; Cunningham and Sinclair 2001). James Clifford cautions that 'we should be wary of constructing our working definition of a term like *diaspora* by recourse to an "ideal type"' (1994: 306).

All diasporas do not have homeland myths at the centre of their consciousness, contrary to William Safran's suggestion (1991). The term is frequently conceptualised as being limited to powerless transnational ethnic communities, but the 'black Atlantic' (Gilroy 1993) includes politically marginalised communities in North America and Britain as well as the ruling elites in many Caribbean states. Often viewed through the lens of migration from the southern to the northern hemisphere, 'diaspora' tends to be limited to 'non-white' peoples who remain distinct as minorities in their countries of residence. But even though some European immigrants like the Irish may find it relatively easy to assimilate into 'white' host countries, their cultural identity frequently remains resilient – especially in music and dance forms. The presentation of Macedonians, Greeks and white Rhodesians as diasporas by contributors to this book challenges Asian, African and Latin American postcoloniality as exclusive markers of diasporic status.

A transnational group's non-dominant position in global cultural contexts generally remains a key indicator of its status as a diaspora; the global English or French are usually not treated as diasporas since their languages and cultures have privileged places in the transnational media and other mechanisms of globalisation-from-above. Similarly, the pronouncements of the Roman Catholic Church's hierarchy have relatively easy access to the purveyors of global discourses like CNN and Reuters. But those of primary Muslim institutions do not enjoy equal visibility; hence the conceptualisation of the multi-ethnic, worldwide Muslim *ummah* (community) in diasporic terms by Peter Mandaville in the present collection. Valerie Alia's chapter presents the circumpolar settlements of the Inuit as constituting a diaspora; she also extends the term to the dispersal of indigenous peoples from their traditional homelands but who remain within the borders of specific countries. These nuances underline contemporary scholarship's insufficient exploration of the numerous manifestations of diaspora and the present prematurity in setting hard limits to its definition.

Diasporas are frequently described as 'imagined communities' (Anderson 1983). Asu Aksoy and Kevin Robins present a more fundamental challenge to the use of this concept as the basis of studying diasporic communication by critiquing its tendencies to essentialise diasporas. Anthony King points out in his chapter that Anderson's work was limited to the concept of political community; however, a number of other authors in the collection apply the notion of 'imagined community' to emphasise the diasporic connections facilitated by various media and the simultaneous consumption of the same content by members of a transnational group.

Diasporas are presented in several contributions to this volume as deterritorialised 'nations'. The concept of nation has long been linked to a singular ethnic group's placement within a particular geographic location. This notion is integral to the mythical lore of many groups, establishing strong emotional links to a particular landscape that serve to exclude others' overlapping territorial claims. Forced or voluntary migrations diminish the physical links of those who leave the homeland, but they take with them the mythical and linguistic allusions to the ancestral territory, which they invoke in nostalgic reminiscences. Some hold on to a hope of eventual return. This creates the demand for cultural products that maintain and ritually celebrate the links of the diaspora with the homeland. The dispersed settlements of transnations[2] also exchange symbolic goods and services, including media content, among each other, thus sustaining global networks.

Homeland politics forms a major topic for the media of some diasporas, especially those consisting largely of first-generation migrants. Ties to the former country remain strong in these cases and individuals seek out the most current information, especially in times of crisis. Events in the news are passionately debated by Rhodesians living around the world, as King discusses in his chapter. Amir Hassanpour and Michael Santianni show how media are used to mobilise support for the homeland causes of the Kurds and Tibetans, respectively. The increasing ease of air travel around the world is encouraging peripatetic tendencies among diasporics, some of whom frequently travel back and forth returning with video recordings of their travels in the old country – which are watched in ritualised ways by the migrant community, as Dona Kolar-Panov demonstrates.

Identity

The diasporic migrations of the last few centuries were largely influenced by colonisation and trading connections as well as by the steady improvements in transport and communications. There also appears to have been a connection between the economic involvement of northern powers in southern countries and the more recent human flows from the latter to the former. Saskia Sassen (1996) indicates that economic links ranging from 'off-shoring' of production, foreign investment into export-oriented agriculture, and the power of multinationals in the consumer markets of developing countries has often resulted in the mass movement of people. Organised recruitment of workers by governments or employers has also stimulated emigration:

> Ethnic links established between communities of origin and destination, typically by transnational households or broader kinship structures, are crucial after a flow has begun, and ensure its persistence. These recruitment and ethnic links tend to operate within the broader transnational spaces created by neocolonial processes and/or economic internationalization.
>
> (Sassen 1996: 77)

The mass migrations of the 1700s and 1800s led to new economic growth in the countries of the 'New World' (while simultaneously displacing indigenous economies). These included movements of slaves from Africa, indentured labourers from Asia and settlers from Europe. Following the lifting of restrictions on race-based immigration in the 1950s and 1960s, Asians and Africans began to emigrate in larger numbers to North America, Australasia and Europe. There has also been substantial migration from Latin America into the United States. These movements have created diasporas that are layered by periods of immigration, the extent of integration into receiving societies and the maintenance of links with the land of origin as well as with other parts of the transnational group. This layering has resulted in the wide variations of connections and attachments that such worldwide communities have to each other. Retention of ancestral customs, language and religion, marriage patterns, and particularly the ease of communication between various parts of the transnational group help determine its characteristics.

This anthology discusses some of the complex historical, social and cultural dynamics within specific groups and in their relationships with other groups that help shape the identities within diasporas. Mandaville views these communities as being continually 'constructed, debated and reimagined'. The twice-displaced Fiji Indians have recreated their culture under different historical and geographical conditions; Manas Ray explores how this contributes to the distinctions between Indian diasporas in Australia. Not only are there multiple types of linkage between the homeland and the diaspora, settlements of particular communities residing in various parts of the world also develop intricate networks among themselves. Hamid Naficy points to an 'interethnicity' between various Middle Eastern communities such as Palestinians and Jews living in Los Angeles that is aided by the consumption of overlapping television content. Stuart Cunningham and Tina Nguyen highlight the hybridity of Vietnamese cultural production in the West. Liza Tsaliki shows how Greeks with an Anglophone background, knowledge of American television and Internet savvy use a unique form of 'Greenglish' to communicate among themselves in Internet chatgroups. Hong Qiu offers the category of the 'knowledge diaspora' consisting of Chinese university students and professionals living in the West, who communicate through online magazines.

In an essay on the Chicano diaspora, Angie Chabram Dernersesian notes that

> these identities will be encountered from particular social and historical locations, from situated knowledges, from ethnographic experiences of rupture and continuity, and from a complex web of political negotiations with which people inscribe their social and historical experiences and deliver their self-styled counter narratives. I do not think we need to celebrate the transnational movement for its own sake. Just having a transnational identity is not something to be romanticized or something only we have: *everyone* in the world has one, thanks to the global culture of communications and the far reaching grip of capitalist formations.

> (1994: 286)

However, we do need a better understanding of the cultural, political and economic impacts that the social dynamics of transnational groupings have on their members and on others.

Diasporas are often viewed as forming alternatives to the structures of worldwide capitalism, but in many instances they are participants in transnational economic activity. From the banking network of the Rothschilds, originating in eighteenth-century Europe, to the more recent global businesses like the Hinduja Group, diasporic families have been leading players in global transactions. At 450 billion dollars, the annual economic output in the early 1990s of the 55 million overseas Chinese was estimated to be roughly equal to that of the 1.2 billion people in China itself (Seagrave 1995). Indeed, Joel Kotkin writes that 'global tribes' will 'increasingly shape the economic destiny of mankind' (1992: 4). Thomas Sowell (1996) asserts that similar patterns of economic achievement of some ethnic groups in Australia, the United States, Asia and South America point to the importance of the cultural capital that they bring to these lands. However, studies that focus primarily on the capitalist characteristics of certain diasporas tend to de-emphasize the vast disparities in wealth, education and social status within these communities. Ray's chapter underlines the social disjunctures between the Fiji Indian immigrants to Australia and some of those who arrive directly from India.

Commentators writing from cultural studies and postcolonial perspectives have tended to view diasporas as ranged against global and national structures of dominance – of the empire striking back. Jon Stratton and Ien Ang suggest that for the postcolonial immigrant to Britain 'what the diasporic position opens up is the possibility of developing a post-imperial British identity, one based explicitly on an acknowledgement and vindication of the "coming home" of the colonized Other' (1996: 383–4). The diasporic site becomes the cultural border between the country of origin and the country of residence – Homi Bhabha's 'third space' (1994). This is the zone of intense, cutting-edge creativity born out of the existential angst of the immigrant who is neither here nor there. She is Abdul JanMohammed's 'specular border intellectual' who, 'caught between two cultures . . . subjects the cultures to analytic scrutiny rather than combining them' (1992: 97). Guillermo Gómez-Peña seeks to oppose 'the sinister cartography of the New World Order with the conceptual map of the New World Border – a great trans- and intercontinental border zone, a place in which no centres remain' (1996: 7).

While the globally dominant Eurocentric cultural structures, particularly media conglomerates, are being vastly strengthened, there has emerged over the last few decades a variety of voices from the South and from diasporas that attempt to present other world views. Ella Shohat and Robert Stam have explored a 'constellation of oppositional strategies, which taken together have the potential of revolutionising audio-visual production and pedagogy' (1994: 10). They refer to the aesthetics of resistance in the New Cinemas of Cuba, Brazil, Senegal and India as well as to diasporic films made in Canada, the United States and England. Just within the South Asian diaspora, one finds a list of accomplished authors that includes Hanif Kureishi (England), Salman Rushdie (India/England), V.S. Naipaul (Trinidad/England), Bharati Mukerjee (India/ Canada/United States), Jhumpa Lahiri (England/United States), Michael Ondaatje (Sri Lanka/Canada), Shyam Selvadurai (Sri Lanka/Canada), Moez Vassanji (Kenya/Tanzania/Canada), Rohinton Mistry (India/Canada), Anita Desai (India/Canada), Anita Rau Badami (India/Canada) and Cyril Dabydeen (Guyana/Canada). Such diasporic artists appear to be at the cutting edge of modernity and cultural life in their countries of settlement. But whereas they do provide other ways of viewing the world, they do not all present stances that actively resist dominant global discourses.

Space

The concept of space is key in the study of diaspora. Doreen Massey views it as 'the simultaneous co-existence of social interrelations at all geographical scales, from the intimacy of the household to the wide spaces of transglobal connections' (1994: 168). The debates around the issues of globalisation, cultural identity and the use of new communication technologies have significantly influenced the study of human geography (see Mitchell 2000). Anthony Giddens (1990) suggests that new media have succeeded in 'emptying' time and space, allowing social relations to be 'disembedded' from their locations and to be carried out at long distance. Manuel Castells (1989) distinguishes the 'space of places' from the new 'space of flows' that occur in global networks. Massey (1994) highlights the 'power geometry' in which various social groups have hierarchical relationships and different levels of access to global capital, goods and mobility. Arjun Appadurai (1996) sees the global cultural economy as characterised by fundamental disjunctures between what he identifies as five dimensions or 'scapes' of 'global cultural flow': ethnoscapes (people), mediascapes (media content), technoscapes (technology), finanscapes (capital) and ideoscapes (ideologies).

These new ways of conceptualising the relationship of people with landscapes have challenged normative notions in which human identity and community have tended to be linked to the territory 'originally' occupied by a group. The naming of an ethnic group is usually based on such a homeland, and its members will often continue to be linked to this ancestral location even after centuries of living in diaspora. But the dynamics of travel involve a shaping and reshaping of cultural space and the relationship that people have with it (Clifford 1997). The processes of transnational tourism, pilgrimage, migrant labour, business and scholarly travel, exile and emigration/immigration continually rub up against the global system of national borders. Governments strive to control such traffic and the activities of foreign nationals within their borders; they generally tend to discourage the links of immigrants with their homelands or with other parts of diasporas. Notwithstanding the predictions of the declining influence of borders under pressures of globalisation (e.g. Appadurai 1996), the spaces of nation states largely continue to remain exclusive. Nevertheless, diasporas present a significant challenge to this territoriality by seeking to produce their own transnational spaces.

The roots of the contemporary political map of the globe are to be found in colonialism. European space was extended to cover the planet: the sway of Spanish, Portuguese, British, French, German, Italian, Dutch and Russian expansion was imprinted on the world not only through territorial appropriation but, more significantly, through the symbolic renaming of places with nomenclature drawn from the coloniser's culture. The system of nation states, which has origins in seventeenth-century Europe, was stretched across other continents, replicating European forms of governance around the world. This included the separation of related peoples' common identities and relationships by marking out fixed (although not completely immutable or impermeable) national borders, which were to be maintained even after independence. European cartography symbolised the hegemony of Europe: the continent was placed at the centre of the upper half of the world map. Colonial educational systems helped ensure that this global arrangement was accepted by all peoples as 'natural' (Blaut 1993).

Transnational media's emergence in the nineteenth century, in the form of news agencies, occurred within the colonial context. The British Reuters, the French Havas and the German Wolff agencies divided the world among themselves by operating a news cartel, which involved exclusive presence in the respective spheres of colonial influence. Transnational telegraph, telephone and transport links to colonies were constructed to serve the colonial metropolises. Formal telecommunications linkages between neighbouring countries in Africa or Asia ruled by rival colonising powers were rare; direct connections between southern continents were almost non-existent. Media content in the form of news and entertainment materials flowed largely from North to South, further reinforcing Northern world views.

The colonial arrangements of global space were therefore linked to the configuration and exercise of power. Much of this spatialisation was engendered by what Edward Said (1979) calls the 'imaginative geography' of orientalist science that supported the imperialist enterprise; it presented justifications for the conquest and colonisation of non-European territories.[3] The academic discourses were complemented by travellers' literature (Said 1979; Egerer 2001). Media materials produced in North America and Europe further reinforced orientalist world views. Even though the influence of this cultural imperialism did not produce a completely monolithic global culture that was devoid of local colourings (Tomlinson 1991), it did disseminate the products of Northern cultures extensively and intensively in the South. Western materials, particularly those of the Anglo-American cultural axis, have wide distribution even in other parts of the North. The dominance of the English language and Hollywood is apparent in Tsaliki's chapter on a Greek diasporic chatgroup.

The cultural power of British colonialism has been such that African and Asian children being educated in many former colonies tend to know more about the fauna and flora of England than that of their own countries. They are steeped in the details of British history. The old imperial capital of London remains central and the rest peripheral in many minds around the Commonwealth. But the contemporary cultural production of diasporas is increasingly challenging this imaginative geography. Claudia Egerer gives the example of the writing of Hanif Kureishi, who is of Pakistani ancestry and lives in England:

> Kureishi's London is a city in which the geography of the colonial past is superimposed on the modern English capital, producing its postcolonial present. This London is a hybrid city where the local and the global co-exist uneasily, a locality saturated with contradictory meanings that escape easy appropriation and which as such may well serve to 'produce new forms of knowledge, new modes of differentiation, new sites of power'.[4] This London – no longer the metropolis of imperial England and not yet a postnational, global city – may serve as a metaphor for the power of transformation engendered by the population movements ultimately set in motion by colonialism.
>
> (Egerer 2001: 16)

Whether diasporic cultural workers are involved in the complete rearrangement of dominant cultural mappings is debatable since Eurocentric world views still remain globally hegemonic. Whereas diasporas' imaginings of space do not necessarily displace the dominant geography what emerges is the coexistence of a multiplicity of cultural cartographies supported by vibrant bodies of literature and other intellectual and artistic forms.

The contemporary 'New World' is also the site of diasporic reimaginings. Stuart Hall presents another way in which colonial space is transformed in the 'territory' of the Caribbean 'Third (New World) cinema'.

> The Third, 'New World' presence, is not so much power, as ground, place, territory. It is the juncture-point where the many cultural tributaries meet, the 'empty' land (the European colonizers emptied it) where strangers from every other part of the globe collided. None of the people who now occupy the islands – black, brown, white, African, European, American, Spanish, French, East Indian, Chinese, Portuguese, Jew, Dutch – originally 'belonged' there. It is the space where creolizations and assimilations and syncreticisms were negotiated.
>
> (Hall 2000: 30)

Caribbean film, reflecting and itself being a site of hybridity, is here a cultural engine that re-maps the spaces previously marked out by imperialism. Hall emphasises that the heterogeneity expressed here speaks not only against colonialism's hierarchical and essentialist human geography but also stands in contrast to the notion of diaspora that necessarily includes a return to the 'original' homeland, a dream that usually involves the displacement of other peoples (ibid., 31).

Instead of dwelling on physically reversing historical migrations, much of the cultural production of diasporas involves the (re-)creation of alternative imaginative space alongside existing mappings. In the face of the homogenising forces of globalisation, diasporas, as deterritorialised nations, are seeking ways of 'reterritorialising' and 're-embedding' their identities in other imaginings of space (Lull 1995: 159). Displaced from their homelands, they find that 'Ethnicity is the necessary place or space' (Hall 1997b: 184) from which they can speak to counteract dominant discourses. Hall views this process as operating on the terrain of 'the global postmodern' (ibid., 184), which 'is an extremely contradictory space' (ibid., 187): whereas he acknowledges the danger of extreme nationalism in ethnic assertion he also identifies the immense opportunities for the empowerment of the local, in contrast to the polarised scenario of Benjamin Barber's 'jihad vs. McWorld' (1995). In this vein, Santianni's chapter in this book explores the 'retextualisation' of dominant global discourses brought about by diasporic reassertion.

The novel appropriations of space by diasporas involve what Lawrence Grossberg calls the 'spatialisation of being' (1996: 179). He identifies 'space as the milieu of becoming', the existential site of human transformation. Drawing from the work of Gilles Deleuze and Félix Guattari, he suggests that we must rethink the production of reality, the coming into being, in terms of dynamics that operate spatially. Spatial materialist (Deleuzean) philosophy proposes that

> reality must be understood as continually mutating within and across the space of existence. What is crucial is that it is the becoming that is real. Its reality is not defined by the points it connects but by the in-between or 'milieu' which it traverses.
>
> (ibid., 180)

According to this view, diasporic reality is effected through the transformation of existence: (hybrid) transnations have their being in the existential location of the 'milieu', not on a physical territory. It is this 'in-between space' (Bhabha 1994) that mentally bridges the homeland and the new location, where the diasporic artist engages with the frontiers of modernity to make a place for herself.

Migrant communities endeavour to make homes (even if 'temporarily') in milieux that are away from the home(land). John Macgregor Wise (2000) asserts that the marking out of a space as one's home involves the infusion of that place with one's own rhythms. (Re)territorialisation occurs through sounds and movement – cadencies and action. The languages, accents and rituals spoken and performed in a space establish cultural connections to its occupants and give it an identity. The rhythmic repetition of these actions is key:

> It is the pattern of sound, of light, of meaning that constructs the space. Patterns are the result of repetition. 'Every milieu is vibratory, in other

words, a block of space-time constituted by the periodic repetition of the component'[5] . . . It is the rhythm (which is different from mere meter), which is the organization that fends off chaos. It is the rhythm, a sympathetic vibration or resonance, which opens up one milieu onto another.

(Wise 2000: 302)

Diasporas (re-)create home by instilling such resonance into the spaces they occupy: they do it with their languages, customs, art forms, arrangement of objects and ideas. Their electronic media reterritorialise the diaspora through the resonance of electromagnetic frequencies. However, the milieux that diasporas seek to create are not bounded by the borders of nation states – their rhythms resonate transnationally to mark out non-terrestrial spaces that stretch out intercontinentally.

The 'supraterritoriality' (Scholte 1996) of diaspora is created and sustained by transforming a milieu: it is not a physical place but an existential location dependent continually on the resonance of cultural practices. Diasporas account for space as an existential location as they seek to redefine and transform their existence from under the historical conditions of colonialism and/or the contemporary exigencies of globalisation-from-above. These dynamics of spatialisation are imaginative; they usually do not necessarily involve the appropriation of territory but they necessarily engage in the rethinking of dominant cartographies. The diaspora exists virtually in the relationships maintained in a transnational milieu, held together by and in the '"space of flows" – in mass media, telecommunications, computer connections and the like – [which] is a realm where religions, nations, classes, genders, races, sexualities, generations and so on continuously overlap and interrelate to produce complex and shifting identities and affiliations' (Scholte 1996: 597). Contributors to this volume illustrate how these spaces, brought into existence by diasporic relationships, are maintained through various forms of transnational communication.

But diasporic space is not monologic. Watching live television from the homeland does not automatically suspend time and space, as Asu Aksoy and Kevin Robins demonstrate in their chapter. Diasporic media networks hardly negate the day-to-day existence in a location where one also interacts with other cultures and consumes local media content. Santianni explores how diasporic Tibetan Buddhist media deliberately seek to create solidarity outside the ethnic community. Hybridity, in its multifarious forms, constantly challenges the notions of essentialism and exclusivity that often tend to accompany the traditional conceptualisation of diaspora. We also need to recognise that the mere existence of diasporic media also does not mean that all of a group's members, or even a majority of them, have access to them. William Ackah and James Newman point to the differential and contradictory uses of new media in a Ghanaian transnational community.

The media of diasporas

Naficy's chapter in this book suggests definitions for 'ethnic', 'transnational' and 'diaspora' television: ethnic television largely produce local shows focusing on minorities within a country of settlement; transnational media import materials produced in home countries; and diaspora programmes are made 'usually by local, independent, minority entrepreneurs for consumption by a small, cohesive population which, because of its diaspora status, is cosmopolitan, multicultural, and multilingual'. However, the latter conception of a 'decentalized global narrowcasting' that is limited to a metropolitan locale does not fit all diasporic experiences. For example, Hassanpour's chapter describes an audience for live programming which is scattered across continents and Cunningham and Nguyen show how sophisticated video programmes produced by North American Vietnamese communities are exported back into Vietnam. There is significant growth in intercontinental traffic of media products emanating in diasporic locations as distinct from those produced in the homeland.

Nevertheless, a substantial portion of television content watched by diasporas remains what Naficy defines as 'transnational'. The 'geolinguistic regions' (Sinclair 1997) centred around Mumbai (formerly Bombay), Hong Kong, Cairo and Mexico City, the major centres for Hindi, Chinese, Arabic and Spanish film and television production respectively, are the foci not only for contiguous regions where these languages are spoken but the cultural hubs for worldwide diasporas. The commercial success of 'Bollywood' is comparable to that of its American counterpart in Hollywood, which it seeks to emulate. It contributes significantly to India's status as the producer of the largest number of films every year. And since the vast majority of these are musicals, there has grown over decades a massive recording industry centred around Mumbai. The late introduction of television in India has resulted in this medium's use of Bollywood film, reviews, retrospectives, music, gossip and so on as fodder for entertainment programming. Whereas the extent of Indian film's transnational distribution is much smaller than that of Hollywood, it has significant penetration in South Asia, South-East Asia and Africa. The Indian diaspora remains the mainstay of audiences and of distribution networks in these regions as well as in Western countries where cinemas exclusively showing Indian films flourish in cities with significant populations of South Asian origins. Bollywood has reciprocated by frequently including in film plots the presence of key characters who are 'NRIs' (non-resident Indians). Indian diasporic print and broadcast media productions are replete with references to Bollywood, to which aspiring NRI performers travel to find stardom. Ray's chapter demonstrates the overwhelming influence that it has had on the diasporic consciousness of Fiji Indians over several generations.

Heather De Santis discusses how Mexican and Brazilian television networks Televisa and TV Globo capitalise on the advantages of their own large domestic audiences and the geolinguistic regions – Spanish-speaking Latin America in the case of Televisa and the string of former Portuguese colonies scattered around the planet in that of TV Globo. Of increasing importance for Televisa is the Hispanic population of the United States, which is growing rapidly and is relatively affluent. But it is also significant that either Univisión and Tele-mundo, the Spanish-language networks in the US, is available on almost every cable system in Latin America. Miami has emerged as a major production centre for entertainment programmes, which are exported to Spain, Mexico and other Latin American countries. The picture that Latin Americans see of American society is very different from that presented by mainstream US tele-vision like the CNN and by global television news agencies. Univisión and Telemundo seek out Hispanic perspectives on national news stories and adhere to Latin American news values that favour greater analysis than that offered by mainstream American television.

Diasporic media have frequently been at the leading edge of technology adoption due to the particular challenges they face in reaching their audi-ences. The relatively small and widely scattered nature of communities they serve has encouraged them to seek out technologies that allow for narrowcast-ing to target specific audiences rather than those that provide the means for mass communication. Marie Gillespie notes about the Indian community in Southall, England, that many families obtained VCRs as early as 1978, 'well before most households in Britain', in order to watch Hindi films on videotape (1995: 79). This is probably true for other parts of the South Asian diaspora, which has high rates of watching Indian films on video – and now DVD tech-nology. Cunningham and Nguyen and Kolar-Panov's contributions to the book show the viability of 'small media' like video in diasporic communication (also see Preis 1997). Hong Qiu's chapter explores innovations carried out by Chinese 'knowledge diasporas' in their development of online magazines.

The arrival of Ku band satellites and digital compression technology enabled a vast increase in the number of radio and television channels that can be beamed over large distances directly to buildings equipped with pizza-sized satellite dishes. Whereas developing as well as developed countries had expressed fears that digitally broadcasting satellites (DBSs) would erode their sovereignty by transmitting foreign programming to their populations in unregulated manners, this technology provided remarkable opportunities for diasporic communities. Ethnic broadcasters, previously having limited access to space on the electromagnetic spectrum in Northern countries,[6] found much greater options opening up for them through DBS. Diasporic use of this tech-nology grew exponentially, well ahead of many mainstream broadcasters. Among the earliest buyers of digital satellite dishes in Canada were Italian and German communities who wanted to receive television, radio and teletext news transmissions of Europlus, a Europe-based service which carries content from public broadcasters in Italy and Germany.[7] Even as mainstream net-works in Europe were making plans to introduce digital broadcasting, Rome-based OrbitTV had begun providing extensive programming via DBS to Arab communities in Europe and the Middle East by 1994.[8] Mainstream direct-to-home (DTH) networks, such as SkyTV in Britain, DirectTV and DISH in the US, and ExpressVu and Star Choice in Canada, have realised the viability of ethnic channels and have made them a part of their offerings.

Adoption of the market model of mainstream broadcasting appears to belie the cultural studies view of diasporic media resisting dominant structures and discourses. Diasporic television networks carry out similar types of market research, programming schedules and advertising (e.g. Dávila 2001). Apart from certain differences in the modes of narrative, the only major difference seems to be in the languages and cultures of the content. But the very advantage that DBS offers, i.e. of enabling broadcasts to widely scattered audiences, inhibits local programming. Many ethnic-oriented services tend to be at the receiving end of one-way flows of material, either from home countries or locations with significant diasporic populations. Additionally, the fairly expensive hardware and subscription costs generally do not allow the less well off in the transnational communities to receive the programmes. Naficy and De Santis's chapters discuss the commercial pressures on the television systems of the metropolitan Middle Eastern market in Los Angeles and the intercontinental Hispanic market, respectively. On the other hand, Kolar-Panov indicates that the personal nature of diasporic Macedonian video letters helps them elude commodification. Tsaliki states that advertising is strictly prohibited in the Greek chatgroup, Katsika, which is protected as non-commercial space. Chinese online magazines have also resisted commercialisation, according to Qiu.

A feature of many of the new technologies is their potential in overcoming some of the hierarchical structures of traditional broadcast media. The extensive use by diasporic groups of online services like the Internet Relay Chat, e-mail, Usenet, Listserv and the World Wide Web is allowing for relatively easy connections for members of communities residing in various continents. As opposed to the broadcast model of communication which, apart from offering little access to minority groups, is linear, hierarchical and capital-intensive, online media allow easier access and are non-linear, largely non-hierarchical and relatively cheaper. The ability to exchange messages with individuals on the other side of the planet and to have access to community information almost instantaneously changes the dynamics of diaspora, allowing for qualitatively and quantitatively enhanced linkages. Mandaville's chapter discusses the use of the Internet by some Muslims to bypass traditional structures of religious authority and Tsaliki looks at the modalities of self-regulating discourse in a Greek diasporic chatgroup. However, Ackah and Newman address the lack of broad access to this technology as well as its deficient usage in a Ghanaian diaspora. Their chapter's example of the prominent placement of a telephone in the address page of a website illustrates vividly the continued dependence on the older technology.

Whereas the dispersal of Internet technology among diasporas is far from uniform, individuals who have access to it tend to make innovative use of it to establish transnational connections. Diasporic websites are assembling global directories of individuals, community institutions and businesses owned by members of diasporas. Some sites have hypertext links to homepages of alumni associations. Listings of forthcoming festivals and cultural events are also provided for those travelling to other parts of the diaspora. The availability of online versions of newspapers from countries of origin and the diaspora further enhance intercontinental connections. Global online technologies also offer some unique advantages for diasporic groups. For example, a worldwide registry would be extremely useful for the medical purposes of locating matches for human marrow donors – who are generally limited to one's own ethnic group. Similar databanks would facilitate global genealogical searches and in looking for adopted children's biological families. Members of endogamous groups are already using the medium to register themselves in matrimonial sections of diasporic websites.[9]

Usenet allows for ongoing discussions between individuals with common origins in newsgroups like soc.culture.germany, soc.culture.pakistan and so on. Discussions range over topics that include culture, literature, entertainment, politics and current events in the countries of origin and settlement. Newsgroups enable the participation of users with common interests, located around the world; these have been termed 'virtual communities' (Rheingold 1993b). However, the notion of virtual or electronic community seems more pertinent when speaking either of a freenet that networks a particular geographic locality or a diasporic group that is linked together by more than a single issue, sharing a symbolic universe that includes a broad variety of cultural markers (Mitra 1997). Indeed, cyberspace is often conceived of as a 'place' where the users electronically reconstitute the relationships that existed before migration. Discussing the participation of Indian immigrants on soc.culture.india (sci), Ananda Mitra writes:

> There is a presupposition that most members of the Indian community would access the network and would chance upon these general messages and thus re-establish contacts with people they might have known before. This signifies that the community produced by, and around, sci is a representation of the allegiances that existed before the diasporic experience occurred. For instance, when one encounters a message that refers back to a college in India there is an effort to find, in the virtual community, familiar relationships that have been severed by the process of geographic movement but can now be re-established in the virtual space of the Internet.
>
> (ibid., 63)

This is echoed in Tsaliki and King's respective discussions in this book. Whereas one is tempted to view the virtual reassembling of global diasporas within electronic chatrooms, this conceit belies the reality of the vastly differing levels of access enjoyed by members of communities as well as the inability of the individual newsgroups to support the coherence of more than a handful of discussions. Ackah and Newman draw our attention to the continued importance of travel and first-hand human contact in the lives of diasporas, criticising the tendency to eliminate space completely and to locate transnational communities exclusively within cyberspace. Pilgrimage, the traditional mode of bringing together members from global religious communities, continues to retain an enormous vibrancy among Muslims, Hindus, Christians and followers of other religions in the age of the diasporic chatroom, as witnessed in the periodic mass gatherings at holy places. Aksoy and Robins also point out the cognitive dissonance experienced by Turkish migrants in Britain in negotiating the discourses of watching satellite television from the homeland and their own lived reality.

After 11 September 2001

The suspected Middle Eastern perpetrators of the attacks of 11 September 2001 in the United States are alleged to have used the Internet to coordinate their transnational terrorist network. Consequently, the intercontinental media links of diasporas are coming under growing suspicion by Western governments. This highlights a fundamental contradiction in the dominant discourses on globalisation, which have favoured the free movements of good and services but generally not of people – especially those with origins in Southern countries. Petra Weyland (1997) illustrates the differential global spaces occupied respectively by the mostly Euro-origin male managerial class, their dependent wives who travel with them to various postings around the world, and the migrant Filipina domestic maids who serve them. As governments seek to prevent terrorism by more tightly sealing national borders, transnational movement is becoming problematic for potential emigrants from non-Western states. Additionally, the loyalty of minority ethnic groups living in Western countries is becoming suspect and their transnational connections and relationships are coming under scrutiny. The multiple and hybrid identities of diasporic members are under renewed pressure to conform to the mythic notion of a monolithic populace of the traditional nation state.

The long-term effect of such retrenchment of attitudes on the media of diasporas remains to be seen. Hassanpour's chapter describes the ongoing struggle that Kurdish satellite television has had with governments in Western Europe. The media of the transnational groups who are perceived as being linked to terrorist organisations will most likely find it even more difficult to operate. The only Internet service provider which supplied the Somali diaspora with online connections to the homeland was forced to close in November 2001 because the US government suspected it of having links to terrorists.[10] Governments have frequently resisted the development of ethnic media, viewing them as obstacles to the integration of immigrants into the host society (e.g. Hargreaves and Mahdjoub 1997) even though ethnic newspapers carry significant amounts of material on civic issues relating to its public sphere (Karim 2002b). However, diasporic media have increasingly become entrenched in the communications structures of various Western countries and it will be difficult to eliminate them without economic costs, especially to advertisers and to cable and satellite companies. There may even be costs for politicians who tend to use ethnic media to reach minority members of their constituencies more effectively.

Whereas governments have the necessary task of preventing terrorism, they also need to understand better the nature of diasporas and their mediascapes. The forces of globalisation and of technological development make it impossible to corral minority groups within borders of countries. Diasporic spaces overlap with other forms of transnational connections. The multiple layering of intercontinental communications networks appears to have become an intrinsic feature of globalisation; diasporic media using satellites and Internet connections are piggybacking on the structures established and maintained by governments and corporations. The 'global postmodern' is a contradictory space, as Hall (1997b) notes: globalisation-from-above and globalisation-from-below do not always work in opposition.

The hybridity of technological and entrepreneurial innovations appears to parallel that of human identity. Transnational 'third spaces' are the liminal sites characterised by a significant degree of creativity. This zone of multiple borders is a frontier of modernity, where new ways of addressing the problems of contemporary social relations are sought at local and global levels. Ray draws our attention to the innovative modalities of interaction between India and the West in the otherwise overly commercialised and formulaic film output of Mumbai. Santianni explores how the Tibetan Buddhist diaspora draws on contemporary universal discourses in order to make alliances with North Americans and Europeans. It appears that the diasporic space where deterritorialised nations are making their home has the possibility for becoming the location for a genuinely cosmopolitan citizenship that would be a logical human outcome of globalisation.

Notes

1 For a fuller discussion on this issue, see Karim 2002a.
2 The concept of transnation is becoming more formalised in policies like those of the Indian government to give a legal status to non-resident Indians (NRIs) and persons of Indian origin (PIOs), thus creating forms of diasporic citizenship which, however, do not hold all the privileges (or obligations) of full citizenship.
3 Spatially constructed power is also produced on the basis of gender and class difference (Massey 1994; Rose 1997).
4 Quotation from Homi Bhabha (1994: 120).
5 Quotation from Deleuze and Guattari (1987: 313).
6 For example, a centre-right French government actively encouraged the country's main broadcast regulator, the Conseil supérieur de l'audiovisuel, to exclude Arabic stations from licensed cable networks (Hargreaves and Mahdjoub 1997: 461).
7 Tony Lofaro, 'New, Mini-Satellite Dishes Appeal to Ethnic Viewers', *The Ottawa Citizen* (5 February 1994), 18.
8 Chris Forrester, 'Orbit Pioneers Space-Age Television' *The European* (24–30 August 1995), p. 29.

9 The collection of personal data on such databanks, however, broaches the issue of privacy on the Internet and its attendant problems.
10 British Broadcasting Corporation, 'US shuts down Somalia Internet' (23 November 2001), news.bbc.co.uk/hi/english/world/africa/newsid_1672000/1672220.stm.

Part 1
Film, radio, television, video

2 Nation, nostalgia and Bollywood

In the tracks of a twice-displaced community

Manas Ray

This chapter examines the process of imagining into existence a sense of nationhood by a specific diaspora of Indian origin (namely the Fiji Indians) in Australia and the role that the Mumbai-based film industry, Bollywood – in its different manifestations – plays in this. The focus of the chapter is to understand how mass images of India can be made to speak and/or represent history far outside the geographical limits of India and the place of viewers in that history. For this I bring together two separate but related journeys. One, I highlight the cultural trajectory of these 'splintered' people – from indenture to subsistence farming to their participation in the urbanisation of Fiji and finally the coup of 1987 that resulted in a big exodus to Western cities and placed the struggle for cultural identity in a new vortex of power. Two, I try to lace this journey with another, that of the images of Bollywood over the decades and how it impacted lives far beyond the shores of India. My aim is not so much a celebration of the ontological condition of the diasporic imagination but to focus on the contingent course of historical subjectivity of this twice-displaced community, a course that has vital links to the changing political economy of Bollywood, its images and image-making over the years.

Different diasporic Indias

The paper addresses two theoretical issues central to understanding diasporic media. First, I argue that the different postcolonial diasporas are not 'splinters' in a transnational world, ready to rearticulate their identity on the lines of extraterritoriality or nomadism; on the contrary, it is the historical subjectivity of a diaspora which holds the key to its cultural life. At one level, there is a need to club the different (postcolonial) diasporas together as those not parties to what Partha Chatterjee calls the 'original historical contract' (1995: 11) that gave birth to the Western nation states. At another level, it is also important to recognise the different historical trajectories of these diasporas. Hence the alienation that postcolonial people face in the multicultural West is multi-layered; merely citing the more visible signs of racism does not register its historical depth. The case of Fiji Indians will amply demonstrate this. Second, diasporic media need to be seen in the context of their politics of its production and dissemination. This is particularly so with Bollywood, which from its inception has situated itself in the locus of contending definitions of 'Indianness' (see Rajadhyaksha and Wildman 1994: 10).

By no means does this chapter seek to analyse media use of *the* 'Indian' diaspora seen as one monolithic whole. In fact, it is the globality of such a concept that needs be contested and read as a sign of ahistoricity and ethnocentrism that so often underwrites the perception of postcolonial societies. This is not to deny that the different Indian diasporas do deploy their notions of 'India' as the broad symbolic horizon for constructing their respective identities. Neither is it to underestimate the crucial role that such pan-'Indianness' (largely derived from orientalist discourse about India) played in imagining a nation into existence during the course of struggle against colonial rule and continues to do so long after the Raj. It is, however, to highlight the fact that for Indians (both inside India and outside) such 'Indianness' – like any other identity concept – is always already fissured. As a matter of *positioning* and not essence, this 'Indianness' varies with different communities, is used at times for contradictory purposes and quite often gives rise to unintended consequences. It may be argued that the different empirical factors like language, region or religion do not by themselves hold the key to cultural difference. It is the positioning of communities in postcolonial space that underpins the cultural lives of different Indian diasporas and sets the course for possible futures.

In an era of the global spread of corporate capital and great demographic shifts, one of the key projects of political modernity is faced with serious crisis: instead of the 'nationalisation of the ethnic' that Western nation states banked their hopes on, we now face the opposite scenario, 'the ethnicisation of the nation' (see Zizek 1997). The yearning for 'roots', as it is called, has become a common phenomenon for both the majoritarian white community as well as the different diasporas in different ways. As a result, the notion of shared public space is increasingly challenged by a different ordering of space – namely a criss-cross of different primordias tied together by the universal function of the market – what has been termed 'public sphericules' (see Cunningham and Sinclair 2001: chapter 1).

For the Fiji Indians, if it was legislated racial discrimination that compelled them to leave Fiji, in Australia they find themselves in the middle of a new entanglement of different, contesting imaginings of 'roots'. Migration to Australia from mainland India has mostly been of the professional category. The social composition of India being what it is, this also means that the Indian representation in Australia is largely from the upper castes, many of whom are unwilling to give up their historical memory of unquestioned superiority *vis-à-vis* the lower castes. As far as the Fiji Indians are concerned, the romantic construction of India (and Indians) – derived most significantly from the movies – faced in Australia for the first time the rude shock of caste discrimination through their interactions with 'compatriot' Indians. This has resulted in a change of focus of cultural antagonism – from the native Fijians, the mainland Indians now constitute the community's 'other'.

One of the results of this process is that Bollywood is taking new significance in their lives. Historically, the bond between them and India has been one of imagination. With time, as memory of 'roots' – the *real* India – was fading away, films took over the responsibility of constructing an empty, many-coloured space through its never-ending web of images, songs, 'dialogues' and stars. In the new political context of Australia, this empty space would be shorn of even the pretence of a referent – it is space unto itself, a *pure* space, so to say. Bollywood reciprocates this gesture by placing the diasporic *imaginaire* at the very heart of its new aesthetics.

Indenture and beyond

The Fiji Islands were declared a British colony in 1874 when a group of indigenous 'chiefs' signed a Deed of Cession with the British. Five years later the first Indian indentured labourers arrived in the coolie ships from India, the labour for the sugar plantations and other enterprises that would make the new colony pay without exposing the indigenous population to the harmful consequences of an industrial economy (Jayawardena 1980; Kelly 1991). By the end of indenture in 1919, 60,965 Indians had come to Fiji as indentured labourers (see Mishra 1979 and Lal 1983). They called themselves *girmitiyas* (from the English word 'agreement', a reference to the labour contract). The British called them 'coolies', so did the indigenous Fijians (the word has an interesting twist, since the word for dog in Fijian language is similar: *kuli*). By 1986, the Indian population was in the majority in Fiji (348,704 compared to 329,305 ethnic Fijians) (Lal 1992: 337) and the country's economy was based on Indian management and labour.[1]

North Indian representation in Fiji constituted around three hundred castes (mostly agrarian, with Brahmin cultivators constituting around 10 per cent) from two hundred villages. The Muslim presence was 13 per cent (Lal 1983). The *lingua franca* that developed among Fiji Indians (known as Fiji Hindi or Fiji Buli) reflects many different dialects, with occasional European and Fijian words. South India came into the picture only after 1903. However, even as latecomers, the total number of South Indians going to Fiji between 1904 and 1917 was 14,536, constituting 23.8 per cent of the Indian population when the indenture period was over. The reason for such bulk migration is the different system under which they went – the *Kangani* system – where the village-head corralled his village people and took them to the colony. In their new destination, the South Indians were moved around and scattered in different plantations and as such they had to adjust to the *lingua franca*. This was a matter of great effort on their part, since the languages of the South emanate from the Dravidian family of languages and are entirely different from Hindi which is part of the Indo-European group of languages. The Gujeratis first came in large numbers in 1920s and 1930s as shopkeepers, moneylenders, artisans, sonars (goldsmiths) and in numerous other trades and services. There were occupational as well as residential differentiations. Mostly they lived in urban areas with little social interaction with the rest of the Indian community. Utilising the discipline of the 'lines', the Indians in Fiji in course of time have made much of what today's Fiji is – economically speaking – with their labour and management. This is a huge achievement given the way they began their journey.

Unlike mainland India, Fiji was governed by British Common Law with no room for separate laws for different religious communities. However, this did not mean that for Fiji Indians the social system of Indian villages that reinforces compliance with accepted rituals gave way to the impersonality of a secular order. This could not have happened, given the built-in conditions of inequality of a plantation regime. For the indentured population, re-creating 'motherland' in its social, cultural and religious manifestations became part of their wider political struggle. The culture that evolved, the fashioning of 'little India' as it is called, was not so much an expression of the desire to return, or idle nostalgia, nor a docile willingness to replay on a minor scale a mammoth original. Rather it was as an active attempt to yoke an identity in the face of little or no recognition as cultural or political beings.

Jayawardena observes that the complete proletarianisation of Indians in Guyana meant near total loss of home traditions while the Fiji Indians could maintain cultural traditions because of isolated subsistence farming in post-indenture (1980: 436). With time, the population become more scattered and professions diversified. This re-emphasised the need to preserve their culture and religion in order to provide support and solidarity among themselves. Culturally speaking, the passage from indenture to post-indenture can be seen as one of 'amnesiac recollection' to an active bid to construct a 'national memory' (Kelly 1998: 840). And what initially had provided fodder to the construction of national memory (in spite of its many divides like north Indians versus those who came from the south, Hindus versus Muslims, Gujeratis *vis-à-vis* the rest) were the folk traditions of North India and, particularly, the ancient epic Ramayan (or better, the popular version composed by Tulsi Das in the sixteenth century, *Ramcharitmanas*). This epic – along with other cultural expressions of the *bhakti*[2] movement – not only provided the cultural and moral sustenance to the community; in the very process of doing so, it also paved the way for the overwhelming popularity of Hindi popular cinema amongst Fiji Indians.

From the Ramayan to Bollywood

Unlike India, in indenture Fiji there was no class of gentry to put through a nationalist sieve the various cultural forms that emerged in the encounter with colonial modernity and selectively adopt and combine the reconstituted elements of the supposedly indigenous tradition.[3] In the absence of any philosophical tradition, what prevailed at the beginning was the reminiscences of numerous local cultural traditions of the villages of India. The traditions of village India that survived were basically derived from *bhakti* – the devotional songs (*bhajans*) of such composers as Kabir, Mira and Sur Das. But over and above anything else what inspired their imagination was Tulsi's *Ramcharitmanas*. Very early on, reciting, singing and enactment of the Ramayan was revived amongst the Indians of Fiji. This bound together a cultural community to brave the chains of bondage in the fissiparous environment of plantation capitalism where everyone was an individual unit of production and daily existence was measured by work hours.

The Ramayan was shorn of deeper philosophical meanings. Its primary function was to serve emotional satisfaction and not individual spiritual enlightenment. The reasons for an overwhelming emotional identification with the epic is directly related to the predicament of an indentured diaspora. The central god character, Ram, was banished for 14 years. For Fiji Indians, it was for at least five years. Ram's banishment was for no fault of his; similarly, it was not the fault of the Indians that they were extracted from their homeland and subjected to inhuman physical labour in this remote island.[4] The triumphant ending of all ordeals provided a kind of moral strength to withstand the brutalities of indenture. If Ram could survive for 14 years, surely the Fiji Indians could do so for five years. The Ramayan thus was used to heal the wounds of indenture and provide a cultural and moral texture in the new settlement.

There is another reason for this strong identification and this involves the question of woman and sexual virtue. Throughout the phase of indenture and even later, the paucity of women *vis-à-vis* men was one of the primary social concerns among the *girmitiyas*. In a situation where many men lived without wives of their own, women were expected to serve two contradictory functions: they were at times forced by circumstances and even by violence to leave one man for another while the pressure was on them to comply with the standards of a good, chaste woman (Kelly 1991, chapter 9).

Hence one of the central moral thematics of Hindi cinema – namely the image of the devoted wife, the heroine struggling to be chaste – had a special appeal to the Fiji Indians, given the peculiar existential circumstances of indenture. A strong emotional identification to the Ramayan and other expressions of *bhakti* movement, a constrained cultural environment, continued degradation at the hands of the racist white regime, a disdain for the culture of the ethnic Fijians, a less hard-pressed post-indenture life and, finally, a deep-rooted need of a dynamic, discursive site for the imaginative reconstruction of motherland, all of these factors together ensured the popularity of Hindi films once they started reaching the shores of Fiji. This was because Hindi film deployed the Ramayan extensively, providing the right pragmatics for 'continual mythification' of home.

The two Indian epics – Ramayan and Mahabharat – helped Bollywood fuse the history of the nation and the history of the family. In the Indian narrative tradition, family history is not strictly demarcated from social history. In the Mahabharat, the battle between the Kauravas and the Pandavas, two branches of the same family, engages vast social, political and cosmic forces, all of which are then sought to be compressed within a single philosophical framework; in the Ramayan, Ram's relationship with Sita is largely determined by his obligation to his family and, more importantly, his social *dharma*.[5]

Of the two epics, the Ramayan is again privileged because of its elaborations of the familial self and the focus on the duties and sufferings of *sati* – the chaste wife. Also to be taken into account is the fact that in North India, Ramayan's popularity far exceeds that of Mahabharat. The usual character stereotypes of Hindi films – the suffering but faithful wife (Sita) who is also a loving and somewhat indulgent sister-in-law; courageous, dutiful and detached husband (Ram); the faithful brother (Lakshman); and the vengeful, evil villain (Ravan) – are mostly drawn from the Ramayan. Bollywood would experiment with these role models, bring in other stereotypes (like that of the frolicsome Krishna of the Radha-Krishna *bhakti* motif popular in eastern India; or that of *dosti* – the friendship between two adult males which will be posited against heterosexual love for creating emotionally charged moments in the narrative). But never would Bollywood transgress the moral limits of the Ramayan.

Vijay Mishra (1985; 1992) points to the various underlying drives structuring the epics, invoking mythic figures from the epics as the substratum from which the various Bollywood character-types emerge. The traffic between the epics and Bollywood is, however, complicated by the role of music and romance. Music functions to transform the epic narratives by foregrounding a romantic repertoire. Romance is absolutely crucial for Bollywood – it is defined by romance. Here Bollywood draws more from the Radha-Krishna trope (of love, desire and erotica) of *bhakti* than it does from the epics. Bollywood, operating within the moral and social limits of the epics, extends its narrative scope by negotiating with other folk and emerging popular traditions.

Hindi cinema established its traffic to Fiji in the late 1930s. By then the period of indenture was over, the Indian community as independent cultivators had lost the solidarity that characterised life on 'the lines' of indenture, and linguistic and religious identities were differentiating. Hindi cinema's primary impact in Fiji was to bond through meta-narratives with which all the different groups of Fiji Indians could identify. In this cinema, the Fiji Indians found the most lively expression of their yearning for roots and bid to reconstruct an imagined homeland culture in an alien surrounding – at once simplified, quotidian and concrete but with a long tradition. And since in Hindi films *nation* is imagined in familial terms, the physical distance between mainland India and Fiji did not interrupt this 'work of imagination'. Evidently the folk traditions borrowed from the villages of India did not come in the way of Hindi cinema's popularity; on the contrary, by simplifying these traditions in a remote island with very little scope for other kinds of cultural traffic, the folk culture actually prepared the way for the unprecedented popularity of this quasi-globalising mass culture.

As Fiji started urbanising, the local Indian village cultures began to recede in influence, at least in the public cultural spaces of the cities. Once in place, Bollywood created its own public and psychic platform for people to interact.[6]

The gossip columns, the 24-hour Hindi service, the occasional visits of singers and stars from Mumbai – all this went into constituting the culture of a community which harboured no illusion of return but, for reasons of identity and cultural make-up, yearned for a romanticised version of India that Bollywood amply provided. The genealogy of unprecedented popularity of the mass cultural tradition of Bollywood in Fiji thus lies in the diasporic rediscovery of 'little' traditions that the *girmitiyas* brought with them and preserved over a century.

The cult of Bollywood that the Fiji Indians re-produced in Fiji is not a case of mimicry, since repetition is inscribed in the very mode of Bollywood's being (see Appadurai 1998). Once Bollywood is made the mainstay of cultural life (which to a very large extent is the case with Fiji Indians), it of necessity repeats its entire cultural ecology – its 'insiderism' (Rajadhyaksha and Wildman 1994: 10). This 'insiderism' constructs a sense of mythological nationhood with very tenuous links with the actual geography of a nation. Hence living in the realities of Fiji and participating in the life of Bollywood is not a case of split existence, since such a split is postulated on a divide between the real and the imagined, something that Bollywood disavows.

Fiji Indian cultural ecology in Australia

Despite their recent arrival in Australia and the structural deficits they face in employment, the Fiji Indians have re-established themselves with a cultural dynamism that is out of all proportion to their numbers and which can be sourced to their embrace of the cultural repertoire proffered by Bollywood. In Sydney, the professional Fiji Indians are scattered all over the city while those in blue-collar jobs tend to concentrate in one or two regions. In the immediate years after the coup, they concentrated in the Campsie region of Sydney. Latterly, Liverpool and to some extent Bankstown are the two suburbs to where a majority of the working class Fiji Indians have moved. All these suburbs, with a number of big Indo-Fijian grocery shops, garment houses, movie halls, auditoriums and nightclubs, have emerged as the different nodes of Fiji Indian cultural life, complete with beauty contests (where participants come from all over Australia, New Zealand and Fiji), bands specialising in Hindi film music, music schools for filmy songs, DJs, karaoke singers, film magazines and community radio programmes. Numbers of Fiji Indian singers of Sydney have brought out several CDs in India. These are mostly popular Hindi film songs and a couple of *ghazals* (light classical North Indian music that has roots in the Mughal courts).

Brisbane's Bollywood cultural life, very much like in Sydney, is mostly a Fijian Indian affair. It has one regular band, Sargam, but relies on Sydney bands for major occasions. There are no nightclubs and no established tradition of karaoke. Public performances, far less in number compared to Sydney, are hosted in rented auditoria. Like other Indian communities, for the Fiji Indians of Brisbane the relation to Bollywood is mostly restricted to renting

Hindi videos, though as a community they are undoubtedly the highest consumers. The reason for Brisbane's lack of a public face for Bollywood culture
is partly due to the composition of the Indian community with a preponderance of the professional class. But primarily it is a factor of size. With a
population of less than ten thousand, the Fiji Indian community does not have
the resources to support an ongoing Bollywood cultural economy and, with
immigration having dwindled to barely a few hundred every year, there is no
sign that the Fiji Indian presence in Brisbane will increase substantially. The
absence of a public culture of Bollywood impacts on the identity politics of
second-generation Fiji Indians. In general, the young Fiji Indians of Brisbane
prefer to portray themselves as much less 'out-going' *vis-à-vis* their Sydney
counterparts, less experimental about Bollywood ('interested in the professional
part of singing and not merely remixes'), less hyped and much more rooted in
the values of Indian culture. As a young woman active in Brisbane's Fiji
Indian cultural world puts it: 'We are more Indians. In the way we mix with
people, our morals and culture, the way we dress – in every way, we are truer
to our Indian ways. For Sydney, India is a commodity to be bought and sold;
for us, India is a way of life' (Aiyasha, interviewed April 1998).

Inter-communal discord and cultural assertion

The ethnic, caste and class differences between mainland Indians and Fiji
Indians has given rise to intracommunal tensions and rivalries which are
neither new nor restricted only to Australia.[7] Many mainland Indians exhibit
deeply entrenched casteist attitudes and view the indentured past of the Fiji
Indians as a non-negotiable barrier. On the other side, Fiji Indians often characterise mainland Indians with the same kind of negative attributes that they
were wont to use for ethnic Fijians. Both realise the need for a united front to
deal with Australian racism but both view each other as an obstacle to better
acceptance by the 'white nation'. Mainland Indians now constitute an *other* for
this community, just as the ethnic Fijians did back in Fiji.

Such rivalry between the two communities has seen the reassertion of
culture and ethnicity by Fiji Indians. This involves a positive mobilisation of
indenture history and an emphasis on a Hindu way of life in a Western
context that bears similarities to Gillespie's account of self-construction of
identity through the positive assertion of ethnicity (1995, 8–11). The dominant
racism of white Australia, the ostracisation by mainland Indians, the need of
the older generation for a platform to socialise and to reflect (which will also
function as a moral regime for younger people) have together fed into a resurgence of religion and revival of folk traditions, neglected in today's urban Fiji.

One of the most creative methods of adaptation is the assertive construction of a cultural community around *Ramayan katha* and *bhajan mandalis* (small
gatherings for devotional songs) which paved the way for Bollywood's popularity. For the last couple of decades, these traditions were mostly on the decline
in urban Fiji. Once in Australia, these have regained their popularity as a

platform to unite the community and act as a moral regime for young people. Significantly enough, in the Hindu religious traditions devotion and erotica are rarely separate departments of life and one very often evokes the other. This is particularly so with the *bhakti* tradition from which Tulsi Das's *Ramcharitmanas* emanates. In the *bhakti* taxonomy, *shringar* is the highest form of devotion – the erotic bond between the devotee (a woman) and the deity (a man). In one of the forms of *shringar*, the female denies herself, her family, all bonds and social constrictions and pursues the love of Krishna. Radha is the epitome of this love and devotion. The trope of Radha and Krishna puts together social transgression, erotica and devotion. As the supreme expression of desire and pathos, it has for centuries provided inspiration for *bhajans* (devotional songs). It has also served Bollywood as a source of much of its music, narrative and allegory. This means that cultural and religious assertion of tradition has not been in opposition to Bollywood; in fact, in a Western diasporic context, it provides young Fiji Indians with the cultural capital to appreciate Bollywood better.

The Fiji Indians, with a long tradition of attachment to *bhajan* and other devotional songs, have been influenced by the recent boom in the devotional music market in India. Coming in contact with mainland Indians has not only meant digging up casteist and indenture memories; it has, more positively, opened new possibilities for creative expressions by exposing the community to the wider world of Indian music and dance. There are many more Indian dance and music (especially classical) schools in Sydney than was the case in Fiji. The result has been quick to materialise: from a receiver of Indian cultural artefacts, the community has become a producer. In the field of devotional music, however, this exposure is impacting the community in a significant way. For more than a century, Fiji Indians were used to singing the Bhojpuri (from the district in Bihar called Bhojpur) style of *bhajan* called *tambura bhajan*. Now this is giving way (at least for a section of the community) to the more classically oriented *bhajan* of Anup Jalota, Hari Om Sharan, Anuradha Paudwal and others through audiocassettes produced in India. The CDs of some of the *bhajan* singers of the Sydney community are clear proof of this trend.

Fiji Indian youth culture and post-Zee Bollywood

The most dynamic aspect of Fiji Indian youth culture centres on the use of Bollywood to negotiate a kind of parallel cultural platform to the dominant Western pop culture. This can be understood through grasping the enormous changes that Bollywood itself has undergone in recent years, especially since the advent of Zee TV. Zee programming has branded itself as a halfway house between the transnational (Asian) Star TV brand and traditional Hindi film, creating a hybrid genre that refers strongly to Western-style music and dance. Such types of dance and music are now also the mainstay of Bollywood, especially of the new genre of 'teenage romance' that has come into being in the liberalising India of the 1990s. DJ Akash of Sydney explains the implication of such music for young diasporic Indians in the following terms:

> Ten years back a young Indian would listen to his music in a very low volume. He would consider his music to be very 'tacky' and would have felt awkward to play it publicly in a western context. The contemporary Bollywood music, by blending Indian melody with Western beats, has changed all this. Nowadays if you go down the streets of Sydney very often you will hear Indian music blasting. Young people no longer consider the Bollywood songs as curry music. It no longer sounds strange to the average westerner.
>
> (Akash Hussain, interviewed May 1998)

Arguably because of this hybridisation of Bollywood music, it manages to signify something special to the diasporic young Indians. Asked about the continued influence of Bollywood music, a young Fiji Indian performed this analysis:

> Bollywood has got the potential. It has got feeling. When you are happy you have something to sing, in love you sing, when you are sad you sing. You can relate to it. Consider a hit song of 1997, 'Dil To Pagal Hai' (my heart has gone wild). It is about love and affection with which a young person can immediately identify. All those who are in love would buy the CD for their girlfriends; they would send requests to the radio channel for the song to be played. We relate to it in two ways: i) visual part – i.e., what the main guy and main girl did in the movie, and ii) the meaning of the lyric. Compared to this, Hollywood music hardly has any message that we can relate to. Take *Men in Black* [1997] for instance. We could barely identify with the hit score. The messages of Bollywood with which we are brought up hardly gets conveyed to us there. There is nothing of our own in such music.
>
> (Satish Rai, interviewed May 1998)

Fiji Indian young people use a wholly hybridised genre like the remixes to fashion a discourse of authenticity. On the one hand, they will deploy the remixes as part of syncretic metropolitan culture and thus break out of the cartography that views their culture as ethnic. On the other hand, they perceive these remixes (for them, an essentially diasporic phenomenon) as part of their attempt to promote Indian popular music by making it contemporary; this they will compare to the Indian nightclub crowd which according to them is hooked on unadulterated Western hard rock and heavy metal. A Fiji Indian enthusiast of 'Indi-pop' describes her experience in terms that combine being 'Western' and being 'Indian': as a Westerner, she prefers Indi-pop to traditional Indian popular music (which for her is 'a bit too romantic and at times unacceptably melodramatic'); she is also 'far more of an eastern person' *vis-à-vis* her Mumbai counterpart:

> When I went to India, I found that kids are not thrilled with remixes. To be honest, I got the impression that they are quite wary of this kind of experiments; they think that it is corrupting the original music scores. On the other hand, I found night clubs in Bombay [*sic*] are more influenced by Hollywood than Bollywood. I was shocked to find many Indian girls dancing to heavy metal and hard rock. This is pretty aggressive by Indian standards. I haven't seen any girl of Indian origin doing that sort of dance in Sydney . . . Kids in Bombay go to night clubs to become western. Here we go to assert our eastern identity. The basic difference lies there.
>
> (Saroni Pratap, interviewed May 1998)

Apart from remixes of popular scores, bhangra as a dance beat serves an important role in the deployment of Indian popular music for the purpose of being 'agreeably different' in a Western context. Originating in rural Punjab as a harvest dance, bhangra's potential to provide the right kind of beat for clubbing was first explored by the Punjabis of Southall (Haq 1997). Fiji Indians were not exposed to bhangra in Fiji. But in the last ten years, it has gained great popularity amongst the young Fiji Indians of Australia. In recent years, on every Wednesday night Sydney community radio 2 SER plays bhangra-pop. Bhangra did not come to Australia from India; rather, it came from London. In fact, it can be argued that the recent popularity of bhangra-pop in India with the rise of such stars as Daler Mehendi is very much a case of the diaspora re-working the homeland.

Diasporising Bollywood

Bollywood has not only coped with the challenges of globalisation but taken advantage of the new situation by enlarging its terrain. This it has achieved by creating a spectatorship aware of the specific requirements of the diasporas as well as those living in India. A globalising world of communication and capital flow, instead of imposing a hegemonic cultural world order, has triggered a politics of space whereby the diasporas of a particular community dispersed world-over are networked to the homeland culture to such an extent that the traditional divide of outside/inside loses much of its analytical purchase. In contemporary Bollywood, it is interesting to see how the inscription of the citizen consumer, its ideal contemporary spectator, has offered spaces for assertion of identity for Bollywood's diasporic clientele *vis-à-vis* the host culture and, in the case of Fiji Indians, with the mainland Indian communities as well.

It can be argued that since the emergence of the super-genre of the 'social' in the 1960s, Bollywood underwent its next major change in the late 1980s and early 1990s coping with the tides of globalisation. Earlier Bollywood was not governed by consideration of community 'out there'; community was securely at home. Hence representations of abroad could only take the form of the travelogue. For instance, towards the later part of the super-hit *Sangam* (1964), the couple goes on an exotic tourist-album honeymoon trip to the West. The exotic locales of such narratives provided not only visual pleasure but constructed a site for marking self's absolute difference from the *other* (one that lies outside the imagined boundaries of home). As compared to this, the diasporic Indian (popularly known as the non-resident Indian or 'NRI') is now very much part of contemporary Bollywood's address. In the new troping of the home and the world, those who are brought up outside India have *India* inside them very much as the *West* is inscribed in the heart of India. This enmeshing of identities has enabled Bollywood to address the moral and cultural alienation that diasporic youth feel with Hindi films made to 'standard formula', while it also offers them the difference they want *vis-à-vis* Hollywood.

With consumption acquiring a different inscription, recent Bollywood has offered for its diasporic youth clientele a trajectory of 'Western-style' glamour, wealth and liberty, but on its own terms. Bollywood manages the ensuing alienation with the mass audience of India by the sheer strength of its vast repertoire, which even now has a large space for films of earlier eras. For the new Bollywood too, it is not as though it merely mimics Hollywood. Rather, the semiotics of exchange with Hollywood have in recent years taken an interesting turn.[8] The biggest hit in recent years, *Kuch Kuch Hota Hai* (1998), for instance, completes this India–West circuit by not venturing to go abroad at all; instead, it creates a virtual 'West' within the bounds of India. In fact, in terms of *mise-en-scène*, the film has internalised the West into India to the extent that it does not even have to announce that it is the West. Thematically, once the tomboy character of the heroine is established, the rest of the narrative concentrates on bringing to the fore her femininity. The framing of the woman as powerless, and above all a wife and a mother, and at the same time allowing her a certain space, a freedom for the pleasure of her subsequent disciplining, has been the general narrative-ethical guideline since the early days of the 'social' in the 1950s. *Kuch Kuch Hota Hai* does not alter the terms of what one might call the 'Sita' trope, but pushes it to accommodate a decisively urbanised, globalised (basketball-playing, baseball-cap-wearing) female prototype; neither is her subsequent realisation of a more feminised, 'Indian' self jarring to her earlier posturing. In fact, such realisation will only act to make her a more holistic woman. In a similar vein, the other female protagonist of the film, the Oxford-returned, guitar-strumming girl, who can also quickly switch to singing Hindu religious hymns – and to whom the hero gets married but who dies at childbirth – is not a 'vamp from the West' (as earlier films of similar narrative would almost certainly portray her to be) but a nice, pleasant woman who happens to wear Westernised clothes in a sexualised sense. This then would be internalised in the Indian imaginary as not someone who represents the West (since 'west' is very much in India) but simply as someone who has lived in the West.

Bollywood representation establishes the 'India' community as a national but global community. To ritually assert, as Bollywood characters often do, that one is part of such an ideal community, it is important that one knows what one is part of. This involves returning to India and seeking sanctions from the original patriarchal order. *Dilwale Dulhaniya Le Jayenge* (1995) is a remarkable instance of such re-working of the traditional patriarchal moral scheme. The film begins with the memorable montage of the heroine's father: as a Punjabi farmer, he is straddling past the mustard fields of Punjab; then through dissolve, he is seen journeying past Big Ben and Westminister (wearing his Punjabi *ajkan*), and finally feeding grains to the pigeons in the city square of London and remembering ancestral Punjab in a voice deeply laden with nostalgia. The father is the epitome of a *darshanic* figure, bestowing sanction within the orbit of his *darshan*.[9] The narrative then moves from the domestic space of the heroine in London to the continent with the couple and finally reaches rural Punjab, where the heroine is supposed to have an arranged marriage with a local boy. Once the couple reach rural Punjab, the film changes gear and becomes unusually slow. The gaze is fixed on the details of the marriage rituals, staged in a static, ornate fashion. The point of view is of the hero, who witnesses the preparations but from a remove. It is important that the occasion is not contested since the pleasure lies in its staging. The spectatorship at this point is clearly diasporic.

The action takes place at the very end of the film, when the heroine's father throws the hero out of his house and the proposed son-in-law starts beating the hero in a typical vendetta fashion. The hero does nothing to defend himself but significantly once his father is hit by one of the men of the heroine's father, he plunges into action and manifests aggression to defend his father. It is at this point that the heroine's father gives sanction to the hero: defending the father means by logic of mirroring defending the future father-in-law or, in a broader sense, the father principle, the originating source of authority. It is interesting for the elaborate carnival of identity where there is a kind of secret strategy to hold it at bay until one can actualise it on one's own terms, on terms of that freedom that the West has given but which needs to be ratified in the ancestral home. As a form, it has been clearly invented by contemporary Bollywood and has of late been repeatedly deployed as major device to bring the West and the East to one place. It is also a ploy to reinscribe the narrative space firmly within the *darshanic* orbit and very much like in old Bollywood, climax comes in the form of defending the *darshanic* object.

Conclusion

I have sought to show how negotiation with the 'culture of motherland' became for the Fiji Indian community part of a much broader question of negotiation with (post-)indenture definition of the self. Needless to mention, this negotiation could not remain the same from the early days of 'extraction' and the physically arduous schedule of indenture through post-indenture life of subsistence agriculture, diversification of occupation and differentiation of the community to entry into a Western context of late modern times with the option of 'multi-plicity of forms of life and conscious adoption of lifestyles' (Dean 1996: 213).

The situation has been made more complex by the recent changes in the Western landscape of the 'social'. Here I go by the definition of the *social* provided by Nicholas Rose: a large abstract terrain of collective experience, the sum of bonds and relations between individuals and events within a more or less bounded territory governed by its own laws. Rose argues that ever since global capital attained prominence, the *social* in the west has been undergoing a transmutation in favour of the *community* – not one but a series of communities with different aims and constituencies but nonetheless basically constituted of self-monitoring, self-governing subjects (Rose 1996). However, the norms of such particularised communities of the contemporary West can barely negotiate with the religio-civilisational norms of the 'narrative communities' of a postcolonial formation. In the vortex of power and positionalities of the multi-cultural west, every ethnic community *owns* an identity (see Rouse 1991, 1995). As an ethnic community, the Fiji Indians are attracted to new forms of association and intimacy of the West but written in this attraction also is the sign of resistance. Together they feed a sense of imagined nationhood kept alive by continuously transforming and reconstructing its constitutive myths. Bollywood, as it caters to the changing market patterns of home and abroad, serves this dual purpose extraordinarily well.

The literature of transnationality is not known for its interest in investigating the different histories of postcolonial dynamics 'back home' as they manifest in the new imaginings and politics of community. Rather its main concern is to write diaspora as an enigmatic excess and privilege the aleatory nature of diasporic temporalities: the *true* people are the liminal people. It may be argued that what Bhabha does is to route the experience of the South Asian intellectual-in-exile through the discourse of black counter-hegemonic culture. This intellectual-in-exile syndrome, however, occupies only a minor part in the South Asian diaspora in general. This is not to say that South Asians escape the problem of 'othering' in the West, nor is it to suggest that they would like to give up their own identities and become 'assimilated' in the dominant cultural order without a trace of difference. Perhaps a change of emphasis is in order here. Rather than celebrating the master narrative of diaspora as a 'slip-zone' of indeterminacy and shifting positionalities, one focuses on South Asian diaspora's widely agreed ability to re-create their cultures in diverse locations and locates the element of the liminal within the nitty gritty of this changing history. Scholars have often counterposed the reality of hybridity against the illusion of 'nameable groups' (see, for instance, Kelly 1998, Geschiere and Meyer 1998). I would like to revise this understanding somewhat and explain hybridity as the *nameable* held under the sign of erasure. The shift is one of emphasis.

Notes

1 John Davies describes Fiji's crisis of 2000 as a tragedy of 'separate solitudes'. Nothing could be more apt. He holds the Fiji Indians squarely responsible for this absence of cultural dialogue: their condescending attitude towards Fijians, their consumerist ways, economic domination and media power. The culture of indigenous people needs to be safeguarded from the globally massive Indian culture, he warns. Towards this he advocates a series of positive discriminations, including the abolition of Hindi from the list of Fiji's official languages (Davies, 2000). Davies's analysis is off-track in crucial ways since the latest crisis is a fallout of the disintegrating native Fijian social order and the rise of its middle-class leadership as has been argued by several scholars (e.g. Lal 2001 and Teaiwa 2000).

2 The literal meaning of the word *bhakti* is 'devotion'. On a broader social plane, however, it refers to the popular social and aesthetic movement that spread across India from the twelfth century onwards. Mostly a gesture against authoritarian rule, it was spearheaded by the subaltern classes.

3 Partha Chatterjee (1993) discusses this process in detail in the context of nineteenth-century Bengal.

4 Interviews with Manas Ray, Canberra, May 1998.

5 The word *dharma* in the early Vedic times referred to religiously ordained duties, rules and customs to be performed or followed for general well-being and being virtuous. During the colonial times, the meaning of the word was further corrupted to mean an equivalent of the Western notion of religion.

6 For a very innovative discussion of the fantasy space that cinema theatre creates in urban Nigeria, see Brian Larkin 1998.

7 For an early account of such communal discord between Fiji Indians and mainland Indians in Vancouver, see Buchignani 1980.

8 I thank Ravi Vasudevan for an insightful discussion of textual strategies of what I call 'diasporic Bollywood'.

9 Madhav Prasad explains the *darshanic* gaze in the following way: 'Contrary to voyeuristic relation, in the *darshanic* relation the object gives itself to be seen and in so doing, confers a privilege upon the spectator. The object of the *darshanic* gaze is a superior, a divine figure or a king who presents himself as a spectacle of dazzling splendour to his subjects' (1998: 75–6).

3 Scattered voices, global vision

Indigenous peoples and the new media nation[1]

Valerie Alia

> Inuit are nomads . . . [and] rejoice in the ability to compare opinions abroad, as they did when traveling at will . . . the hamlet is the new iglu, and the Internet is the new Land.

Thus the Nunavut journalist Rachel Qitsualik offers a cultural context for understanding the openness of Inuit and other indigenous communicators to technological innovation and change. On a global scale, indigenous peoples are using radio, television, print and a range of new media to amplify their voices, extend the range of reception and expand their collective power. The international movement of indigenous peoples has fostered important social, political and technological innovations, producing organisations such as the Inuit Circumpolar Conference (ICC) and World Council of Indigenous Peoples (founded in the 1970s but with roots going back to the early 1900s) (Minde 1996).[2] Although culturally distinct, the world's indigenous communities have collectively experienced many of the elements of diaspora. Small numbers of people are scattered over great distances, some far from their homelands, as in Oklahoma – where survivors of forced relocation landed at the end of the 'Trail of Tears', and the high Canadian Arctic, where Inuit were moved from northern Quebec. Some reside in homelands newly 'legitimated' by dominant governments – as in the instances of Nunavut Territory and Greenland Home Rule.

Starting from Arjun Appadurai's idea of 'mediascapes' and 'ethnoscapes' – new flow patterns of media and people – John Sinclair and Stuart Cunningham observe that 'whereas flows of people often have tended to be from . . . the periphery . . . towards the "centre", media flows historically have travelled in the other direction' (2001: 2). This is not always the case with respect to indigenous media. Although dominant-society media made early incursions into indigenous communities, the main movement in Canada has been from 'periphery' to 'core' – with indigenous media originating in remote arctic and sub-arctic communities and moving gradually towards the urban centres. The most recent example of this pattern is the transformation of Television Northern Canada (TVNC), based in the minimally populated northern regions, to the Aboriginal Peoples Television Network (APTN) that covers all of Canada and is moving towards globalisation.

The poverty and distortion of mainstream coverage have made it imperative for indigenous people to develop their own news outlets.[3] They are using satellite, digital, cable and the Internet to strengthen their culturally and linguistically diverse voices and disseminate information to a rapidly expanding global audience, simultaneously maintaining or restoring particular languages and cultures while promoting common interests. Their progress is consistent with Ien Ang's idea of the 'progressive transnationalization of media audiencehood' (Ang 1996: 81). However, 'transnationalisation' implies a unidirectional crossing of national boundaries and should be extended to account for instances of internal colonialism and boundaries between ethnicities and regions. The alternative is a fluid, constantly changing crossing from boundary to boundary and place to place – the *inter*nationalisation of *indigenous* media audiencehood and media production, which I have called the New Media Nation.

Pathways to broadcasting

The first indigenous broadcasts in North America were heard on Alaskan radio in the 1930s, but despite Alaska's nearly 30-year head start, Canada is presently the world leader in indigenous broadcasting. The US has moved all too slowly to support indigenous media. There are about 30 Native American radio stations nationwide as compared to several hundred in Canada. In 1985 Australia's first exclusively aboriginal station began broadcasting at Alice Springs. There are now stations at Brisbane and Townsville and an indigenous community television station at Alice Springs, and the National Indigenous Media Association of Australia (NIMAA) has a membership of 136 community broadcasting groups. Indigenous broadcasting is more recently arrived in New Zealand, where 21 Maori radio stations are linked to Ruia Mai – the national Maori radio service founded in 1990.

Canada's first aboriginal language radio programme (in the Inuit language of Inuktitut) went on the air in 1960. In 1967 the Frontier Package brought radio into 17 communities in the western Arctic and Kenomadiwin Radio began broadcasting in northern Ontario from a travelling van. In northern and remote communities, news media often begin as 'alternative' services. Northern Ontario's Wawatay Communications Society started as a trail radio rental service to trappers out on the land, with the small, high-frequency transmitters forming a community-based emergency communications system. Canada now has several hundred local stations, eleven regional networks, an emerging national radio network, at least six television production outlets and APTN, the Aboriginal Peoples Television Network.[4] Most technological and programming breakthroughs were in the north – in the Northwest Territories, Yukon, the northern regions of the provinces, and Nunavut.

Radio, the most grassroots of media, is well adapted to oral cultures, nomadic and remote-community life. Where indigenous languages are threatened, indigenous-language programming is the main attraction, with talk radio providing a forum for social and political dialogue. Conway Jocks, the founder, talk-show host and former station manager of CKRK-FM in the Mohawk First Nation of Kahnawake, Quebec, observes that 'talk radio' forges the communication links in ethnic neighbourhoods, small towns and aboriginal communities from the farthest Arctic coasts to the outskirts of major Canadian cities, sending hundreds of languages through the air' (Jocks 1996: 174). Most North American talk radio is AM, but in indigenous communities, the less costly and more easily established FM and trail radio dominate. Radio is a medium of linguistic and cultural continuity, and sometimes of survival. During the crisis of 1990, when Quebec police and Canadian military troops clashed with Mohawk people at Kanehsatake, CKRK-FM in blockaded Kahnawake was the sole connection with the outside and an essential link between the communities. At the same time, Mohawk broadcasters inside Kanehsatake were trapped in their community radio station. Marie David and Bev Nelson provided on-the-spot news and commentary which kept the community informed and helped maintain morale. The situation recalled the 1973 Lakota siege at Wounded Knee in South Dakota, where Lakota women kept the local radio station going under tense and sometimes life-threatening circumstances (Crow Dog 1991).

From the 1970s to the 1990s there was 'a quiet revolution' in Norwegian Sámi radio (NRK), broadcasting from studios at Karasjok. In 1992 it issued a mission statement saying, 'NRK shall in the coming years be one of the most important tools in the preservation and development of Sámi society' and would encourage Sámi 'to want to be Sámi' (Solbakk 1997: 190–1). The Sámi journalist, John T. Solbakk, hopes Norway's new policy will help create 'an activist radio'. Sámi in Finland, Norway and Sweden are represented by a Finland-based service which broadcasts in three languages – North Sámi, Inari Sámi and Skolt Sámi. While Danish people sent and controlled the early broadcasts in Greenland, Kalaallit were soon involved, and by the 1950s programmes were broadcast in both Danish and Greenlandic. Hans Lynge recalls that 'the radio broadcasts quickly became as necessary a part of life as food'. In 1978, a year before the launch of Greenland Home Rule, Kalaallit-Nunaata Radioa (KNR, Greenland's national public broadcaster) became an associate member of the European Broadcasting Union, establishing exchange programmes with Faroe Islands Radio, Radio Iceland and Canadian Broadcasting Corporation (CBC) Northern Service. Today, KNR employs about 120 people and has its own television building and news departments in Nuuk, North Greenland, South Greenland and Copenhagen, with a daily radio newscast in Copenhagen for Greenlanders living in Denmark.[5] Supporting its hopes of eventually providing most of its programming in Greenlandic, KNR's Greenlandic-language radio programmes increased from 2,454 in 1989 to 2,613 in 1995. In the same period, television programming showed a more striking shift, from 126 Greenlandic-language programmes in 1989 to 239 in

1995. Greenland also has a handful of privately owned radio and television stations.

The first Native American-owned and operated radio station in the United States, KYUK radio and television in Bethel, Alaska, began broadcasting in 1971. It is the only station broadcasting in the Yup'ik language and the only Inuit (Alaskan Eskimo) television news service in the US (see Alia 1999). Its television service, KYUK-TV, was launched in 1973, followed by the news-paper, the *Tundra Drum*. KYUK originated in the conditions of the Alaskan bush. 'The region had no electronic media [of its own] and could not reliably receive transmissions from elsewhere' (Smith and Cornette 1998: 29). Despite lively productions, enthusiastic audiences and the continuing need for media outlets in the state, the government of Alaska 'has been steadily reducing its commitment to public broadcasting in the state, to both Native and non-Native stations' and rural Native stations 'with few other options for raising money feel the squeeze most acutely' (ibid., 31). Perrot laments the scarcity of indigenous media in Chukotka in the Russian north, seeing the post-Soviet shift as 'le passage de la propagande à l'anomie' (1993: 149). After years of having their place marked by a symbolic empty chair and flag, Siberian Inuit attended the 1989 ICC General Assembly in Sisimiut, Greenland, and became full ICC members three years later. Recently, the ICC opened a Chukotka office, and there are tentative indications of journalistic progress and cultural revival amidst devastating environmental and economic conditions. In 1998, the ICC passed Resolution 98–14 establishing an ICC Communications Commission with a global and pan-indigenous mandate of improving communications 'be-tween Inuit and other aboriginal and non-aboriginal peoples' as well as among Inuit of ICC's member regions in Siberia, Alaska, Greenland and northern Canada.

Re/presentations on film

Nanook of the North is widely considered to be the first 'documentary' film, although John Grierson first applied the term to Robert Flaherty's 1926 film, *Moana*. Shot in northern Quebec (Nunavik) on the Ungava Peninsula in Hudson Bay, *Nanook* was the first full-length, filmed representation of indigenous people. Ironically, Flaherty's fictionalised story and characters would be consid-ered unacceptable by today's understanding of 'documentary'. 'Nanook's' 'wife', 'Nyla', was played by Alice Nuvalinga, grandmother of the former Pauktuutiit (Inuit Women's Association) president, Martha Flaherty. Just before the final credits, Massot's 1994 film about Flaherty, *Kabloonak*, tells us that 'Nyla's' real-life son is no longer alive, but neglects to mention his living descendants. The filmed construction of Martha Flaherty's grandmother as a romanticised sex object is reminiscent of the 'Indian princesses' documented by Gail Guthrie Valaskakis. Among them, Sakajawea or Sakakawea, a Hidatsa word meaning 'bird woman', transformed in popular imagery, such as a 1920s cleaning and dyeing advertisement, into 'an "ageless" and "shapely Indian princess with perfect Caucasian features, dressed in a tight-fitting red tunic, spearing fish with a bow and arrow from a birch bark canoe suspended on a mountain-rimmed, moonlit lake"' (Valaskakis 1995: 11).

Ann Fienup-Riordan examines the portrayal of Eskimos as 'noble survivors in a hostile land' (1995: 4), by actors from every cultural group except that of the people being portrayed. Such 'Eskimos' included Anthony Quinn, Yoko Tani, Gloria Saunders, Lotus Long, Joan Chen, Meg Tilly and Lou Diamond Phillips. In Canada in the 1960s, indigenous filmmakers began to make their own representations of aboriginal experiences and people. In 1969 – the year the Anik satellite system was launched, propelling aboriginal television into the northern day and night – Canada's National Film Board (NFB) produced *These Are My People*, directed by Michael Mitchell. He came out of the NFB's Challenge for Change programme, which helped to reshape Canadian indigenous communications and pave the way for TVNC. Canada's first national indigenous television documentary, *Sharing a Dream*, would not appear until 1988. The Iqaluit-based Nunatsiakmiut Film Society, which fostered Inuit film and television, merged with the Inuit Broadcasting Corporation in 1982. Today, there is a strong international body of indigenous films and an international network – the First Nations Film and Video World Alliance with members from Canada, Vanuatu, Mexico, the United States, Greenland, Australia, New Zealand and the Solomon Islands (First Nations Film and Video World Alliance 1993). The roster of indigenous filmmakers is rapidly growing. Sherman Alexie's 1998 feature film, *Smoke Signals*, featured Canadian actors Tantoo Cardinal and Gary Farmer (who co-starred with Graham Greene and Margo Kane in the 1989 film *Powwow Highway*). Métis director Gil Cardinal's 1998 made-for-television film, *Big Bear*, chronicles the life of the eponymous Cree chief, played by Gordon Tootoosis, co-starring Tantoo Cardinal and the dancer and actor Michael Greyeyes.

Medicine River, a 1996 Canadian television-film based on Thomas King's novel, features un-hectic pacing, trickster-humour, and a way of allowing a character's awareness to unfold without the abrupt conflicts taken for granted in Hollywood. The protagonist, Will, is a prominent, white-identified photojournalist who returns to his remote Alberta 'reserve' after a 20-year absence. Asked to help photograph a community project, he first refuses, saying, 'I don't do people'. While it is hard to imagine a working photojournalist saying this, the idea is pivotal: as he photographs the community's elders, Will is drawn back (and forwards) into his culture and community. His return from diaspora is made vivid by the replacement of his blonde, urban, corporate lover with an equally independent but community service- and motherhood-oriented woman from his home community. King equates loss of culture with diaspora, and cultural continuity with a return from diaspora to birthplace. The Oglala Sioux, Black Elk, took a more flexible view: 'Your world has a centre you carry with you'. He travelled from the Black Hills of North Dakota to Chicago, New York, Paris and London, declaring, 'wherever you are can be the centre of the world' (Clifford 1989).

My favourite film in recent history is *Grand Avenue*, a pilot for a US HBO (Home Box Office) series based on short stories by Greg Sarris, the former Chairman of the Federated Coast Miwok Tribe and a Pomo-Miwok from Santa Rosa, California and professor of English at UCLA. Shot mostly in an urban neighbourhood, the film counters stereotypes while allowing a range of remarkably cast indigenous actors to create subtly drawn and finely nuanced characters. A mix of voluntary and involuntary exiles, they hold on to tradition and each other in the diaspora of a multiethnic city. It is unfortunate that, despite winning the Best Feature award at the American Indian Film Festival, *Grand Avenue* has had limited distribution since its release in 1996 and has been shown in theatres only in Europe. The Inuit Broadcasting Corporation (IBC), the National Film Board, and Words and Pictures Video coproduced the 1998 documentary *Amorak's Song*, narrated by Martin Kreelak, whose 80-year-old father is at the film's centre. *Amorak's Song* had its world premiere in Baker Lake (Nunavut) in June 1998. In December 2000, the first full-length feature film produced, written, directed and acted by Inuit in Inuktitut premiered in Igloolik, Nunavut. *Atanarjuat* came out of Igloolik's independent film studio, Isuma Productions, was directed by Zacharias Kunuk, and featured an all-Inuit, all-Igloolik cast. In 2001 Kunuk received the Golden Camera Award at Cannes.

In the decades following the 1990 Hollywood film *Dances with Wolves*, Graham Greene has become one of several new indigenous 'hot properties'. Along with culturally neutral casting in several films and television shows, he has become one of the new generic 'Indians' playing a range of roles once given to non-indigenous actors such as Anthony Quinn. Greene, who is Oneida from Ontario's Six Nations 'reserve', has featured as Yahi in *The Last of His Tribe* (1992), as a 'local tribesman' in *Clearcut* (1992), as Lakota, and as a member of several unidentified indigenous cultures. Similar roles are given to Tantoo Cardinal, Gordon Tootoosis and Floyd Red Crow Westerman – an American Indian Movement (AIM) activist and singer-songwriter whose satirical 'Here Come the Anthros' illuminates the experience of many a scholar and community. While it is cause for celebration that talented indigenous actors are finally playing a range of roles (including those cast without reference to culture), it would be a mistake to assume inherent 'authenticity'. There is a need to distinguish between cultural authenticity (a construct of questionable credibility), fair and accurate representation and equality of opportunity in the workplace and marketplace.

Media, culture and technological change

The arrival of satellite-transmitted television in the 1970s marked an international breakthrough: using Telesat's Hermes Anik satellites, Canada became the first country to develop a domestic telecommunications satellite system, and indigenous people were among the first creative users. Early projects included crossovers such as the experimental interactive audio project carried by satellite across northern Quebec (Nunavik) which linked eight radio stations, run by the Aboriginal Communications Society Taqramiut Nipingat Incorporated (TNI), then affiliated with a land claims lobby group, the Northern Quebec Inuit Association.

The 1977 document *Ikarut Silakkut: Bridges-Over-the-Air*, 'described a new cross-cultural contact space' for Inuktitut-speakers of the circumpolar countries, a circumpolar cross-border short-wave radio service (Roth 2000: 251–2). In 1978, the Anik B satellite carried programmes developed by Project Inukshuk – the start of Inuit-produced television. In 1980 the Canadian Radio-television and Telecommunications Commission (CRTC) struck a committee to consider proposals for satellite television services in northern and remote communities. Headed by François Thérrien, it included John Amagoalik, the first indigenous leader in Canada to help set national communications policy. The committee emphasised the role of broadcasting in preserving and maintaining aboriginal languages and cultures and sought nothing less than a 'New Broadcasting Universe', declaring,

> Immediate action must be taken to meet the needs of the many Canadians who believe that, as regards broadcasting, they are being treated as second-class citizens . . . We cannot stress too strongly the immediacy of the problem: alternative television programming must be provided from Canadian satellites with no further delay.
> (Canadian Radio-television and Telecommunications Commission 1980: 1)

The government responded by funding Inuktitut programming in northern Quebec and the Inuit Broadcasting Corporation (IBC) in what is now Nunavut, and the CRTC licensed the private satellite distribution service Canadian Satellite Communications Inc. (CANCOM), with the stipulation that it make a substantial contribution to indigenous programming. A concerted pressure group strategy by indigenous communities and their supporters led to the 1983 launch of the Northern Broadcasting Policy and Northern Native Broadcast Access Program (NNBAP) with a commitment to fund 13 Aboriginal Communications Societies. Linked to an umbrella organisation, the National Aboriginal Communications Society (NACS), they would become regional centres for radio, television and print media services.

> At exactly 8:30 p.m., an Inuktitut voice signals the start of the world's largest aboriginal television network . . . The vision of TVNC became a reality with a montage of Inuit, Dene, Métis, Gwich'in, Kaska, Tuchone, Tlingit and non-aboriginal faces beamed to 22,000 households from Northern Labrador to the Yukon-Alaska border . . . TVNC is a non-profit consortium which aims to use television for social change.
> (Thomas 1992: 20)

The Anik satellite system brought high-quality telephone service to 25,000

Inuit in 57 communities and transmitted 16 hours a day of English-language television programming over CBC. Concerned about the relationship of television to the cultural marginalisation of northern aboriginal people, Valaskakis nevertheless predicted more indigenous language programming than ethnocide in Canada's future. Current developments would seem to support her optimism.

By contrast, television in the Sámi countries is more dream than reality. 'What should one say about something that doesn't exist?' (Solbakk 1997: 195). Solbakk considers the monthly half-hour for adults and weekly half-hour for children scarcely a beginning. His 1995 presentation to the Sámi Parliament, calling for a coherent media policy, is still under consideration. Despite many advances and slowly increasing government support, indigenous broadcasting in Australia also remains far behind that of Canada. Nevertheless, indigenous media are the fastest growing in Australia and include print, radio, film, video and television, multimedia and online services. As elsewhere, radio is the most advanced. In 1998 more than a thousand hours of indigenous radio went out weekly over indigenous and non-indigenous community stations the Australian Broadcasting Corporation (ABC) and the Special Broadcasting Service (SBS); of 94 licensed stations, 80 were in remote communities. Australia's equivalent to Canada's NNBAP and NACS is BRACS, the Broadcasting for Remote Aboriginal Communities Scheme, developed in 1987 to deliver satellite radio and television to 28,000 people. BRACS serves about 50 indigenous media associations, broadcasting on non-indigenous community radio in the language of each community's choice. In 1993, ten years after its conception, NIMAA was officially recognised and incorporated, representing 'the collective of Indigenous media bodies Australia-wide' with a goal of increasing 'availability of culturally appropriate and effective media service for Aboriginal and Torres Strait Islander peoples'.[6] In 1996 Australia established the National Indigenous Radio Service (NIRS), a satellite service somewhat akin to TVNC in Canada. ABC also produces two national indigenous programmes.

Please adjust the colour: the Aboriginal Peoples Television Network

In 1991 the world's largest aboriginal television network was born. TVNC's mandate was to broadcast 'cultural, social, political and educational programming' in English, French and several indigenous languages, to Canada's northern indigenous people, via satellite to an audience of approximately a hundred thousand. Its leaders represented the 13 aboriginal communications societies and a handful of associate member organisations. In early 1999, after several years of successful broadcasts, the CRTC granted TVNC permission to become a national aboriginal television service – the Aboriginal Peoples Television Network (APTN). APTN is run and produced by aboriginal people for a nationwide, multicultural audience who receive it as part of their basic cable television packages. The October/November issue of *Aboriginal Voices* ran a cover photo of APTN's first chair, the Inuk journalist Abraham Tagalik (a veteran of IBC and TVNC), headlined: 'Please Adjust the Colour On Your Set'. APTN is licensed to broadcast 120 hours of programming a week in English, French and up to 15 indigenous languages. Some indigenous-language programmes have English subtitles, making even the most culturally specific material widely accessible. In Whitehorse, Yukon on 10 September 2000, just after APTN's first anniversary, I tuned in midway through an Inuit current affairs magazine featuring mini-documentaries on northern Nunavut Day celebrations and a skidoo race captured with energetic and creative, experimental camera work and editing.

Strictly speaking, it is illegal in Canada to deny access to APTN; the law requires cable companies to carry it on their regular cable packages in all communities of more than a thousand residents. In reality, the placements of APTN in low-priority spots and slowness to upgrade cable services prevent many eligible people from watching. I was unable to find it on the channel selector, or by channel-surfing in my Toronto hotel room. Not all channels are accessible, especially in hotels with older television sets or in certain neighbourhoods; the array of cable companies exacerbates the problem. The experience was repeated at the grand old government/railroad hotels in Calgary and Ottawa. In Ottawa, I phoned the Chateau Laurier's service line to ask why I could not access APTN and was told, 'We don't get it; I don't know if it's a corporate decision or what'. Similarly, at the Palliser in Calgary, Alberta, no one seemed to know why APTN was unavailable. In my cross-Canada travels in 2000 and 2001, the only hostelries with APTN access were family-run bed-and-breakfast homes in Toronto's Annex neighbourhood and in Whitehorse. Recent information shows APTN on channels in the 60s, 70s and 80s in such major Canadian cities as Toronto, Vancouver and Halifax.[7]

The incomplete access comes as no surprise to observers of the debates over licensing. There was strong and organised resistance to APTN from cable operators and broadcasters who considered the idea of a mandatory, national channel carried on all cable services in the country anti-democratic. With some exceptions (e.g. CANCOM and WETV), cable operators wanted APTN to be licensed on an optional distribution basis, like other fee-based Canadian services (Roth 2000: 262). Roth considers the location of APTN on cable systems' channel grids a major obstacle to consumer access, a position underscored by my own experience and the observations of APTN Communications Director Noel Habel. He said many hotels and some residential areas cannot access the network because 'a lot of cable companies buried it at the tail end of their channel listings; a whole section of Toronto can't get it yet – Rogers took over MacLean Hunter and they've got old cables'. Older television sets have too narrow a range to accommodate a service often located above channel 60.

These difficulties aside, there are indications that APTN is reaching a wide range of locations and people, and will continue to expand its audience in future. While lobbying efforts are likely to increase, Habel said, 'Our main focus is on programming at this point, and establishing routines so the public can access the network on its website. As far south as the state of Virginia in the US, people are calling for our programme guide'. The network plans eventually to 'go global' and broadcast internationally. A CRTC decision of 5 January 2001 provided a head start in that direction, permitting APTN to increase its international television programming content from 10 to 30 per cent. With this decision,

> APTN improves its capacity to share with Canadian audiences the diverse perspectives, lives and cultures of aboriginal peoples around the world, including Australia, New Zealand, Central and South America, Greenland, Northern Europe, Asia, Hawaii, Alaska, and the continental USA.[8]

Besides broadening its international base, APTN is working to diversify its Canadian base. Since 2000, services have devolved to the head office in Winnipeg, with a minimally staffed office remaining in Ottawa close to Parliament. In its regional centres, personnel and programming APTN maintains strong ties to its northern roots, and the highest profiles remain those of the northern Aboriginal Communications Societies. Although within Canada in general Yukon is still the most marginalised northern region, its aboriginal communications society, Northern Native Broadcasting Yukon (NNBY), holds a key national position. I have come to think of Yukon cultural and media production as akin to the Wizard of Oz – using props and pulling strings behind the scenes to give this small territory a larger-than-life presence in the outside world.

APTN is addressing the need to promote itself to viewers for whom the initial thrill of its mere existence is displaced by a hunger for more original programming and better production values. To expand its audience requires active promotion and competitive production. Not coincidentally, the CRTC granted APTN permission to air infomercials, in the same ruling that expanded its global offerings.[9] An APTN staff member said he thinks the move from TVNC to APTN was especially difficult for Inuit, because the increased broadcasting in other aboriginal languages has meant a loss of Inuktitut programming. As creators of the dominant indigenous broadcaster, IBC, Inuit were core participants in the founding of TVNC. Although their role is somewhat diminished, Inuit are unlikely to stay on the media margins as APTN programming continues to reflect the dominance of the communications societies which were the backbone of TVNC. The situation merits further study of Inuit experiences and perceptions. In addition to expressing concern about Inuit participation, the staff member said APTN's nationwide mandate, by definition, dilutes established northern (TVNC) programming – one of the downsides to globalisation. APTN staff also said some indigenous viewers have a hard time finding when their language is on the air. This is partially remedied by a situation some consider detrimental – the airing of many programmes three times a day. Although partly due to lack of programming and funding, the repetition helps to bridge cross-country time differences. The current daily, weekly and speciality offerings include regional, national and international programming in English, Inuktitut, Cree, North and South Slavey, Chipewyan, Dogrib, French, Northern and Southern Tutchone, Gwich'in and other languages.

Areas for future study: the effects of national policies on indigenous media

The communications policies of different countries have restricted or enhanced the development of indigenous media. Indigenous people have been among the beneficiaries of Canada's broad support of multicultural institutions and minority media. The result is a multiplicity of public voices which, to my knowledge, is unique in the world. Such policies are not without their costs. With a focus on creating communications outlets and infrastructures, the development of transport came second. One explanation is the involvement of the United States, whose keenness to establish transport networks in northern Canada increased during the Second World War and the Cold War. However, American involvement is insufficient explanation, because Canada has long involved itself in language and minority rights and particularly in communications – thus the distinction of its National Film Board, the Canadian Broadcasting Corporation, the Aboriginal Communications Societies and APTN. While Canada has a longstanding alternative tradition of what Liora Salter calls 'constituency-based services', it has shifted from a regionally inclusive 'right-to-receive-services' approach to enshrining the rights of women, First Nations (indigenous) peoples, and multicultural and multiracial ('visible minority') communities. The 1991 Broadcasting Act specifies the right of all Canadians to be fairly portrayed and equitably hired in public, private and community broadcast media.

By contrast, the Soviet Union invested little in indigenous peoples or regional communications and greatly in transport networks in its remote and northern regions. Siberia is today experiencing a crisis, largely due to the change in government and shift away from subsidised transport. Where air travel over vast distances, at bus-fare prices, once enabled indigenous peoples and other northerners to make frequent visits among remote communities, the Russian government can no longer subsidise air travel at such a level. 'Cheap aviation used to hold communities together, and now it's a mess'.[10] There are intimations of progress. Charlie Johnson, chairman of the Alaska Nanuq Commission, told the *Arctic Sounder* newspaper that Alaskan Inuit are pleased at the election of a new governor in Russia's Chukotka province. In December 2000 Roman Abramovich replaced the former governor of Chukotka, Alexander Nazarov, who was 'widely despised for trying to halt the subsistence practices of Chukotka's indigenous people and, according to Johnson, "did everything he could to break down native organizations"'.[11] Revival of subsistence hunting and gathering is a major survival issue in the post-Soviet era, with widespread scarcity of food and fuel. Governor Abramovich has expressed support of Inuit hunting rights and has said he will collaborate with Alaskans on common problems of wildlife conservation. Whether this will enhance indigenous Siberian communication networks remains to be seen.

Except for purposes of medical evacuation and other emergencies, air travel in the Canadian north remains too costly for many, while an elaborate network of communication structures enables people to 'visit' in low-cost broadcast-space or cyberspace from home, or in community centres with public computer access. For an array of reasons which merit in-depth study, the USSR subsidised transport but not communications while Canada concentrated its support on communications-based projects in broadcasting, teleconferencing and satellite technology, and sometimes left transport links to others, or behind. It would be interesting to look cross-nationally, cross-regionally and cross-culturally at such policies to see whether communications and transport are always mutually exclusive or are sometimes linked in the priorities of sponsoring nations.

We have seen the future and it sometimes works[12]

Having negotiated the turn of both century and millennium, we have arrived at an important moment in the history of indigenous media and self-representation. Things are better . . . and . . . not. Along with the exemplary changes come the continuing media carelessness and misrepresentation, and the racism sometimes born of fear of the increasing power of pan-indigenous movements. A succession of errors recently appeared on the pages of one of Britain's esteemed national 'broadsheet', *The Guardian*. Alternating between 'Inuit' and 'Eskimos', the author attempted to use Inuktitut words but got the grammar wrong, and issued 'corrected' information which most Inuit, and most indigenous and other scholars, would dispute. Headlined 'Snowy synonyms and other famous fictional "facts", (based on a half-cited research report) Simon Hoggart's Diary declares,

> Eskimos do not have 36 (or whatever) words for snow, as is almost universally believed and frequently quoted. In fact the Inuit have two. We have far more terms for 'rain' . . . But of course the old Eskimo story will still get trotted out. It's too useful.[13]

The information is inaccurate and misleading: 'There are indeed many Inuktitut words or terms for different forms and conditions of snow. These include snow that is falling, fine snow in good weather, freshly fallen snow, snow cover, soft snow that makes walking difficult' (Brody 2001). With the story is a photograph of a man in what appears to be Invuialuit caribou winter clothing, constructing a snow house. The caption calls him 'an Inuit' and the sculpted figure behind him 'an inuksuit'. *Inuit* is the plural form of the Inuktitut word for human being; the singular is *Inuk*. The singular for the sculpted figure is *inukshuk* (*inuksuit* is the plural) and real *inuksuit* are made of stone, not snow. Clearly, indigenous journalists and spokespeople have their work cut out for them.

Apart from the continuing impact of APTN's daily alternative to 'standard' programming, there are on-going, if intermittent, efforts to improve indigenous–non-indigenous communications – both media-based and interpersonal. In the late 1990s, I participated in the Canadian Nation of Immigrants project, which, though framed in non-indigenous terms, sought to debunk myths of 'others' and create forums for community-wide and media-focused change through dialogue and a set of guidelines for inclusive media coverage. In March 2001 the Anishinabek Nation/Union of Ontario Indians, Huntington University and Indian and Northern Affairs Canada co-sponsored a conference entitled, 'The Aboriginal Beat: Building Bridges Between the Media and Aboriginal Communities', aimed at improving intercommunity relations and news coverage.

Perhaps the most important indigenous publication in recent history was the Toronto-based, internationally distributed magazine *Aboriginal Voices* – founded and published by the journalist and actor Gary Farmer. In 2000 the print version of *Aboriginal Voices* ceased publication due to financial difficulties but transformed itself into a broadcast magazine produced for APTN. In 2001 it is developing a radio magazine as well. Before it ceased publication, Farmer wrote,

> 75 years ago, we were all we had except for Saturday night radio. A hundred and fifty years ago, we were all we had. We must have been a hell of a lot more fascinating. We had to have been great storytellers. We certainly had a lot more time for each other . . . Yet, the amount of information we have at our finger tips is astounding. Access such as we have never had before . . . I wonder about our existence in the future and what communication skills will be required to survive . . . Can we live off our creativity and our ability to communicate?
>
> (Farmer 1998)

In 2001 the Kativik Regional Government (KRG) extended Internet access to all fifteen Inuit communities in Nunavik, Quebec, after other attempts to link Nunavik to the Internet had failed (George 2001: 25). KRG installed a $300,000 (Canadian) satellite dish in Kuujjuaq – Nunavik's major community, connecting all organisations except the regional health board (already linked to a high-speed health and social service network by the province of Quebec). Criticised by private cable owners concerned about losing telecommunications delivery to a non-profit agency, KRG is determined to provide affordable, high-speed Internet access, video conferencing, distance learning, wide-area networks and e-commerce opportunities throughout the region (ibid.: 25, 31).

While radio remains the chosen medium for local communication, the Internet is rapidly becoming the primary outlet for the voices of indigenous individuals and peoples, a forum for discussion and debate and a tool for global and regional constituency-building and cross-border organising. Websites are expanding and increasing, and are likely to continue to do so. CD-ROM and other multimedia technologies can provide storage for important audio and visual material – an effective way to store and transmit oral histories, materials from community and regional archives, music and visual art – resources that are currently available or are being developed in many communities. Jim Bell, editor of *Nunatsiaq News*, thinks the Internet offers a way of 'fighting back' – a chance for aboriginal people to 'send the information the other way' and an antidote to the cultural demolition that has occurred in some other media (e.g. non-indigenous television), described in the famous speech by the Inuk journalist and political leader Rosemarie Kuptana: 'We might liken the onslaught of southern television and the absence of native television to the neutron bomb . . . Neutron bomb television . . . destroys the soul of a people but leaves the shell of a people walking around'.

In the United States, the American Indian Radio on Satellite network distribution system (AIROS) now operates 24 hours a day using the Internet and public radio. Run by Native American Public Telecommunications, it has partial funding from the Corporation for Public Broadcasting and headquarters in Lincoln, Nebraska, with a website and e-mail access, and a video distribution service (VMV) with an archive of Native American videos and public television programmes available to tribal communities throughout the country. In the Sámi world, 1996 marked a turning point in the information explosion. There had been Sámi websites in Finland and Sweden and a few university servers in Norway had Sámi pages. In 1996, the Sámi youth organisations created a website offering daily updates of the Fourth World Indigenous Youth Conference, an experimental beginning which spurred other projects, including websites by the journal *Samefolket (The Sámi People)* and the North Sámi magazine, *Min Aigit (Our Time)*. Most communication is in Swedish, Norwegian and Finnish. North Sámi are better able to promote their own language, using type fonts developed by Apple, which also developed an Inuktitut programme for Canadian Inuit. Dene fonts are now available for downloading for Windows and Mac – in Dogrib, Chipewyan, North Slavey and South Slavey, languages in use in Canada's western Arctic, where the Northwest Territories Community Access Program (CAP) teaches Internet skills and helps communities develop their own websites.

For the Sámi literary scholar Harald Gaski,

'a more or less traditional Sámi upbringing in a contemporary Norwegian society in a way gives a person more than two legs to stand on, because what one gets is a rather confident rooting and foundation in both of the cultures; one stands with both legs in both cultures'

(1997: 199–200).

Grounded in cultural specificities and intercultural commonalities, and committed to the broadest possible dissemination of information, the new media nation shows signs of becoming a force for global sociopolitical change.

Notes

1 The author wishes to thank the Canadian High Commission for funding research undertaken for this chapter, including interviews with indigenous communicators. Excerpts of the interviews are cited in this chapter, which also draws on earlier publications of the author.
2 There are serious omissions from Minde's history, among them the ICC and its link to Sámi politics; the Greenlandic political and cultural movement which led to Home Rule; and the American Indian Movement (AIM).
3 For example, the caption which accompanied a series of photographs released by the Canadian government in the 1940s: 'The Eskimo is a happy, childlike nomad' (Alia 1999).
4 The words 'aboriginal' and 'indigenous' are used interchangeably here, reflecting the preferences of various peoples and locations. In Europe, 'aboriginal' tends to connote Australian people, but the word is in widespread usage in Canada. There is difficulty in adopting any one designation, and it should be noted that some people (e.g. some Native Americans in the US) have expressed other preferences – including the historical misnomer 'Indian'. Apart from culturally specific designations, 'Indigenous' is the term in widest international usage. In Canada and parts of the US, 'First Nations' refers to 'Indian' peoples who are neither Inuit nor Métis (people of mixed ancestry and culture).
5 randburg.com (2001) News and Media: Radio and TV Greenland, online at www.randburg.com.
6 National Indigenous Media Association of Australia (1998) NIMAA: 'The Voice of Our People' press kit.
7 Aboriginal Peoples Television Network, 'APTN Channel Placements (as of 1 December 1999)', Ottawa: APTN.
8 Aboriginal Peoples Television Network (2001) press release. Online at: www.aptn.ca/en/CRTCJan5-01.htm.
9 Ibid.
10 P. Vitebsky (2001) seminar and personal communication, Cambridge University, Scott Polar Research Institute.
11 *Nunatsiaq News*, 'Chukotka's governor supports Inuit hunting', 9 May 2001, 2.
12 With apologies to my father-in-law, the journalist and 'muckraker' Lincoln Steffens, who (were he still alive) might express both delight and horror at the wild array of quotes, misquotes, permutations and misrepresentations which have arisen and continue to arise from his original utterance, 'I have seen the future and it works'.
13 S. Hoggart, "Simon Hoggart's Diary: Snowy synonyms and other famous fictional 'facts,'" *The Guardian*, 22 January 2000: 10.

4 Narrowcasting in diaspora

Middle Eastern television in Los Angeles[1]

Hamid Naficy

Diaspora television as a genre

Middle Eastern television programmes aired in Los Angeles are a constitutive part of the dynamic and multifaceted popular cultures in diaspora produced and consumed by immigrant, exilic and displaced communities in southern California. These programmes are also part of new developments in mass-media institutions and practices worldwide that have resulted in the emergence of so-called minority and ethnic television and video.

Multinational and transnational media conglomerates and television networks from ABC/Capital Cities to NHK to BBC and newsgathering organisations from Associated Press (AP) to Agence-France Presse (APP) to Cable News Network (CNN) have created and dominated a model of broadcasting that might be called 'centralised global broadcasting'. At the same time, massive worldwide political, economic and social restructurings and displacements along with rapid technological advances have ushered in a new model of television that could be termed 'decentralised global narrowcasting'. This latter category, which in the United States is often called 'minority television', is neither homogeneous nor all-encompassing; it includes television produced by various peoples and communities in the USA with varying relationships to both their homelands and host land. As a result, this chapter divides narrowcasting into three categories of television: ethnic, transnational and exilic. Although these categories are flexible, permeable and at times simultaneous, and can merge under certain circumstances, there are distinguishing features that set them apart.

Ethnic television refers to television programmes primarily produced in the host country (in this case, the US) by long-established indigenous minorities. Black Entertainment Television (BET) is an exemplar of this category, most of whose programming centres on the lives and experiences of African-Americans in the United States. The homeland for many of these programmes is understood to be in the US, not someplace else. If ethnic television's programmes inscribe struggles, they are usually intracultural (within the USA) not intercultural (between the USA and geographic other cultures).

Transnational television consists primarily of media imported into the USA or of programmes produced by USA and multinational or transnational media

concerns. Many Korean, Japanese and Chinese programmes fit this category because they are imported from their respective home countries. As such, these programmes locate their homeland outside the United States and they typically minimise the drama of acculturation and resistance. This theory is corroborated by a study conducted by SRI-Gallup Organization for the International Channel Network, which noted that the channel's Chinese, Korean and Japanese viewers 'by far prefer programming produced in their native homeland over programming produced locally within the US'.[2] In some cases, reliance on imports gives a foreign government, friendly to the USA administration, direct access to American homes, thus raising legal and political issues about 'unwarranted' use of American airwaves for propaganda purposes.[3] The Korean-language broadcasts, for example, are produced by Korean Broadcasting Service in South Korea, a government-controlled body, and imported and distributed for broadcast in the United States by the government-owned Korean Television Enterprises. In addition to supplying many self-promoting programmes, the South Korean government provides 'unlimited financial and technical support'[4] that allows Korean-language television in Los Angeles to enjoy a degree of stability and security that producers of diaspora television can only dream about. As a result of such outside assistance, Korean producers of both radio and television programmes have been able to block-book prime-time hours on multiethnic stations in Los Angeles, pushing out other ethnic competitors.

Spanish-language national networks in the United States (Univision, Telemundo and Galavision) are primarily transnational and only partly ethnic, for they are produced primarily by USA or foreign multinational and transnational corporations that import much of their programming from Mexico, Venezuela and Brazil.[5] These programmes, which are often modelled after proven USA or Latin American shows, adequately address neither problems of acculturation nor issues of diversity and specificity of the various Latin American, Central American and Chicano populations living in the United States. Instead, they appear to reinforce, on the one hand, the assimilation and Americanisation of Latino populations and,[6] on the other hand, the 'Cubanisation' of Spanish-language programming.[7]

Diaspora television is made in the host country by liminars and exiles as a response to and in tandem with their own transitional and/or provisional status. Television programmes produced by Iranians, Arabs and Armenians and some of the programmes of the Jewish Television Network (JTN) fall within this classification. These programmes are often produced by small-time individual producers, not media conglomerates of the home or host societies. Thus they tend to encode and foreground not only the collective but also individual struggles for authenticity, legitimacy and identity. Even though ethnic television networks, particularly BET and JTN, are primarily focused on the cultural concerns and personalities of segments of the USA population, they also reach mainstream audiences because their programmes are delivered in English. As such, ethnic television is a form of 'broadcasting'. Transnational and diaspora television, on the other hand, are examples of 'narrowcasting' because they are aired in foreign languages, which limits their reach considerably. Diaspora television, to which Middle Eastern programmes primarily belong, is an example of the decentralised global narrowcasting model. The programmes are produced in diaspora, usually by local, independent, minority entrepreneurs for consumption by a small, cohesive population which, because of its diaspora status, is cosmopolitan, multicultural and multilingual. Such decentralised narrowcasting is thus simultaneously local and global, concerned with both present and past. Taken together, these programmes form a new televisual genre of diaspora or exile television. This is a ritual genre in that it helps the displaced communities to negotiate between the two states of exile: the rule-bound structures of the home and host societies (*societas*) and the formlessness of exilic liminality in which many rules and structures are suspended (*communitas*). The ritual diaspora television genre introduces a sense of order in the life of its viewers by producing a series of systematic patterns of narration, signification and consumption that set up continually fulfilled or postponed expectations. I have elaborated on these generic issues elsewhere (see Naficy 1993). An examination of these programmes reveals Middle Eastern societies – both at home and in diaspora – that are diverse and complex in terms of nationality, language, ethnicity, religion, culture and politics. These societies do not fit into easy dichotomies such as East versus West, coloniser versus colonised, Israeli versus Arab and Shi'i versus Sunni. In fact, diversity is a key determinant of narrowcasting that both distinguishes these programmes from one another and reveals the dense intermingling of Middle Eastern societies and cultures. At the same time, these programmes express certain commonalities that stem from not only historical and cultural affinities of Middle Eastern people but also the production and transmission of these programmes in diaspora.

Production, transmission, consumption

Los Angeles is perhaps the most ethnically diversified broadcast market in the world. KSCI-TV (channel 18), an independent station, provides around-the-clock programming in some 16 languages that is either produced in the USA by ethnic, transnational and exile groups or imported from their home countries. KMEX-TV (channel 34) and KVEA-TV (channel 52), which belong to Univision and Telemundo national networks respectively, offer Spanish-language programming only. The independent stations KDOC-TV (channel 56), KWHY-TV (channel 22) and KRCA-TV (channel 62) also provide many hours of programming in Spanish as well as in other languages. Black Entertainment Television and Jewish Television Network are available from national cable companies with outlets in Los Angeles. Rounding out this televisual menu, local cable companies air locally produced minority programmes on either a lease-access or public-access basis. KSCI-TV claims to provide the most diverse ethnic and linguistic menu of any station in the country.[8] It broadcasts the bulk of the Middle Eastern programmes; the rest are aired by cable carriers and public-access outlets. Table 4.1 lists all of the Middle Eastern programmes aired in 1992 in Los Angeles by broadcast, cable and access channels. The overwhelming majority of these programmes are produced in Los Angeles; Iranians produce the largest number and the most diverse menu of programmes (22 hours per week), followed by Jewish/Israelis (seven hours), Armenians (five hours), Arabs (three hours), and Assyrians (two hours).

Transmission by KSCI-TV and cable carriers is on a lease-access basis,

Table 4.1 Middle Eastern television programmes aired in Los Angeles, 1992*

Programme title	Language	Frequency	Length (in min.)	Broadcast channel
Arabic programmes				
Arab-American TV	Arabic/English	Weekly	60	KSCI-TV
Alwatan ('My Country')	Arabic	Weekly	60	KSCI-TV
Islam	English/Arabic	Weekly	30	KSCI-TV
The Good News	Arabic	Weekly	30	KSCI-TV
Armenian programmes				
Armenian Teletime	Armenian	Weekly	60	
Horizon American TV	Armenian	Weekly	60	KSCI-TV
Tele-USA Armenians	Armenian	Weekly	180	Public access[†]
Assyrian programmes				
Bet Naharin ('Assyria')	Assyrian	Weekly	60	Cable
Assyrian-American Civic Television	Assyrian	Weekly	60	Cable
Iranian programmes				
Aftab ('Sunshine')	Persian	Weekly	120	Cable
Cheshmandaz ('Perspective')	Persian	Biweekly	30	KSCI-TV
Diyar ('Country')	Persian	Weekly	60	Cable
Emshab ba Parviz ('Tonight with Parviz')	Persian	Weekly	30	Cable
Harf va Goft ('Words and Talk')	Persian	Biweekly	30	KSCI-TV
Iran	Persian	Daily	30	Cable
Iran va Jahan ('Iran and the World')	Persian	Weekly	30	KSCI-TV
Iranian	Persian	Weekly	60	KSCI-TV
Jam-e Jam ('Bowl of Jamshid')	Persian	Weekly	60	KSCI-TV
Jonbesh-e Iran ('Iran's Uprising')	Persian	Weekly	60	KSCI-TV
Mardom va Jahan-e Pezeshgi ('People and the World of Medicine')	Persian	Biweekly	30	KSCI-TV
Melli ('National')	Persian	Weekly	60	Cable
Midnight Show	Persian	Weekly	30	KSCI-TV
Mozhdeh ('Glad Tidings')	Persian	Weekly	30	Public access
Negah ('Look')	Persian	Weekly	30	Cable
Pars	Persian	Weekly	60	KSCI-TV
Pezeshg-e Khub-e Khanehvadeh ('Family's Good Physician')	Persian	Weekly	30	KSCI-TV
Shahr-e Farang ('Peep Show')	Persian	Weekly	60	Cable
Sima-ye Ashena ('Familiar Face')	Persian	Biweekly	30	KSCI-TV
Sima-ye Azadi ('Face of Freedom')	Persian	Weekly	60	KSCI-TV
Sobh-e Ruz-e Jomeh ('Friday Morning')	Persian	Weekly	30	KSCI-TV
Sokhan ba Ravanpezeshg ('A Talk with a Psychiatrist')	Persian	Weekly	30	KSCI-TV
You and the World of Medicine	English	Tri-weekly	30	KSCI-TV

Israeli-Jewish programmes[§]

Jewish TV Network News	English/Hebrew	Tri-weekly	30	Cable
The Diane Glazer Show	English	Weekly	30	Cable
Community Affairs	English	Weekly	30	Cable
Jerusalem on Line	English	Weekly	30	Cable
Beyond the Headlines	English	Weekly	30	Cable
Judy's Kitchen	English	Weekly	30	Cable
A Conversation with Robert Clary	English	Weekly	30	Cable
The Goldbergs	English	Weekly	30	Cable
ITN Specials	English	Weekly	30	KSCI-TV
Twenty 2 Forty	English	Weekly	30	KSCI-TV
Israel Today	Hebrew	Weekly	30	KSCI-TV
The Phil Blazer Show	English	Weekly	30	KSCI-TV

Notes

* Reflecting their exilic and diasporic status, there is a considerable flux in the fate of these pro-grammes. This table, therefore, only reflects their status in the latter half of 1992.
† The coverage of cable companies and public-access channels is limited to only a small geo-graphic segment of Los Angeles. To cover the entire area, multiple copies of programmes must be aired by a number of cable companies. As a result, not all Middle Eastern shows are avail-able in all areas. On the other hand, the signal of broadcast channels such as KSCI-TV can reach the entire area.
§ With the exception of *Israel Today* and the *Phil Blazer Show*, all of the Israeli-Jewish programmes are syndicated as a package by the Jewish Television network.

whereby television producers lease time from the station to air their pro-grammes. The cost varies from US$600 to US$2,500 per hour depending on transmission time and channel. Public-access programmes are generally aired free of charge. Some of the Middle Eastern programmes originating from Los Angeles are syndicated via tape (e.g. Jewish Television Network and *Iranian*) and others are transmitted by satellite via the International Channel Network (e.g. *Arab-American TV*, *Emshab ba Parviz* and *Aftab*) to cities across the United States with large Middle Eastern populations. The emergence in the early 1990s of the International Channel Network, run by the parent company of KSCI-TV in Los Angeles and reaching over 13 million households nationwide, has far-reaching potentials for minority programmers. Ethnic and diaspora broadcasters can reach their compatriots in other cities in the United States and aid in cre-ating a kind of national minority identity and an ethnic economy. This wider reach of non-mainstream programming by satellite also creates the possibility for national advertisers such as IBM, AT&T, Toyota, Bank of America, Crest Toothpaste and Metropolitan Life to target minority niche markets. According to the studies commissioned by the International Channel Network, the ethnic communities that it serves are upscale, with a 'higher level of disposable income than the USA population as a whole'.[9] The International Channel Network (whose motto is 'we speak your language') carries Middle Eastern programmes that are Los Angeles-originated and aired and also programmes that are not aired there, such as *Arabic Drama*, *Arabic News*, *Pakistani Serial*, *Ariana* (Afghanistan television) and *Hineni* and *Shalom Show* (both in Hebrew).[10] There are many other large cities with Middle Eastern populations (e.g. Chicago, Detroit, Houston, New York, San Francisco and Washington, DC) that support at least one local Middle Eastern programme, usually broadcast in Arabic or Persian.

There are no reliable, up-to-date statistics on the number of viewers for Middle Eastern television shows. None of the standard rating services such as Nielsen and Arbitron gauge the preferences of ethnic audiences except those for the Black Entertainment Television and the Spanish-language programmes. As a result, it is practically impossible to know with any degree of certainty how many people watch the Middle Eastern television programmes and what they like or do not like about them. The statistics compiled by KSCI-TV on its Middle Eastern audiences in 1987 are unreliable because they seem to be based largely on population figures and not on actual viewership. They are, however, important because they form the basis on which the station determined its lease-access and advertising rates (see Table 4.2). These figures must no doubt be different today due to the tremendous surge in Middle Eastern populations in southern California during the 1980s, from 144,100 to 300,000, making Los Angeles the 'largest and most diverse centre of Middle Easterners in the United States and in the Western world' (Bozorgmehr *et al.* 1996). The popular press's account of the Middle Eastern populations, however, vastly differs from these figures, which are based on the 1990 census data.[11] Complicating the determination of audiences are such factors as generational differences, subethnicity, interethnicity and cross-viewing of Middle Eastern programmes.

By and large, Middle Eastern programmes target the entire family as their primary audience, a fact reflected in the 'magazine format' of most of the programmes, which tries to present something for every family member. The engine of the diaspora television genre, this format consists of news, music, interviews, satirical skits, soap opera serials, cartoons and advertisements. Some families plan their day around their favourite shows, such as *Arab-American TV*.[12] The programmes may target the entire family, but they are often successful only in reaching either the older generations or the recent immigrants. Youngsters and second- or third-generation immigrants are usually left out or only given a nod in the programmes. Communities that support a large number of programmes, however, are able also to sustain specialised programmes. For example, *Diyar TV* targets younger Iranians by specialising in pop music. The entire programme is devoted to interviews with Iranian pop stars in exile, their music videos, and advertisements about entertainers.

Politics, commerce, religion

Under normal conditions, society's established structures tend to differentiate and regulate the roles and status of its members. In the liminality of exile, however, many traditional structures of the self and of group identity come under severe questioning or dissolve entirely. This situation encourages the forging of new or the reconfiguration of old identities and politics. Exilic liminality, therefore, is a period of profound change, one that can breed radicalism

Table 4.2 KSCI-TV's Middle Eastern viewership, 1987 (compiled from KSCI-TV data)

Nationality/language	Weekly household	Weekly viewers
Arabic	42,486	132,756
Armenian	46,350	148,000
Iranian/Persian	69,327	235,710
Israeli/Jewish	27,750	88,800

and extremism of all kinds. For a variety of reasons, the Middle Eastern diaspora television in Los Angeles tends to fall into a conservative form of political and cultural radicalism that is marked by a type of long-distance nationalism and chauvinism driven by longing, nostalgia, fetishisation of the homeland and a burning desire for return. Chief among the reasons for political conservatism is the USA capitalist system and the commercial television structure within which diasporic television must operate. The majority of Middle Eastern television programmes are commercially driven, and programme producers generate their income by selling time to businesses for spot advertisements, which are usually for ethnic products and services or government-sponsored 'ads' for national ideologies. The average income from ads placed in a single programme amounts to several thousand dollars.[13] The ratio of ads to programme matter varies tremendously. Israeli-Jewish programmes, particularly those of the JTN, carry the fewest ads, and Iranian and Armenian programmes contain the most (although not all Iranian programmes carry ads).[14] Although JTN, which packages nearly ten shows a week, carries very few ads for consumer products, it heavily promotes tourism to Israel in its programmes and in its ads for El Al Israel Airlines. It also continually urges its viewers to subscribe and donate funds to the network. From time to time, a list containing donors' names is displayed on the screen.

In the case of certain communities such as Iranians, the amount of money spent on television production, transmission and advertising is large enough to create a thriving ethnic economy that helps not only to consolidate a shared ethnic identity but also to facilitate exchange of information and business transactions among community members. However, despite such a collective economic power, as independent producers unattached to established broadcast networks, Middle Eastern programmers must seek additional funding to augment their income. Some Jewish and Arabic television programmes solicit subscription fees from their viewers. Even producers of commercially driven shows that carry many ads, such as several Iranian shows and *Arab-American TV*, buttress their income by sponsoring music concerts and entertainment banquets (*haflahs*) that generate both additional profits and programmes. Another strategy, with less desirable side effects, is the producers' practice of accepting money for on-air interviewing of celebrities and newsmakers, a practice in which some Iranian and Armenian producers are known to engage. Others are reputed to accept money from their governments at home or from opposition political factions abroad. Such assertions are difficult to substantiate and, at any rate, they shift dramatically over time.

The negative end result of such a tight imbrication of commerce and politics is both the commercialisation of the news and the politicisation of the entertainment shows. This and other factors force the producers into chauvinistic, partisanal politics, which in the case of Iranians has meant a shrill and doctrinaire anti-Islamist and pro-royalist discourse and, in the case of Armenian programmers, a vehement anti-Turkish and anti-Azeri stance. Such politicisation is evident in the preponderance of newscasts that report and music videos that depict acts of violence at home. These factors may also help explain the general disdain that many Middle Eastern viewers, especially youngsters, express about these programmes. Although most programmes tend to hide their political or religious sponsorship or affiliation, some do not. These programmes tend to be less conservative in outlook, some promoting radical change. Less dependent on market forces, they are either semi-commercial or essentially non-commercial, in that they do not carry ads for consumer products. For example, for quite some time, *Horizon Armenian TV*, whose producer was the Armenian National Committee Media Network that promoted Armenian revolutionary aspirations for a free, independent, united Armenia, was non-commercial and was largely sponsored by contributions from the Armenian community. In the past few years, perhaps in response to the collapse of the former Soviet Union, it has changed to a commercially driven format.

The relationship among money, politics, religion and diaspora television is particularly complex for Iranians. The religiously oriented programme *Mozhdeh*, produced by the Assembly of God Church, and the politically oriented programme *Sima-ye Azadi*, produced by the Mojahedin-e Khalq, a guerrilla organisation stationed in Iraq fighting to overthrow the Islamist government in Iran, do not carry ads for consumer products, but they are propaganda programmes for the respective ideologies and practices of their producing organisations. These programmes do not hide their ideologies, allowing them to colonise the programme entirely. However, another higher-quality programme, *Aftab*, much of whose content comes from Iranian government sources, engages in a discourse of subterfuge by emphasising Iranian culture and downplaying Islamist politics.

The only programme that promotes Islam as a religion and a way of life in the US is *Islam*. Produced since 1985 by Islamic Information Service in southern California, the programme appears to have three chief aims: to counteract the negative stereotype of Islam and of Muslims in the USA, to help non-Muslims learn more about Islam, and to help Muslim children in the USA feel better about their faith.[15] *Islam* features lessons and testimonials about various tenets of Islam as well as interviews and discussions with religious scholars and historians about various theological, jurisprudential and political questions. Although not openly sectarian, the programme appears to favour Sunni Islam, which is dominant in the Middle East. The programme also urges viewers to contribute financially to Islamic causes and to vote for legislation favourable to Islamic causes and Islamic values and to Muslim politics worldwide. *Islam* does not carry ads for consumer products, but it promotes a Tape of the Month Club through which viewers may purchase copies of past programmes. The programme is financially supported by contributions the producer collects from the community and from Tape of the Month Club's earnings.

Nationality, nationalism, language

Language is one of the chief markers of nationality and of national identity. Contemporary immigrants in the West have formed what might be called postmodern diasporas, communities created by voluntary or involuntary movements of people who are pushed or pulled across ethnic and national boundaries in response to rapidly changing political, economic and social orders brought on by the dismantling of the party states, the resurgence of radical forms of Islam and the globalisation of multinational capital. However, although physically separated from their 'habitus', these postmodern diasporas have not neglected their indigenous cultures and languages; instead, using electronic media, they have worked actively to celebrate and sustain them. Videos from the homeland and television programmes made in the diaspora are powerful vehicles in this process. However, using indigenous languages to establish differences between the cultures of the Middle Eastern countries and the USA tends to highlight national languages at the expense of regional or local languages and dialects of the homeland. For example, until 1992 nearly all Iranian programmes were in Persian, the national language of Iran. No regularly scheduled Iranian programme has been aired in Kurdish or Turkish, which are regional languages of significant populations in Iran (and perhaps in Los Angeles as well). Thus Iranian programmes have tended to use language nationalistically. Although nationalism demands linguistic purity, professional communication permits its violation in the interest of assimilation. Thus the first regularly scheduled Iranian programme to be aired entirely in English is a medical show, *You and the World of Medicine*, in which physicians advise viewers about various illnesses, their diagnoses and modes of treatment.

Arabic programmes, on the other hand, seem to have favoured a kind of pan-Arabism driven by Egyptian Arabic. Pan-Arabism is particularly strong in the case of *Arab-American TV*, which attempts to appeal to all religions and cultures of the Arab Middle East. Ironically, linguistic pan-Arabism seems to be informed less by a genuine desire for collective identity among disparate Arabs in diaspora than by the desire to counteract the generally negative stereotypes of Arabs in the USA by presenting a united front. However, the television shows that form the resulting pan-Arabist cultural artefact tend to suppress regional differences and the specificities of Arabic cultures, and in the end they may serve to feed the offensive stereotypes. A number of programmes are bilingual, broadcasting in various proportions of Arabic, Hebrew and English.

For example, with the exception of its short local news section, which is in English, *Arab-American TV* is presented entirely in Arabic. This strategy seems to fulfil the different generational needs of its viewers. Elder members who are understood to be more attached to the 'old country', the Arabic language and the politics of their homelands are served their programme segments in Arabic. Younger viewers, on the other hand, who are presumably more focused on their lives in the host country, are served local news (chiefly entertainment news) in English.

Of the Israeli-Jewish programmes, *Israel Today* is entirely in Hebrew. The overwhelming majority of the JTN programme package is in English. However, the use of English does not work to suppress Jewish ethnic identity. In fact, the majority of the news on the English-language *Jewish Television Network News* is about events of interest from either inside Israel or various Jewish diasporas in the world. Likewise, although the entertainment shows such as *A Conversation with Robert Clary* are in English, they tend to highlight famous American Jewish entertainers and celebrities. Such programming presumes that, for Jewish Americans, it is not the language of the broadcasts that constructs ethnicity so much as their cultural and political contents. Perhaps for these viewers other forms of artistic expression such as cinema, literature, poetry and jokes are better able to link language to nationality and ethnicity. One effect of using the English language and national celebrities is that Jewish programmes, with the exception of *Israel Today* and *The Phil Blazer Show*, locate themselves in the present United States. Jewish programmers seem to be less ambivalent about their politics of location and about identifying themselves as American because, unlike most other Middle Easterners in this country, they are relatively confident of their social acceptance and their economic and political power in mainstream America.

All Assyrian programmes, whether produced by Iranian or Iraqi nationals, are in Assyrian, and they tend to work towards preserving and propagating the religious, historical and cultural values and beliefs of Assyrians in their worldwide diaspora. All Armenian shows are primarily in Armenian, with *Armenian Teletime* in Lebanese Armenian and *Horizon* in Eastern Armenian; English-language materials form part of both broadcasts. *Tele-USA Armenians* programmes contain many films, newscasts and television materials in the original language imported from (formerly Soviet) Armenia.

Ethnicity, subethnicity, interethnicity

Middle Eastern populations in Los Angeles are ethnoreligiously very diverse, a diversity that up to now has remained largely repressed by the desire to create a strong national identity in diaspora. For example, although many Iranian Baha'is, Armenians, Jews and Muslims are involved in making Iranian television programmes, there is no programme that espouses openly the religious beliefs, cultures or languages of any one of these four groups. Instead, programmes foreground a kind of essentialist Iranian-ness. Caught in the liminality of exile in a host society that has been generally hostile to them, Iranians have stressed consolidation of nationality from a distance. Internal differences are expressed only behind this harmonious veneer.

However, the veneer is not completely opaque, for submerged ethnicity ruptures through, often in the form of commercials for subethnic products and businesses or interviews with subethnic figures.[16] *Jam-e Jam* and *Iran va Jahan* are good examples of Jewish submerged ethnicity among Iranian programmes, where Jewish businesses are advertised more heavily than in other programmes. Likewise, *Twenty 2 Forty*, an irreverent lifestyle and exercise show packaged by JTN, does not highlight its Jewishness at all, but the presence of Jewish ethnicity is inscribed in the programme in such moments as when the host conducts 'man-on-street' interviews with passers-by about the meaning of the word *kvetch*.

In addition to submerged ethnicity, interethnicity is another operating principle for Middle Eastern programmes not only during their production but also at the time of their reception. Because of the long historical intermingling of societies and cultures of the Middle East, there are many things that Middle Easterners in diaspora share, which allow them to enjoy watching programmes from different Middle Eastern countries. For example, Iranian Jews may enjoy not only Persian-language programmes but also Hebrew- and English-language programmes produced by JTN. Palestinian Arabs may appreciate the Hebrew language programme *Israel Today*, and Christian Copts may benefit from *Arab-American TV*. Interethnicity and multilingualism create intertextuality that tends to be liberatory because it allows both the unforeseen juxtaposition and overlapping of cultures and the transgression of boundaries that have divided Middle Eastern peoples. The consumerist-driven postmodernity is neither entirely liberatory nor is it universally celebrated. From certain vantage points, fragmentation and decentring may be considered to be disempowering, but the potential for interculturalism, intertextuality and transgressive juxtapositions that the postmodern diaspora offers can be regarded as its empowering and redeeming rewards.

Notes

1 This chapter is a reprint of 'Narrowcasting in Diaspora: Middle Eastern Television in Los Angeles,' in *Living Color: Race and Television in the United States*, edited by Sasha Torres. Durham, NC: Duke University Press, 1998. It has been revised slightly and is reprinted here with permission and payment for copyright.

2 'Cable TV's Perfect Niche Marketing Vehicle', 1991, p. 3.

3 David Holley, 'South Korean Ownership of TV Firm Admitted', *Los Angeles Times*, 11 February 1986, p. B1.

4 Ha-il Kim, 'Minority Media Access: Examination of Policies, Technologies and Multi-ethnic Television and a Proposal for an Alternative Approach to Media Access', PhD thesis, University of California, Los Angeles, 1992, p. 288.

5 For example, 50 per cent of the programmes carried by Univision Television Network, the leader in Spanish-language programming in the United States, which reaches some 60 per cent of the Spanish-speaking audience, is produced in the

United States, with the balance imported chiefly from Mexico and Venezuela; Claudia Puig, 'Univision President Bolts to Rival Telemundo', *Los Angeles Times*, 27 May 1992, pp. D1–2.

6 Victor Valle, 'Latino TV Re-creates USA Images', *Los Angeles Times*, 18 August 1998, p. F1.

7 In the late 1980s, Mexican Americans in southern California charged that both Telemundo and Univision were working to reduce the Mexican influence at the networks, despite the fact that 60 per cent of the 22 million Latin Americans living in the United States are of Mexican descent; Frank Del Olmo, 'TV Dispute Sheds Light on the "Hispanic Myth"', *Los Angeles Times*, 29 May 1989, p. B55.

8 The breakdown of these programmes by language on KSCI-TV is as follows (hours/week, week of 17 May 1992): Arabic 3.0, Armenian 5.0, Cambodian 1.5, Mandarin 9.5, French 2.5, Tagalog/English 5.0, German 0.50, Hungarian 0.50, Hindi/English 1.0, Persian 15.5, Italian 0.50, Japanese 14.5, Hebrew 1.0, Korean 22.5, Russian 1.0 and Vietnamese 5.0 (source: KSCI-TV).

9 Quoted from the International Channel Network's publicity material.

10 According to the International Channel Network's literature, by March 1992 the broadcast hours per week devoted to Middle Eastern shows was as follows: Iranian 8.5, Arabic 6.5, Hebrew 4, Armenian 2.

11 For example, the *Los Angeles Times* estimated that the number of Iranians in southern California alone has increased from 200,000 in 1984 to 800,000 in 1991; Charles Perry, 'Nouruz: Have a Happy Equinox', *Los Angeles Times*, 19 March 1992, p. H-1.

12 Brian Clark, 'Arab-Americans on the Air', *Aramco World* (1992), pp. 12–15.

13 In the case of Iranians, for example, producers can expect to earn from advertisements approximately $2,500 for a half-hour show and $5,000 for a one-hour show. From this must be subtracted, of course, the cost of production and airtime rental.

14 Although KSCI-TV has tried to keep ad time in a one-hour programme to twenty minutes, some Iranian programmes, to the chagrin of viewers and station officials, have frequently carried up to forty-five minutes of ads in a one-hour time slot.

15 From *Islamic Information Service News* 2 (1990).

16 On 'submerged ethnicity' in media, see Shohat (1991).

5   Mi programa es su programa

Tele/visions of a Spanish-language diaspora in North America

Heather De Santis

New global patterns of cultural, economic and political flows are characterised by the evolution of new centres of cultural production, new technologies and the spread of new media. Moreover, the task of mapping world cultural flows has to account for the asymmetries and countercurrents between and beyond the traditional centre–periphery power structure of colonial relationships. These developments have allowed previous peripheral players in the transnational export of media content, such as Mexico and Brazil, to develop a strong influence within the transcontinental Latin American cultural market. Furthermore, new patterns of human flows, such as Latin Americans and particularly Mexicans to the United States and Canada, have strengthened the demand for Latin American media products. Deterritorialisation creates new markets for cultural products which cater to the need of diasporic populations to maintain connection to and contact with their homelands (Appadurai 1996: 35). Media corporations, such as Mexico's Televisa and Brazil's Globo, are fulfilling this need and in essence creating Latin American audiovisual space by offering a historically dominated people the heightened ability to exchange cultural goods like television programming which bear shared cultural representations related to identity, such as language, history and religion, allowing for a connection to the wider Latino community.

The Latin American diasporic groups in Canada (mostly Chileans, El Salvadorians and Mexicans) and the USA (mostly Mexicans, South/Central Americans, Puerto Ricans and Cubans) form parts of the new audiences for television emerging from Mexico and Brazil. Keeping in mind Ulf Hannerz's question, 'to what extent do the peripheries talk back?' (1997: 13), this chapter provides an initial exploration of the use of Spanish-language programming particularly from the Latin American geocultural region by Spanish-speaking audiences in Canada and US. It will begin with a discussion of the concept of geocultural markets, the roles language and culture play in the connection of peoples worldwide, especially diasporas, and will provide a brief historical description of the emergence of key production houses (Televisa and Globo) which have been instrumental in the provision of programming for this language community. Moving into a more local focus, I will then provide a brief profile of Latin American populations in Canada and US and describe the availability of Spanish-language programming for these populations. Finally, this chapter will explore what all this means for diasporic Latin American groups and their relationship to the geocultural community at large, their homeland(s) and their new home(s).

The diasporic market language and culture

Many of the Spanish-speaking communities in the United States and Canada consist of foreign-born, as well as both Canadian- and USA-born, individuals, who are all connected to the larger Latin American community worldwide through real and imagined links. Cohen explains these ties that extend through the local and global:

> all diasporic communities settled outside their natal (or imagined natal) territories acknowledge that the 'old country' – a notion buried deep in language, religion, custom or folklore – always has some claim on their loyalty and emotion . . . a member's adherence to a diasporic community is demonstrated by an acceptance of an inescapable link with their past migration history and a sense of co-ethnicity with others of a similar background.
>
> (1997: ix)

The diasporic link this chapter explores is language, therefore to some extent I am grouping communities with different national affiliations together (for example Cubans and Mexicans) which within a Canadian or USA context would not normally identify with one another. Moreover, I am referring to some individuals who may be of Latin American descent who may not consider themselves linked to a 'homeland' other than the USA or Canada. The Mexican community in the USA is an interesting example here because of the border relationship that infiltrates its history. In fact, Cohen argues that Mexican-Americans are not a diasporic community, rather a border culture that has developed from frontier societies bleeding into one another to create a new, complex intermediate identity (1997: 190). I will employ the broader, simpler use of 'diaspora' as defined above, which refers to groups in Canada and the USA connected by the Spanish language who identify with an external homeland (Spanish/Portuguese-speaking nation states of the Americas) and/or the larger Latin American geocultural community worldwide.

The linkages between nations of the Latin or Spanish-speaking world have led numerous thinkers, such as Straubhaar (1997), Hannerz (1997), Tracey and Redal (1995) and Collins (1994), to argue that the United States, while undoubtedly the world leader in the trade of cultural products, is no longer the dominant force it once was as new regional centres of cultural production emerge. The seminal studies on international flows of television programming conducted for UNESCO by Tapio Varis (and Kaarle Nordenstreng for the first) in 1973 and 1984 were some of the first to identify that while a few major exporting nations dominated the supply of programming, exchange between regions was becoming increasingly important (Wildman and Siwek, 1988: 40). Mexico in particular stands out (with Brazil and Miami) as a centre of programming production for the Latin world. A common language is certainly one of the key factors in determining the countries to which Mexico exports. As Collins has noted, 'Clearly a particular language community will, all other things being equal, tend to prefer information content encoded in its own language' (1994: 135). Moreover, the high cost of dubbing and/or subtitling can be a disincentive for export beyond linguistic regions for those production centres (in poorer regions) without reasonably priced translation facilities. New centres of production, however, such as Mexico City, Brazil and Miami, have increasingly developed their production infrastructures and they now are able to dub and/or translate at reasonable costs that facilitate export to non-Spanish-speaking markets. These and other new technologies have cut production costs by one third to one quarter in the past 30 years making it easier for smaller markets, such as the Spanish-speaking market, to develop and become self-reliant (Straubhaar 1991: 44).

Bonds within communities extend beyond language to cultural ties that a number of thinkers, including Straubhaar and Sinclair, refer to as 'regionalisation' of market links. These supranational (connections within Latin America and Europe) and subnational (Quebec) links can be described as 'geocultural' (Straubhaar 1997: 291). These markets go beyond

> language to include history, religion, ethnicity (in some cases) and culture in several senses: shared identity, gestures and nonverbal communication; what is considered funny or serious or even sacred; clothing styles; living patterns; climate influences and other relationships with the environment. Geo-cultural markets are often centred in a geographic region, hence the tendency to call them regional markets, but they have also been spread globally by colonisation, slavery and migration.
>
> (Ibid., 1997: 291)

In this sense, language and cultural similarities become as crucial as geography and borders in the creation of a community (Cunningham and Sinclair 2001: 3). Therefore, programming can translate into a foreign market that shares similar cultural values, beliefs and ideas. This interdependence of regional programming has made it easier for exchanges of programming from within the Latin American geocultural region which includes (but is not limited to) Mexico, South and Central America, some Caribbean countries, the Latin-based cultures of Europe like Spain, Portugal, Italy and their satellites around the world, and to some extent France, Quebec and other communities within Canada, as well as those Latino groups in Australia and Asia (Macao, Goa and so on). Studies reveal audience preference for local programmes or programmes imported from the Spanish-speaking world community, such as soap operas (telenovelas), comedy shows and other entertainment programming (Sánchez-

Ruiz 1999). These programmes are not only in Spanish, but contain cultural references that are accessible to Latin American audiences.

Hoskins *et al.*, who use an economic lens to view this phenomenon, explain that market expansion and increased sophistication within industries have contributed to the development of 'regional platforms'. They argue that these shared characteristics of common borders, geographic proximity, language and level of industrial development allow for a 'lower cultural barrier between nations within the subsystem' (1991: 218). This understanding of a 'barrier' between nations has also been referred to as the 'cultural discount', whereby viewers in export markets are alienated from foreign programming by the culture of the home market expressed through styles, beliefs, culture and social patterns. This reduction in value affects the popularity of the show but, most importantly, it affects the price which foreign broadcasters are willing to pay (Hoskins *et al.* 1994: 143–4). Therefore programming which can translate into a foreign market that shares similar cultural values, beliefs and ideas becomes extremely profitable to export. It usually has recouped its numerous production expenses within the home market (such as fees to technical and creative personnel, the cost of set-creation and the amortisation of the costs of production apparatus and infrastructure), leaving only the cost of the film or videotape on which the programme is recorded to cover in exportation (Collins 1990: 16). With more advances and more reasonably priced video technology, this second-stock copying of domestic programming has made it even cheaper for a developing exporter such as Mexico to increase the outward flow of product within the Latin American cultural region.

Globo and Televisa

Undoubtedly, USA programming continues to be popular in most television markets; however, regional markets have become increasingly intradependent. Exchanges of programming now occur more frequently within the Latin American region. Also, many exporters have had success by adapting local programming to a USA format (such as telenovelas) which work better with audiences when the content is local (Straubhaar 1991: 50). All of this means that US programmes are often shown outside of prime viewing times, while shows from Mexico, Brazil or other exporting countries from within the region occupy key time slots. This demonstrates that the cultural discount (or cultural affinity) is a competitive advantage for Mexican products within the geocultural region (which includes both nations and the subnational level, such as the Hispanic community in the United States). The increased availability of cheap programming from Latin American transnational production powerhouses like Televisa in Mexico and Globo in Brazil make it easier for broadcasters to import shows for this particular geocultural audience. These two transnationals have enjoyed great success both domestically and across the Latin American region because they have been able to incorporate themselves into the international cultural export economy. While English-language products, particularly from the USA, dominate most of the world's popular entertainment markets, the Spanish language has been the key to Globo's and Televisa's success. Spanish is the second most widely spoken European language after English, with Mexico as the world's largest Spanish-speaking nation. Portuguese is the world's fourth most widely spoken European language with Brazil as the world's largest Portuguese-speaking country. Language has proven to be their comparative advantage with strong domestic market success as their starting point for the development of market niches that now extend throughout the world.

Both Mexico and Brazil have strong domestic markets and production infrastructures facilitated by many years of government regulation. Economies of scale have also worked in Televisa's and Globo's favour – with large domestic populations and heavy penetration of television sets. For example, Brazil has an estimated national audience of 100 million viewers that can support a vibrant domestic production infrastructure. As a result, Brazilian viewers have become accustomed to, and support, indigenous programming which has 'made a contribution to national integration, spreading among Brazilians a feeling of Brazilian-ness' (Marques de Melo 1995: 315). Domestic success, in turn, facilitates the transformation of national television corporations into transnational corporations. For example, Televisa and Globo have turned their home-market platform into international success. Collins observes

> Home market size is undoubtedly among the factors which contribute to the success or failure of information content producers in their national markets, but the relevant unit of analysis seems not to be the size of a single national market (or strictly the size of the market of a state) as has usually been argued hitherto, but rather the size (and wealth) of the whole language community within which a media enterprise or enterprises is located.
>
> (1994: 315)

The size of the eventual market contributes to the overall success of a programme which may not recoup its production costs in the home market. Since 1970, Televisa has not only been the leading Latin American programming exporter, but has also become the dubbing centre for USA programming in the region. This has resulted in the prevalence of Mexico-accented Spanish which has further opened markets for its own television output (Sánchez-Ruiz 1999). In 1997 total Mexican audiovisual exports were US$112.5 million with US$43.9 to the USA; US$43 to Latin America; US$8.1 to Europe; and US$17.5 to other countries (Toussaint 1999: 3). This success has been tied to Televisa's hold on four domestic channels (2, 4, 5 and 9) and the development of satellite communications through which it has added regional subsidiaries such as Eurovisión in Europe and Univisión in the USA, which is its most lucrative market outside Mexico (Sánchez-Ruiz 1999). Globo began exporting in 1975 to Portugal, then began dubbing its programming into Spanish to reach other Latin American audiences. It now exports to 20 countries including the international Spanish-language market, as well as Germany, the USA and Canada (Marques de Melo 1995: 327). Globo and Televisa are now the two largest television channels in the world outside the USA (Sinclair 1997: 161) and their success has increased access to Spanish-language programming for both the Latin American geocultural regional and diasporic communities located in the USA and Canada, to which we will now turn.

Spanish-language television in the US and Canada

Spanish-speaking Latin American diasporic groups in Canada are small communities compared to other minority or diasporic groups. Using the most recent Canadian census figures, 187,335 people identified themselves as being of Latin American descent in 1996 (which does not include Cuban-Canadians who totalled 4,265). The two largest groups of Latin Americans are from Chile (33,835) and El Salvador (24,125), owing to large numbers of refugee migrants, followed by Mexicans, who make up the third largest group (23,295) of the total Latin Americans. The highest concentrations of Latin Americans are in Ontario (743,425), Quebec (244,740) and British Columbia (117,895) (Statistics Canada 1996). Using the 1996 census, the population from Latin America only accounts for 0.63 per cent of the total Canadian population. Out of this total, 73 per cent identified Spanish as their mother tongue. We can therefore assume that the market for Spanish-language programming in Canada exists, but only to a limited degree.

While the Canadian market for Latin American programming is comparatively small, the Spanish-language market in the United States is significant. There are 31.5 million Latinos in the USA who account for 11.5 per cent of the total population (including Cuban-Americans). This population is expected to constitute 24.5 per cent of the total population by 2050. Latin Americans are concentrated in California (10.1 million) and Texas (5.9 million), with significant populations in New York (2.2 million) and Florida (1.2 million). Mexican-Americans constitute the clear majority of Latin Americans accounting for 64 per cent of the total Latinos. Other groups include South/Central Americans (20 per cent), Puerto Ricans (11 per cent) and Cubans (5 per cent).[1] 72.8 per cent of the largest group, Mexican-Americans, do not speak English well or not at all (Smith and Edmonston, 1997, 376). If we consider that Spanish is the second-most common language used in the USA after English and that according to the 1992 census more than half of USA Latinos speak Spanish (Rodriguez 1997: 185), we can assume that the demand for the Spanish language is significant.

Data on Latinos and television in the USA tells us that almost 100 per cent of Latino households in the USA have a television set and the average home has 2.3 sets. Research into Latino viewing patterns in the USA shows that 74.5 per cent of Latino homes receive cable or satellite television service (Tomás

Rivera Institute, 2000). Latino households also report higher viewership rates than anglophones in the USA – half of households report watching between one and three hours a day. Interestingly, the majority of Latinos watch television in both Spanish and English; however, viewing patterns differed for those born in the US and foreign-born Latinos. Latinos born in the USA report that they tend to watch English-language programming or programming in both languages, whereas foreign-born respondents watch programming in both languages and have higher rates of respondents who watch primarily or exclusively Spanish programming. Therefore the primary demand for Spanish-language programming comes from immigrants who make up 40 per cent of the total USA Latino population. DeSipio forecasts, 'Thus, if these television language patterns were to continue and if immigration were to slow, the demand for Spanish-language programming could decline over time. At present, however, the Spanish-language audience increases with new immigrants to the United States' (1998: 4). This data reveals that the diaspora is using Spanish-language programming. Moreover, news is the most widely watched programming in Spanish with 74 per cent of Latinos reporting that they watch news on Spanish-language television (DeSipio 1998: 5). While news is more likely to be produced locally, studies show that Spanish-language news programming is more focused on news from Latin America than English-language news (see Rodriguez 1997). We can infer that Latinos in the USA watch this programming out of interest in events in the Latin American region.

Overall, Spanish-language programming in the United States is now commonplace in most major television market areas. Univisión, Televisa's USA arm, has supplied imported programming from Mexico to USA cable systems and affiliates since 1967 (formerly known as the Spanish International Network). Recent data shows that through its increased ownership of stations (11) and affiliates (19), Univisión has increased its reach to over 92 per cent of Spanish-speaking households (Karim 1998: 10). The second largest Spanish-language network is Telemundo, which is owned by a consortium of Venzuelan and Colombian broadcast companies. It is available in 62 markets in the USA and reaches 7 million Hispanic households. The company estimates that it is currently available in 85 per cent of Hispanic households. There are also numerous speciality channels available to USA viewers by both cable and satellite systems including Spanish-language channels and programming offered by Fox, Discovery, CBS ESPN, MTV and CNN en Español.

Not all ventures into Spanish-language television services in the USA market have been successful – NBC cancelled its Canal de Noticias en Español, as did *TV Guide* its Spanish-language version in June 2000, without corporate explanation. It appears, however, that overall availability is on the rise as mainstream broadcasters become more attracted to the size and wealth of the growing USA Latino market. For example, in the autumn of 2000, Home Box Office (HBO) launched HBO Latino, a new mulitplex channel for films, sports and original Spanish programming. With 11.5 per cent of the total USA population, this community is the sixth largest Spanish-speaking community in the world and certainly the most prosperous (Sinclair, 1997: 161). It is estimated that the buying power of Latinos in the USA is equivalent to that of 25 per cent of Mexico's population and equals that of Mexico's working force (Robina-Bustos 1995). Some estimates put its worth at almost US$400 billion. Furthermore, this population within the United States is growing quickly with an estimated population of 100 million by 2050 (Tomás Rivera Institute, 2000) and becoming increasingly affluent (Karim 1998: 8). Therefore it can be assumed that the demand for Spanish-language programming in the USA and its availability can only increase. To this extent, DeSipio has observed that the 'richness of the Latino audience in terms of numbers and habits of watching television than other populations make it a rich prize for programmers' (1999: 18).

The availability of Spanish-language programming in Canada pales by comparison, as does data on viewership from the Latin American community in Canada. Currently, there are two widely available channels that offer limited Spanish programming. The Telelatino Network (TLN), launched in the autumn of 1984, is Canada's only quasi-national Hispanic broadcaster. It reaches over three million households across Canada and is carried by all of the major Canadian cable systems (although it is not always part of basic cable packages) and is available on Star Choice and ExpressVu, Canada's licensed DTH satellite systems. Spanish-language programming constitutes 50 per cent of the 165 broadcast hours per week (the other half is Italian) and originates from Univisión, Telemundo, Televisa and CNN en Español, among others. While most of the programming is imported, there are community programmes that address news, current events and community activities in Canada. CFMT Television, an Ontario-based multilingual television system that is available across Canada via cable, carries one Spanish-language programme, *Latin Vibes*, which is produced locally. Local stations in large cities with hispanophone populations also carry a limited amount of programming, such as CJNT in Montreal (3 hours per week) and Shaw Multicultural Channel in Vancouver, but the market is narrow. Digital services, such as Rogers and LookTV, currently offer ethnic programming, but not in Spanish. This may change as the technology allows further channel expansions through cable lines.

The president of Telelatino has commented on this narrowness of the market: 'Canadian ethnic services serve relatively small niche audiences and in some cases ethnic specialties [*sic*] already compete with over the air multicultural broadcasters and mainstream broadcasters doing ethnic programming too'.[2] For this reason, ethnic broadcasters in Canada have lobbied the Canadian Radio-television and Telecommunications Commission (CRTC) to block non-Canadian ethnic services like Spanish-language broadcasters from the USA. So far, their efforts have been successful and, it can be argued, this has resulted in less available programming for Spanish-language audiences. Survey data on audiences for Spanish-language programming is currently not available; however, some audience research shows that non-French, non-

English-speaking audiences in Canada report a high interest in gaining access to more programmes with international content (Kirpitchenko and De Santis 1999: 18). In this light we must consider that Canadian viewers can also access USA Latino channels through the satellite black market. By using USA addresses, Canadians owning compatible satellite dishes can subscribe to USA Direct Broadcast Services (DBSs) that are not licensed to broadcast in Canada. This market also includes satellite dish owners who have been able to unscramble USA and/or European satellite services with their own personal devices. While it is difficult to measure this market, we must consider that Canadians have access to Spanish-language and other programming through USA DBS which offer, in some cases like PowerDirecTV, up to 30 USA and international Spanish-language channels. Certainly, the debate surrounding access to USA and international Spanish-language channels is one that will grow more complex over time as Canadians have increased access to international programming due to technological development, and if the Spanish-speaking community in Canada grows.

In both Canada and the USA, Latinos tend to be targeted as one media market for television programming. While Latinos generally tend to identify with a national origin (Cuban, Mexican, Puerto Rican and so on), their language unifies them into one visible group distinct from the English-speaking mainstream. Spanish becomes the central means of identifying the Latino community which is perceived as one ethnic minority community. This grouping glosses over cultural differences that clearly exist between Spanish-speaking communities; however, for audience marketing strategies, language overpowers ethnicity. Rodriguez explains that the:

> nexus of the notion of a unitary Hispanic market, and so a national USA Hispanic audience, has two interconnected elements: language and ethnicity. The Spanish language became, in commercial terms, a proxy for race, class and national origin and the symbolic core of the transformation of Latinos into a national ethnic 'Hispanic market.'
>
> (1997: 188).

This link between language and ethnicity becomes the point of interaction for the linguistic community *vis à vis* television programming. The information is clearly more accessible from the viewer's point of view. However, Rodriguez argues that it is more than a matter of accessibility; rather, the production and consumption of Spanish-language programming becomes a means of reinforcing and expressing one's Latino identity (1997: 189).

Geocultural region as imagined community

The availability of programming from one's own geocultural region is relevant because television is a unique medium that serves to create and reinforce cultural communities. Even though watching television is a domestic activity experienced within the confines of one's household, individuals watch simultaneous broadcasts along with other households. Therefore the 'very act of watching with other households across the region, nation or globe makes it a social act' (Cunningham and Jacka 1996: 18). It becomes a joint ritual across the cultural community shared by a large number of participants in varying groups. Benedict Anderson's notion of the imagined community describes this contrived connection: 'the members of even the smallest nation will never know most of their fellow members, meet them, or even hear of them, yet in the mind of each lives the image of their communion' (quoted in Sinclair 1997: 11). Television is thus geared to imagine its audience as members of a community by addressing the audience directly in the first person and inviting the audience to participate in some kind of shared activity. It becomes the community's forum and means of communication across vast distances (Cunningham and Jacka 1996: 18). This connection provided by television transcends geography and allows viewers to share information that reinforces the sense of cultural community within the nation and the nation state. While the entire geocultural community may not watch the same show simultaneously, it may watch the same programmes which are shown first in the country in which they are produced and then distributed to other countries within the geocultural region, allowing them to connect with a common cultural source.

There are a number of research schools that consider the use of media, such as television, to be more than a passive activity. The uses and gratifications line of audience research argues that viewers make an active choice about what programming they watch based on a particular social or psychological need. These needs vary from information to entertainment, but also encompass a need for reinforcement of personal identity and connection to the community. Ang (quoting McQuail) suggests that this includes 'finding models for behaviour, identifying with valued others, gaining insight into oneself . . . gaining a sense of belonging, [and] finding a basis for conversation' (1990: 159). Programming from one's geocultural community provides this personal cultural reflection, but also reflection on the larger community regardless of where the viewer lives. Reception analysis also offers insight into the ways in which viewers construct meanings from programming at the moment it is being viewed. Viewers are producers and consumers of content as they interpret programming subjectively through the lens of their cultural circumstances. Communities of viewers who share the same lens, such as a geocultural community like Latin Americans, actively connect themselves to the larger community by the process of viewing the same programming. Ang explains,

> Such communities or subcultures do not have to be physically united in one location, but can be geographically dispersed and can consist of many different types of people who do not know each other, but are symbolically connected by their shared interest in a media product.
>
> (1990: 161)

Therefore television not only provides the virtual connection for geocultural groups, it can also reinforce existing cultural values of the community.

Deterritorialisation and hybridisation of identity

This projection of Latin American identity and values on the global scene is a result of the growth of the Spanish-language market worldwide and the success of exporters like Televisa and Globo. The result has been the 'Latin-Americanisation' of cultural industries as opposed to the days when Latin America was exclusively an importer of consumption goods. The Latin American community can now connect via television programming internationally, and is therefore starting to overcome its history of cultural dependency. Sinclair argues that through this linguistic and cultural connection and media corporations, such as Televisa in Mexico and Globo in Brazil, 'a kind of Latin audiovisual space is in fact being created' in spite of less lucrative markets on the platform created by Spanish colonialism (1997: 160). This new space has allowed for communications exchanges within the Latin American geocultural region not only to become commonplace, but also to be expected by members of the community.

In this line of thinking, we can challenge the notion that the centre–periphery flow of knowledge that is characterised by symmetries of input and scale is a one-way flow to the periphery from the centre. In this instance, using cultural products as our example of knowledge flow, he argues that world cultural flows have become more intricate and complex than the domination by a centre over a silent periphery (Hannerz 1997: 13). While we may not be able to ascertain here whether the peripheries are talking back per se, we can clearly conclude that their transnational conversation is being heard. The presence of Spanish on Canadian or USA airwaves provides a sense of connection for migrants to the Latin American community worldwide, but it also gives the diasporic community a presence on their host country television system. By flipping through the channels in a major USA city, one would find both English and Spanish channels (and perhaps others depending on the system), as well as bilingual channels. This linguistic hybridity of television stations reflects the hybridity of the identities of some migrant Latin Americans who find themselves between two cultures in what Homi Bhabba calls the third space. In this space, a hybrid subject negotiates cultural difference between home and host (Cunningham and Sinclair 2001: 9). Furthermore, the presence of different languages and cultures on television also reminds all citizens of the diversity of the cultural reality of their communities. Tomlinson describes this reminder of diversity:

> as global communications collapse physical distance – in this context bringing the subordinate cultures into direct proximity with the dominant one – so collapses the cultural distance necessary to sustain the myths of identity. It is as though the cultural pluralism which western modernity

exported to the rest of the world – and which destroyed the certainties of tradition – now returns to undermine its own certainties.

(1997b: 147)

The stable identity of the West (Canada and the USA) is confronted by the periphery on its own turf in a reverse cultural imperialism scenario. While we are only dealing with cultural and linguistic matters and not discussing cultural imperialism writ large, we can conclude that formerly 'unquestioned cultural assumptions and self images' based on geographic, economic and other binary oppositions may be challenged (Tomlinson 1997b: 106).

Mexican cultural theorist Garcia Canclini has characterised this penetration of global cultural influences on our local cultural experiences as deterritorialisation. Everyday life activities are no longer only local – they encompass cultural experiences from around the world (Tomlinson 1997b: 118). These cultural experiences reflect on the identities of all citizens, so that there 'is no longer any stability in the points of origin, no finality in the points of destination and no necessary coincidence between social and national identities' (Cohen 1997: 175). Moreover, groups which form part of a diaspora are deterritorialised in the sense that they must negotiate a hybridised identity based on the ties to the locale they chose to leave or were forced to leave (the homeland) and the locale in which they settled. Part of the means of informing this new identity is through media and cultural products. Appadurai argues that deterritorialisation creates new markets for cultural products that cater to the need of diasporic populations to maintain connection to and contact with their homelands. In his framework for global processes, he describes two streams of cultural flow which are relevant to our discussion here: ethnoscapes, which refer to the persons who constitute the shifting world, such as diasporic peoples; and mediascapes, which refer to growing capabilities of private and public interest to produce and disseminate information around the world, particularly images which constitute narratives of the other. He describes the point of convergence between ethnoscapes (diasporic communities) and mediascapes (global or geocultural television programming) as a point of disjuncture (Appadurai 1996: 35–8). To this end, television images blur the lines between fictional and realistic landscapes so that the audience constructs imagined worlds based on external perspectives and imaginations.

It is through the imagination that the geocultural Latin American community around the world can remain connected regardless of geographic limitations. Television programming feeds this imagination and provides the images and references transnational groups need to reinforce their sense of connection to a distant homeland, as well as their new connection to the 'host' state. The data presented here clearly reveals this need: USA Spanish-language audiences are tuning into Spanish-language programming (and more so for recent arrivals and immigrants than those born in the USA, which is logical if we assume that as immigrants acculturate they become more interested in local culture and information). Some of this programming is produced locally in the USA (particularly news), but a large portion (drama, comedy and variety) is produced in Brazil and in Mexico and other Spanish-speaking countries. As this audience continues to grow, more research will be needed to determine audience-share differences for local and imported programming. The existence of a debate within the Canadian broadcasting community, on the question of increasing consumer access to USA-based 'ethnic broadcasters' such Univisión, reveals that there is a desire from ethnic communities for greater access to these services. While it may be too early to tell whether or not these communities are talking back, it is clear that they are talking and listening to one another at unprecedented levels, facilitated by new media and emerging technologies. We can only expect this conversation to grow louder and more complex as access to Spanish-language programming for Latin American diasporic groups increases with the evolution of new distribution services and the further production and global dissemination of programming from transnational production houses like Televisa and Globo.

Notes

1 Tomás Rivera Institute (accessed 4 March 2000), 'Latino facts and statistics'. Available online at www.trpi.org/facts.htm.
2 Canadian Radio-television and Telecommunications Commission (accessed 27 February 1999), 'Transcript/Public Hearing for Third Language and Ethnic Programming'.

6 Diaspora, homeland and communication technologies

Amir Hassanpour

This chapter examines the media in the diaspora of the Kurds. While there are thousands of non-state peoples around the world, the Kurds of the Middle East are distinguished by their division among the four neighbouring states of Iraq, Iran, Syria and Turkey. These states have perpetrated genocide, lingui-cide, ethnocide and ethnic cleansing against their Kurdish populations. State violence against the Kurds has fanned the flames of nationalist movements that seek self-determination, statehood or autonomy. This nationalism is also present in the Kurdish diasporas in the West, which are sites of nation and state-building activities. The tradition of building political and cultural move-ments, governments, parliaments, armies or media in exile is rather old and well documented (Olson, 1999). What invites more reflection is claims about the enhanced ability of non-state entities to engage in disrupting the modern nation state's centred sovereignty and replacing it by decentred power centres (Luke 1997: 14). These theoretical claims about the demise of sovereignty confer on new media technologies unprecedented power in disturbing moder-nity's world order.

The case of Kurdish diasporas, especially those formed in the West, is also distinguished by the geostrategic significance of the countries that rule over the Kurds. Western powers, especially the USA, Britain, Germany and France, have vital interests in the region, and intervene in the political, cultural and media activities of the Kurds. This chapter focuses on a diasporic satellite tele-vision channel, which turned into a site of struggle between Kurdish diasporas, on the one hand, and Turkey, its Western allies in NATO and the European Union, on the other hand.

Territory and the nation state

Communication technologies enable human beings to define the contours of space and time. While the control of space is crucial for all species, it is in human societies that relationships with space are socially and politically con-structed. Physical space is divided, owned, monopolised, leased, sold, conquered, destroyed, scorched, bombed, closed, opened, assembled and dismantled. It is at the same time idealised, deified, humanised, utopianised, idolised, worshipped, sanctified, ethnicised, cleansed and purified. Space is divided ideologically into heaven and hell, eternal and ephemeral, or worldly and celestial; it is also divided into categories such as earth and sky, land and sea, terrestrial, sub- and extraterrestrial. Of all these diverse constructions, however, the appropriation of space by the state and the nation is more lasting and universal. While a state without territory is not possible (Oppenheim 1955: 451), the control of large territories and diverse populations is also not possible without a state. Modern nations, states and their territories are constructed as indivisible. Thus the nation state claims undivided sovereignty within its borders. Violation of the territorial integrity of the state is treated as treason, often punishable by death.

Poststructuralists reject these modernist constructions of sovereignty, and argue that in the emerging postmodern world the nation state is immersed in a crisis of governance: it is losing its ability to exercise undivided sovereignty. According to one observer, the sub- and supra-national nuclei of decentralised power already exercise power, in so far as sovereign states cannot determine for themselves what laws will be, for whom and why (Luke 1997: 8, 12, 14). The modern world order is, thus, changing because national and international borders are eroding, and nations and nation states are withering away.

Others envision a global civil society in which the actions of non-state actors allow theorists to challenge the representation of the state as a pure presence and a sovereign identity reflecting a coherent source of meaning (e.g. Marden 1997: 51). Here, the main concern is not the loss, real or imagined, of state sovereignty. The problematique is, rather, to deny the state a single coherent sovereign presence. This may, then, bring into play other modes of sovereign being besides the privileged figure of the state. Once the irreducibility of the state is abandoned, it will be possible to see alternative sources of sovereignty; closure may give way to new openings (ibid). These claims about the parcelisation of state sovereignty in the postmodern era are of special interest for the study of new diasporas and their communication media. If it is true that modernity's centred sovereignty is being replaced or even displaced by decentred power centres, one may assume that non-sovereign diasporic communities will probably be in a position to exercise certain sovereign powers so far monopolised by the nation state. This has indeed occurred, to a limited extent, in the Kurdish diaspora since the mid-1990s. I intend, however, to argue that this event does not support poststructuralist claims about a radical shift in the exercise of state power.

The Kurds: a non-state nation

The Kurds are often described as the largest stateless people of the world, and the fourth largest ethnic people of the Middle East, outnumbered by Arabs, Turks and Persians. However, despite their contemporary non-state status, they have a long experience in exercising state power. Much of Kurdistan was, until the mid-nineteenth century, under the rule of Kurdish principalities and mini-kingdoms. The short-lived Kurdish Republic of 1946, formed in north-western

Iran, was an experiment in modern state building, which contrasts with previous, feudal, forms of governance. In the wake of the First World War, which changed the face of the Middle East, the Kurds were forcibly divided among four modernising states: Turkey, Iraq (under British rule until 1932), Syria (under French rule until 1946) and Iran. All these nation states pursued a policy of denying them self-rule or even (except for Iraq) the status of a minority. The architects of these states used modernist, Western concepts of governance for setting up unitary structures of rule. The indivisibility of the nation, state and territory, borrowed from the West, was the most important concern of the state. The current Constitution of the Turkish Republic, for instance, is quite clear about indivisibility and integrity: 'This Constitution, determining the eternal existence of the Turkish Homeland and Nation and the indivisible integrity of the Grand Turkish State is entrusted for safekeeping by the TURKISH NATION to the patriotism of its sons and daughters' (Republic of Turkey,1995: 1; emphasis in the original).

Coercion much more than consent was the means of nation-building especially in Turkey and Iran. In fact, the modernisation of the Turkish state coincides with the creation, according to Mark Levene (1998), of a zone of genocide from 1878 to 1923. In this zone, which continued to exist after 1923, the Armenian nation was eliminated in a series of massacres leading to the genocide of 1915, and the Kurds and Assyrians were subjected to numerous genocidal and ethnic cleansing operations (see Levene 1999). The assimilationist policies of Turkey, Iraq and Iran led to numerous Kurdish revolts seeking independence or autonomy. The last major revolt in Turkey began in 1984 led by the Kurdistan Workers Party, known as PKK, its Kurdish acronym. This organisation originally sought the formation of an independent socialist Kurdish state, although by 1999 its agenda changed to cultural autonomy. The revolts were sparked by the coercive policies of the state, turned into civil wars, and were put down through military operations. These operations, involving genocide and ethnic cleansing, led to the loss of the lives of millions, the destruction of several thousand villages and the forcible movement of populations. While the majority of the displaced population resettled in the region, some were able to escape into Western countries, especially after the defeat of the autonomist movement of Iraqi Kurds in 1975.

The Kurdish diasporas in the West

The Kurdish diasporas in the West are of fairly recent origins. They are products of internal wars and a changing world order; almost half of the Kurds living in the West were part of the labour force that some European countries, especially Germany, recruited from Turkey in the 1960s. The rest are mostly refugees of various wars, which erupted in the last quarter of the twentieth century. While in Turkey, Iran, Iraq and Syria the advocacy of self-rule was equated with secessionism and treason punishable by death, the Western diasporas offered the Kurds considerable freedom for propagating Kurdish sovereignty. The absence of freedoms of assembly and expression in the Middle East was in sharp contrast with the Western diasporas, where everyone was entitled to freely publish, assemble, lobby and publicise the nationalist cause.[1] Early activism in the diaspora, however, involved little more than publicity, political recruiting within the community, limited publishing and political and diplomatic networking. In the 1960s and 1970s the most visible activities were the annual congresses and publications of the small circle of the Kurdish Students Society in Europe. The Kurdish political parties of Iraq and Iran conducted some of their activism through the Kurdish Students Society in Europe, which acted as an organ of the 1961–75 autonomist movement of Iraqi Kurdistan. Until the mid-1980s the population of the diaspora came mostly from Turkey and Iraq.

Accurate figures on the size of the Kurdish diaspora are unavailable. According to one estimate by Institut kurde de Paris, they number 1,065,000 in the following countries: Germany 550,000, France 120,000, Sweden 80,000, Norway, Denmark and the Netherlands 60,000, Italy and Greece 15,000, the USA 10,000, Russia and the Caucasian countries 150,000, Lebanon 80,000 (*Courrier international* 1999). There are Kurds in countries such as Britain, Spain, Canada, Australia and Finland, and in Eastern Europe. However, the remarkable numerical increase in the size of the Kurdish diasporas did not visibly enhance their impact on interstate politics.

The international borders which have divided Kurdistan since 1918 continue to separate them in exile. In spite of the freedom of assembly in the diasporas, Kurds from the four Middle Eastern countries have failed to unite in pan-Kurdish projects for creating an independent Kurdistan. No doubt, the idea of creating a single Kurdish state is widely shared by nationalists. In practice, however, the complex task of political organising as well as the formidable goal of creating a Greater Kurdistan have contributed to the reproduction of the borders in the diaspora. For one thing, the targets of the Kurdish nationalist movements are four different states with conflicting policies and interests. Another factor is the close ties that bind the diaspora with the country of origin. Eight decades of incorporation of the Kurds into four countries with different political systems has created a diversity of agenda and political cultures. Also, the division of Kurdistan has created linguistic cleavages, including three alphabets, terminological problems and criss-crossed dialects. Here we see a reproduction, rather than erosion, of the borders of the nation states, even extraterritorially among diasporan communities that have risen to eliminate these borders.

State-building in the diaspora

Political activism in the diaspora is shaped, to a large extent, by developments in the political situation of Kurdistan. From 1958 to 1979 activism was centred on the politics of Kurdish nationalism in Iraq. This was due to the fall of the Iraqi monarchy in 1958 and its replacement by a republican regime, which allowed open Kurdish nationalist activism (1958–61). The suppression of the movement in 1961 led to armed resistance, intermittent war and extensive repression (1961–75, 1976–91). In Iran, the fall of the monarchy in 1979, and the advent of an armed autonomist movement against the Islamic regime, gave prominence to the Kurds of Iran. Intially overshadowed by the nationalist cause of the Kurds of Iraq and Iran, the Kurds of Turkey moved to gradually occupy the centre stage after the PKK took up arms against Turkey in 1984. Although the UN-sanctioned Gulf War brought the Kurds of Iraq into the centre of world politics in April 1991 (their televised Great Exodus to the mountains, the creation of the Safe Haven, the formation of a Kurdish autonomous government in the haven and continued USA conflict with Iraq), the PKK remained a main player in the politics of the region.

A radical turn in diaspora politics occurred in the mid-1990s, when steps were taken towards establishing the founding organs of a Kurdish state in exile. These institutions of state rule were the Kurdistan-Parliament-in-Exile, the Kurdish National Congress and a satellite television channel called Med-TV. Med-TV was the crown of the sovereign state in exile, and attracted the most concentrated opposition of Turkey. All these initiatives were by the Kurds of Turkey, whose political activism was dominated by the PKK. The legislative organ of the Kurdish state, Kurdistan-Parliament-in-Exile (KPIE), opened in the Hague in April 1995. It included Kurds from all parts of Kurdistan, including some of the former Kurdish members of Turkey's parliament who were persecuted by Ankara and were able to escape into Europe (Gürbey 1996: 27). According to one of its representatives, 'this parliament in exile is a first step towards the creation of a national parliament . . . Our aim is not to remain in exile but to go back to Kurdistan and to set up a Kurdish national parliament that will represent all Kurds' (Kutschera 1995: 12).

Preparations for elections and the opening of the parliament did not go smoothly. Germany had tried, according to parliament sources, by all means available to prevent the organisation of the elections, and actually succeeded in several cases in forbidding the political meetings or festivals that were a cover for the elections (ibid.: 12). Under Turkey's diplomatic pressure, Belgium did not allow the parliament to convene its meetings in Brussels. The United States and Turkey both protested against the Netherlands for allowing the 'terrorist group' to convene their meeting in the Hague. Ankara recalled its ambassador to the Netherlands for consultation, and asked the NATO Council to convene an extraordinary session to discuss Ankara's grievance.[2] A senior Turkish diplomat revealed that Turkey called a NATO meeting arguing that the Netherlands had threatened the territorial integrity of a member state by allowing the KPIE to convene its meeting in the Hague.[3] According to an Agence France Presse news report, thousands of Turks coming from the Netherlands, Germany and Belgium (25,000 according to police, 100,000 according to organisers) demonstrated in the Hague against the Kurdish parliament.[4] Ankara declared that it would stop future military purchases from the Netherlands.[5] One goal of these actions was to warn other European countries not to tolerate Kurdish activism directed against Turkey. Turkey adopted a similar policy towards other countries which allowed the KPIE to hold meetings on their territory. For instance, Ankara helped the Chechen rebels in order to obstruct Russia's support of the Kurds and allowing the KPIE to hold offices and meetings in that country.[6] In spite of Turkey's efforts to prevent the work of the parliament, the KPIE succeeded in holding sessions in Austria, Russia, Denmark, Italy and Belgium, often with the support of local parliamentarians. In its seventh session (April 1997), the parliament decided to return to the homeland of Kurdistan.[7] The successful launching of the satellite television channel Med-TV was followed by the formation of the Congress in Amsterdam in May 1999. Its main goal was to form a national parliament and a government.[8]

Kurdish national television: Med-TV

The non-media organs of the state-in-exile were dwarfed and, at the same time, bolstered by the launching in 1995 of the first Kurdish satellite television channel Med-TV. The channel was licensed in Britain to a group of Kurdish citizens[9] in 'response to calls over recent years, particularly from the Europe-wide Kurdish diaspora, for a television station of its own' (Med-TV: 1995: [6]). The licence for the channel was issued in London by the Independent Television Commission (ITC), which requires the licensee to comply with British broadcasting codes including 'due impartiality in the treatment of matters of political controversy or public policy'.[10] Broadcasting began with a daily menu of three hours, which was gradually expanded to eighteen hours a day by late 1997. Med-TV's office was in London but most of the production work was undertaken in their studios in Brussels and Stockholm. The channel got its name from the Medes who, according to Med-TV, established one of west Asia's ancient civilisations and were the ancestors of the Kurds.

Programming was quite diverse, including three newscasts a day, in two dialects of Kurdish and in Turkish. Leaders of Kurdish political parties from all parts of Kurdistan frequently participated in debates. Viewers from Kurdistan and Europe participated in live talk shows and debates through the telephone. This inter- or pan-Kurdish dialogue had never occurred in the media. Entertainment and cultural programming included film, drama, music, theatre, science and so on. Children's programming was extensive including Kurdish language-teaching, play and cartoons. Religious programming was provided for the majority Muslim population as well as minorities.

Med-TV worked as the national television of the Kurds. It threatened the Turkish state's single coherent sovereign presence in politically and culturally significant ways. For instance, Article 42 of the Turkish Constitution stipulates that no language other than Turkish shall be taught as mother tongue to Turkish citizens at any institutions of training or education. This article has been implemented with utmost force, making many disobedient teachers, textbook-writers and publishers, and students pay a high price (Chyet 1995).

Ankara has even used diplomatic power to prevent Kurdish education outside its borders, in Denmark and elsewhere (Skutnabb-Kangas 1981: 279–80). While Kurds have individually resisted the ban on education by secretly teaching themselves and their children to read and write in their language, Med-TV provided such instruction to millions of viewers on a daily basis. For example, the programme *Roj Baş Mamosta* (Hello, Teacher!) consisted of a classroom setting where a teacher instructed children in their native tongue, using a blackboard, books and other teaching materials. Children's programming promoted one of Kurdistan-Parliament-in-Exile's slogans, which called on the Kurds to learn their language.[11] Equally serious was Med-TV's violation of another provision of Article 42, which requires that training and education shall be conducted along the lines of the principles and reforms of Kemal Atatürk, founder of the Republic of Turkey.

Although Turkey repealed in 1991 the law that banned the use of non-Turkish languages like Kurdish, the constitution and various laws allow the government to suppress the language. Broadcasting in Kurdish and even speaking in the language in public places is still illegal. Symbolic violence, i.e. making people ashamed of their language, culture and origins, was used extensively against the Kurds, who were identified as retrogressive tribal groups who resist the civilising mission of the Turkish state. Kurdish was declared as a Turkish dialect corrupted by non-Turkish languages. Many Kurdish personal and geographic names were banned and replaced by Turkish names (Akin 1995). As recently as the 1980s, Turkish embassies were trying to extend the ban on Kurdish names to refugees and immigrants in Western countries (Helsinki Watch 1988: 10; Pierse 1997).

It was clear, then, that every second of Med-TV's broadcasting undermined Turkish sovereign rule, as inscribed in the constitution and implemented by all state organs. The logo 'Med-TV', always present in the upper left corner of the screen, was an assertion of Kurdishness. It also asserted, from a nationalist perspective, Kurdish rights to statehood. The logo's colours of red, yellow and green were the colours of the Kurdish flag; moreover, the flag itself appeared frequently in the programming, ranging from news and information to entertainment and culture. The daily menu began with a grand orchestra performing the Kurdish national anthem, *Ey Reqîb* (O Enemy!). The presence of the Kurdish national flag and anthem meant that Med-TV treated the Kurds not as audiences but as citizens of a Kurdish state. Much more than a war of meanings and identities, this was a conflict between two nationalisms – one that has achieved state power and one that struggles for statehood.

In the absence of political freedoms, however, the channel was not able to report directly from Kurdistan. Television reporting requires a crew of at least one cameraperson and a reporter, which is difficult if not impossible to disguise in police states. Also needed in transnational broadcasting are studio facilities and satellite links. Moreover, it is risky for individuals to participate in interviewing, perform music or appear on the screen. However, resistance was extensive. In a society with insatiable hunger for native-tongue television, clandestine reporters and audience members used telephones, fax machines and camcorders, and smuggled videos out of the country.

New forms of violence were used against Med-TV in the Kurdish provinces. Reported cases include the smashing of satellite dishes and the intimidation of viewers, dish vendors, dish installers, and owners of coffee-houses with satellite dishes (for details, see Hassanpour 1997). Diplomacy extends state power beyond its territorial base. Turkish embassies were ordered to collect information on the financial and organisational structure of the channel and its use of the services of Eutelsat. In direct contacts between heads of state, Turkish leaders asked Britain and other European Union countries to take action against the channel. Under the terms of the Council of Europe Convention on Trans-Frontier Television, the ITC provided the Turkish government with information about the licensing of Med-TV. Ankara demanded the revoking of the licence by arguing, among other things, that the broadcasts threaten Turkey's territorial integrity and make propaganda for the terrorist organisation PKK. However, lacking evidence to connect the licensee to PKK or any political organisation, the ITC was not in a position to comply with Turkey's demands. The Turkish embassy also mobilised Turkish immigrants in England to write letters and petitions to the ITC, which repeated Ankara's disinformation against the channel, accusing it of 'terrorism' and 'hate propaganda', and calling for the revocation of its licence. A Med-TV director received threatening letters[8] while another was physically attacked by four men in a train station in Germany. On 14 December 1995 broadcasting was jammed, apparently for the first time in the history of satellite television, when Abdullah Öcalan, the leader of the PKK, was scheduled to announce a unilateral ceasefire.

If the most convenient legal action, i.e. revoking the licence, was not forthcoming, the democratic state still had recourse to other avenues. On 18 September 1996, police simultaneously raided Med-TV offices in London and its studio, Roj NV, in Brussels, while in Germany some Kurdish homes were searched. The London office's files, diskettes and computers were seized in a three-hour search by Special Branch officers.[12] The raid in London was carried out under the Prevention of Terrorism Act. The police stated that the aim was financial investigation.

In Brussels, a 200-strong special forces unit attacked the studio and detained 97 people. Everyone was handcuffed and forced to lie on the floor, forbidden to speak to each other. Five employees of the channel were issued arrest warrants on charges of money-laundering and criminal conspiracy. The special forces took files, mailing lists, videos and computers, damaged the premises, and sealed the studio. The office of the Kurdistan parliament in exile in Brussels, too, was searched. On 9 October police searched houses belonging to Kurds in six Belgian cities. The aim was apparently to seek confirmation from the Kurdish community that Med-TV raised money through extortion. On 27 October the Turkish daily *Hürriyet* wrote that the raids in Brussels followed an agreement between Belgian police and the chief of

Turkey's internal security. The arrested staff were released and rearrested several times from 18 September to 30 October when the last four were released. Med-TV's decision to expand, through cable, its delivery system in Europe invited further Turkish interference in the internal affairs of other countries.

Bowing to pressure from Turkey, France Telecom refused to renew Med-TV's Eutelsat transponder lease when it expired a year later. This was followed by the refusal of Portuguese Telecom to honour its contract. Spanish and German companies followed suit. Then, when the Polish PTT unilaterally breached a contract vetoed by the Polish government, the channel was forced off the air on 2 July. Although Turkey celebrated its victory, Med-TV resumed test transmissions on 13 August, after signing a contract with an American company, Intelsat. Ankara protested the deal and called for USA government intervention. When Eutelsat service, this time leased through Slovakia, resumed in July 1997, it was jammed (1–23 July) and Ankara pressured this country to withdraw the service.

Turkey also mobilised the private sector against the channel. Ankara was apparently involved in the resignation of three lawyers who had been working for Med-TV and in the closing of the channel's bank account.[13] According to one source, several West European banks, legal firms and other companies have refused to work with Med-TV, apparently for fear of alienating the Turkish authorities (Mortimer 1996: 29). Turkey pioneered new forms of sabotage in international broadcasting. During a live studio debate on Med-TV, telephone calls from two guest speakers phoning from their home in Diyarbakir in Turkey were intercepted and replaced with music and electronic jamming.

It is clear from the above that a separation, however limited, between sovereign rule and its territory had already occurred in Turkey. Med-TV, as a broadcaster, and Turkey, as a state, share the same land and population, i.e. northern Kurdistan, in the language of nationalists, or the south-east, in the language of the Turkish state. There is one territorial base and two contenders for loyalty. In spite of the imbalance of power between Turkey and Med-TV on the international level, the channel was not totally helpless. One of its weaknesses, the enormous cost of satellite broadcasting, was in part compensated by running the station along the lines of community television. The dedication of the staff and the voluntary work of many viewers and supporters was a source of strength. It is remarkable that broadcasting resumed immediately after the main studio in Brussels was ransacked and closed down. Med-TV was supported by non-state actors, including human rights groups, anti-censorship organisations, intellectuals and others.

While the silencing of Med-TV required coordinated efforts by several states and market forces, its survival also depended on cooperation among forces of civil society on the global level. The imbalance of power was evident here, too. The interstate system of cooperation is well established, and lavishly funded by taxes including those collected from the viewers of Med-TV. By contrast, while actors in civil society are numerous and potentially powerful, they are scattered and fragmented; they have no embassy networks, no legislative organs and no intelligence and military coalitions. Any non-state institution such as Med-TV would need considerable financial and organisational resources to rally a support that is vital but not automatically available.

Med-TV has seriously challenged Turkey's constitutional stipulation of a pure, sovereign Turkish presence in the country, especially its south-east. It established relations with Kurdish viewers not as members of an audience but rather as citizens of a Kurdish state and, by doing so, it exercised de-territorialised sovereignty. Every day, viewers experienced the citizenship of a borderless state with its national flag, national anthem, national parliament, national television and national news agency. Indeed, every day Med-TV raised the Kurdish flag in about two million homes. It was obvious that Turkey would treat each satellite dish as a Kurdish flag hoisted on the rooftops of every building in the south-east. Government authorities had, in fact, considered banning dishes in Kurdish provinces. The experience of Kurdish citizenship was further enhanced every time the Europe-based Kurdistan-Parliament-in-Exile set its foot on Kurdish homes through the channel's regular coverage. The failure of the Turkish state to silence the channel had given it, at least in the eyes of viewers, more than the semblance of executive power.[14] Many viewers saw Med-TV as the realisation of one of their dreams of sovereignty.[15]

Upon the unexpected arrival in November 1998 of PKK leader Öcalan in Rome, Med-TV was the only channel to devote its entire programming to the event, and played a major role in rallying Kurdish support for his cause. Four months later, the channel also played a crucial role in rallying protest against Turkey's abduction of Öcalan. Med-TV increased its programming from 18 to 24 hours and tried to provide Kurdish perspectives on the events and air the statements and positions of the PKK and its leaders.[16] On 6 March 1999 Turkish Prime Minister Bulent Ecevit urged his European and NATO counterparts to close down Med-TV and a Kurdish newspaper published in Europe.

The ITC announced, on 22 March, that it had suspended the channel's licence for a period of 21 days. Med-TV was given three weeks to convince the ITC to allow the channel to remain on the air. Turkey welcomed the decision and called on the ITC to revoke the licence. The Kurds and others supporting freedom of the press protested with a wave of demonstrations. After three weeks, the ITC was not convinced and, on 23 April, it served a notice revoking the licence to take effect in 28 days. In ITC's words, four broadcasts included inflammatory statements encouraging acts of violence in Turkey and elsewhere.[17] On 29 May Kurdish programmes were aired for six hours daily on Britain's Cultural TV (CTV). All the broadcasts were pre-recorded so that their contents could be checked for compliance with ITC codes. The programmes were produced by a Belgian firm, BRD, at Med-TV's studios. In June, Turkey began pressing Britain to crack down on CTV, claiming that it was making propaganda on behalf of the PKK.[18] Turkey and its

NATO supporters were able to silence Med-TV on the eve of the channel's fourth birthday (July 1999). In late July, however, Med-TV reappeared in the form of Medya TV, this time licensed in France, and with programming that was sensitive to the European standards of impartiality.[19]

Med-TV and uprising in the Kurdish diaspora

In November 1998 and mid-February 1999 the Kurdish diasporas in the West were the focus of media attention throughout the world. Abdullah Öcalan took refuge in Italy in November but was denied refugee status. Turkey's subsequent abduction of the fugitive sparked an immediate wave of Kurdish protests throughout Europe, Canada, Australia, Russia, Iran and Turkey. In the absence of freedom of assembly in the homelands, the diasporic communities staged more active protests. The ability of the Kurds in Europe and other countries to respond to the kidnapping within hours took Western governments and the mass media by surprise. One Canadian source noted:

> It is very difficult to mount a world-wide series of demonstrations – involving a lot of people – without a fairly sophisticated organisation . . . There must be representatives around the world who were contacted through the Internet or through conventional telecommunications. Critical to the whole thing is the media; it is the oxygen by which all demonstrations live.[20]

The solidity of the diaspora was, however, an instance of the powerlessness of a non-state entity versus the state. The event dramatised the powers of the nation state, especially the Western bloc, the architect of the old and new world orders. In spite of all the complex and conflictual relations that constitute the present interstate regime, Öcalan was not able to find an opening in the order where he could seek asylum. The Kurdish citizens of Europe, some of whom gave their lives for Öcalan, were unable to offer him refuge. These non-state actors were very simply dwarfed by the power of the nation state in the postmodern world order. The nation states rather than citizens decide who is treated as a refugee or terrorist. The United States played a crucial role in driving Öcalan out of his rather secure base in Syria, in pressuring Italy not to grant him asylum and in locating and abducting him in Kenya. The hero of millions of Kurds was labelled a terrorist by Washington and its allies. The two sides, the two images and the two politics were worlds apart: freedom fighter and murderer, angel and devil. It seemed that the end result was obvious from the very beginning of the globally televised confrontations between the Kurdish diasporas and the nation states in February 1999.

Conclusions

Although the Kurds of Turkey made extensive use of both the diaspora and the cracks or openings in the interstate world order, they have failed in their efforts to achieve statehood. Using satellite broadcasting and other new communica-tion technologies in the diaspora, they were able to evade the borders of the Turkish state, and to exercise limited sovereignty over the Kurdish population of the country. Their project of building a state was, however, defeated by the nation state system. The experience of state building in the Kurdish diaspora confirms the limited erosion of certain boundaries that divide the powerful and the powerless, and the state and stateless. However, this experience shows that the knots that bind the state to territory cannot be untied by communication technologies. State–territory relations are maintained also by power relations rooted in class, gender, nation, race and interstate alliances. Even some post-structuralists reject illusions of virtual geography or cosmopolitan optimism, which fail to explain, among other things, the continuing trend of nationalist revival, ethnic cleansing and formation of new nation states. These theorists admit the enduring presence of the state but reject state-centrist theoretical frameworks (Marden 1997: 39; Brown 1995).

The abduction of Öcalan to Turkey, made possible by the cooperation of the interstate system, accelerated the PKK's change of direction from pursuing Kurdish statehood to cultural rights, or from secessionism to integration.[21] In the context of a lost war, the Kurdistan-Parliament-in-Exile was dismantled in September 1999, and the Kurdish National Congress was left to work for achieving cultural and linguistic rights in Turkey.

Although the non-media organs of Kurdish statehood were dismantled, its media organ, Medya TV, remained rather intact. However, it took a new turn by adopting the PKK's revised politics of safeguarding the territorial integrity of Turkey and promoting the cultural rights of the Kurds by advocating the democratisation of Turkey's ethnonationalist political system.[22] Med-TV aimed high, acting as the national television of a state-in-the-making rather than simply recreating the culture of officially non-existent Kurdistan in the virtual form of an 'electronic little nation' (Morley 2000: 103). Accordingly, the trans-formation of Med-TV into Medya-TV involved more than a change in name. It was, among other developments, the nationalist movement's abandoning of the struggle for statehood under the pressures of the modernist state order. These dramatic transformations of the turn of the century question techno-logical determinist claims about the egalitarianism of the virtual world as well as postmodernist claims about the emergence of an open, fluid, contingent and uncertain world.

Notes

1 The class and gender limitations of civil society and public sphere have been emphasised by Marxist, feminist and other critical theories. In the West, the market has largely replaced the state as the major regulator of economic, political and cul-tural life. However, the state continues to act as the main agent of surveillance of dissidents.

2 'Turkey angered by Dutch permission for "Kurdish Parliament-in-Exile",' *Turkish Probe*, 21 April 1995.

3 'Turkey condemns the Netherlands at NATO,' *Turkish Daily News*, 12 April 1995.
4 'Manifestation turque contre l'inauguration d'un parlement kurde en exile,' Agence France Presse, La Haye, 23 April 1995 (AFP/J00245/231725).
5 'Turkey severs defence industry ties with the Netherlands,' *Turkish Daily News*, 27 April 1995.
6 For details, see Olson (1999: 96–102).
7 'Preparations for a Kurdish National Congress,' Interview with Yaşar Kaya by Thomas Rutting, published in *Kurdistan Rundbrief*, no. 10, 20 May 1997, translated by *Arm The Spirit*, 21 May 1997 (burn.ucsd.edu/~archive/ats-l).
8 Ibid.
9 This section is based on my previous studies of Med-TV, especially Hassanpour (1999).
10 Jon Davey, Director of Cable and Satellite, Independent Television Commission, London, in response to my enquiry, 13 October 1995.
11 'Kampanya 'bi Kurdî bixwine bifikre bi peyive binivise' destpêkir (The campaign 'read, think, talk, write in Kurdish' began),' *Bultena Parlamenta Kurdistanê li Derveyî Welat*, Hejmar 2, Îlon 1995, r. 15.
12 Ian Black, 'Police raid Kurdish TV in London', *The Guardian* (London), 20 September 1996.
13 My interview with Mr Haluk Sayan, Director of Med-TV, London, 12 July 1995.
14 Unable to take Med-TV off the air, Turkey helped an enemy of the PKK, the Kurdish Democratic Party of Iraqi Kurdistan, to launch a rival satellite channel, KTV, in late 1998. KTV's regular programming began in January 1999 with extensive anti-PKK propaganda.
15 For a report on the channel see Amberin Zaman, 'Swords into rabbit ears: Kurdish rivals launch TV broadcast battle across tense border,' *The Washington Post*, 4 February 1999, p. A24.
16 Andrew Buncombe, 'Diaspora hear the word on Kurd TV,' *The Independent*, 19 February 1999, 12.
17 For a list of Med-TV's breaches of the Programme Code, see ITC website www.itc.org.uk.
18 Ian Black, 'Turks want "pro-Kurd" TV censored by Britain,' *The Guardian*, 21 June 1999.
19 The daily programming in April 2000 was 12 hours (*Medya TV Magazine*, April 2000).
20 Quoted from Don Gracy, advisor to the Senate committee on security and intelligence, in Bruce Culp, "Sophisticated organization behind Kurd protests," *The Ottawa Citizen*, 18 February 1999, p. A5.
21 The PKK leader Öcalan declared in 1993 that the organisation was not seeking separation from Turkey. In 1999, he called for the recognition of the linguistic and cultural rights of the Kurds within a 'democratic republic of Turkey' (Öcalan 1999).
22 Opinion is divided over the nature of the nationalism, ethnic or civic, that underlies the structure of the Turkish state. See Muller (1996) for a discussion of the ethno-nationalist foundations of the state.

7 Banal transnationalism

The difference that television makes[1]

Asu Aksoy and Kevin Robins

A better way of listening: listen to the unexpected, no longer knowing what
one is listening to.

(Elias Canetti 1991: 82)

All across the European space now, Turkish-speaking populations are tuning in
to the numerous satellite channels that are broadcasting programmes from
Ankara and Istanbul. Just like other migrant groups – Maghrebis, Arabs,
Chinese, Indians, Afro-Caribbeans and many more – they are now able to
make use of transnational communications to gain access to media services
from the country of origin. This has been an entirely new phenomenon, a
development of the last decade, which has very significant implications for how
migrants experience their lives, and for how they think and feel about their
experiences. What, then, is this significance? What precisely is the difference
that television makes for those who live in migrant contexts? What is the nature
of their engagement with the new transnational media? These are key questions
that we want to pose in the following discussion, with particular reference to
Turks living in Europe.

We shall draw on research that we have been undertaking amongst the
Turkish-speaking populations in London, in order to see how it is that ordinary
Turkish people are relating to the new transnational media. If we are to understand what it is that they are doing with television, then we have to listen to
Turkish people talking about their responses and reactions to it. Trying to
make sense of what they have to say will therefore be a primary aim of this
chapter. What we then have to recognise, however, is that the interpretation of
what they are telling us is far from being a straightforward matter. For so much
clearly depends on the conceptual and theoretical framework in terms of which
we seek to make sense of these Turkish reflections on transnational media services. Elsewhere (Aksoy and Robins 2000; Robins and Aksoy 2001a, 2001b),
we have argued that the currently prevailing framework – which has been
mainly concerned with how transnational satellite broadcasting systems sustain
new kinds of 'global diasporic cultures' or 'transnational imagined communities' – is deeply problematical. It is problematical, we maintain, because it seeks

to understand transnational developments through what are essentially categories of the national imaginary – and is consequently blind to whatever it is that might be new about emerging transnational media cultures. In our own work, we have sought to move beyond the national mentality and its fundamental categories – those of 'community', 'identity' and 'belonging' – in order to explore alternative possibilities of transnationalism. A second endeavour of this chapter, then, will be to further open up this agenda concerning the appropriate categories for understanding what is happening – actually, what might unexpectedly be happening – in transnational cultural experience.

Migration and diasporic cultural studies

Migration and movement from one country to another, whether in the form of economic migration or asylum-seeking, has involved an experience of separation – the migrant has inevitably left behind his or her home, relatives, friends, surroundings, familiar objects and the everyday routines of everyday life. We shall be moving on to consider what such cultural transition means now for Turkish people living in London. But first – because it provides an important point of reference for our own arguments – we need briefly to consider how the theme of separation and distance has been made to figure in contemporary discourses on migrant identity. Here we are referring to accounts of migrant experience – and the recent literature of cultural, migration and postcolonial studies already contains a great many examples – that have developed around a narrative of migration as exile, loss and longing. We are concerned with a particular imagination of migration, one that has taken (what it declares to be) the drama of separation and the pathos of distance from the homeland as its core issues.

It is essentially an imagination of migration as estrangement, as Sara Ahmed makes apparent. Migration may be considered, she says, 'as a process of estrangement, a process of becoming estranged from that which was inhabited at home . . . It [involves] a process of transition, a movement from one register to another' (1999: 343). Migration involves both 'spatial dislocation' and 'temporal dislocation': it is about separation and distance from the homeland, and also involves the experience of discontinuity between past and present. Through the process of migration, a radical break is assumed to have taken place, and this break is associated with a sense of acute discomfort, involving 'the failure to fully inhabit the present or present space' (ibid.: 343). Ahmed makes it clear that there are ways to redeem the sense of alienation, ways of creating new communities to substitute for the lost community. But it seems that this kind of redemption can only ever be partial, and that the original home will continue to function as a key point of reference. What migration always involves, according to Ahmed, is 'a splitting of home as place of origin and home as the sensory world of everyday experience' (ibid.: 341).

From a somewhat different perspective – actually that of a group analyst working with Turkish-speaking immigrants in London – Seda Şengün develops

a similar argument. For her, too, migration involves a process of estrangement, associated with 'separation from the mother culture' (2001: 68), as she
puts it. 'For the immigrant things once thought to be objectively perceived are
no longer so,' says Şengün. 'There is a completely different reality. The language one always spoke does not make sense to others . . . Everyday things
which are taken for granted are either not there any more or strongly ques-
tioned' (ibid.: 65–66). This experience of cultural dislocation is again regarded
as one of discomfort (potentially it is a 'traumatic experience' (ibid.: 76), we
are told). Like Ahmed, Şengün believes that there are ways of coping with the
'anxiety of separation' (ibid.: 68). But, here again, we find the sense of a deep,
underlying antinomy of 'mother culture' and 'new culture'. 'Sometimes,' says
Şengün, 'the conflict between the new and the old culture and experiences
becomes so intense and unbearable that, as a defence, strong splitting occurs'
(ibid.: 69). Again, it is the image of splitting – this time in a more explicitly
psychoanalytical sense – that is being deployed to describe the migrant's situation 'between cultures'.

While Ahmed and Şengün come out of rather different theoretical contexts
and orientations – one from cultural studies, the other from transcultural psy-
chotherapy – their concerns are remarkably similar. Both of them are
addressing, in their different ways, that sense of loss and consequent yearning
that has seemed to be such an integral part of migrant experience. Each
draws our attention to the ever-present desire to affirm, and often idealise, the
culture of the homeland. This affirmation may often be simple and quotidian.
Şengün tells us that the 'own' culture may function 'like a teddy bear during
the mother's absence': 'Familiar tastes, smells, tunes and gestures provide con-
tainment and comfort, reducing the anxiety of separation. When a migrant
eats food which is specific to his original country, or listens to a song in his
own language, he is immediately linked to his past and his own culture' (ibid.:
68). At other times, in other contexts, holding on to the lost culture may
assume more epic and dramatic dimensions, and involve the invocation of a
'mythic past', as Ahmed (1999: 342) puts it. As an example of this tendency
towards mythologisation, we might cite from Eva Hoffman's acclaimed autobi-
ography, *Lost in Translation*, where the experience of separation is conceived in
terms of a fall from paradise. 'Loss', says Hoffman, 'is a magical preservative.
Time stops at the point of severance, and no subsequent impressions muddy
the water you have in mind. The house, the garden, the country you have lost
remain forever as you remember them. Nostalgia – that most lyrical of feelings
– crystallises around these images like amber' (1991: 115). Nostalgia is, as
Vladimir Jankélévitch (1974: 346) observes, a melancholy brought about by
'awareness of something other, awareness of somewhere else, awareness of a
contrast between past and present, and between present and future' – and
migrations have created the conditions for its most intense and elaborated
forms of expression.

Estrangement from the 'mother' culture, distantiation from the place of
origin, processes of splitting, involving idealisation of, and nostalgia for, the

'homeland' – these have all by now become familiar (if not over-familiar) themes. We have briefly introduced the theoretical – and evocative – elements of what has become something of a conventional stance in diasporic cultural studies. And we have done so in order to be able to go on now and reflect on how it might be possible to move beyond these established and routine tropes. For we ourselves have considerable difficulties with this diasporic agenda. As Roger Rouse (1995: 356) has argued, it involves 'asserting and organising around either revalorised versions of ascribed identities or new ones that the (im)migrants develop for themselves'. This is an agenda that regards individuals as socially or culturally derived and driven – an agenda that works to perpetuate the 'assumption that the possession of identities and processes of identity formation are universal aspects of human experience' (Rouse 1995: 356). Our fundamental problem with diasporic cultural studies is that, in the end, it remains caught up in the mentality of imagined communities, cultures and identities – which is grounded essentially in the national mentality.

In the present discussion, we do not want to enter directly into a theoretical discussion of the categories of culture and identity that are being proposed in these analyses of diasporic communities. Our critique will assume a more oblique form, moving the argument into an empirical frame, via an exploration of certain new developments in migration that cannot be made sense of within this diasporic cultural frame (and may actually be affecting the conditions of possibility of the diasporic imagination). We want to consider new practices that seem to open up alternative, and potentially more productive, dimensions of migrant experience. We are concerned with the kind of developments described by Alejandro Portes and his colleagues, in which 'a growing number of persons . . . live dual lives: speaking two languages, having homes in two countries, and making a living through continuous regular contact across national borders' (Portes *et al.* 1999: 217). Through a 'thick web of regular instantaneous communication and easy personal travel' (ibid.: 227), it is argued, migrants are now routinely able to establish transnational communities that exist across two, or more, cultural spaces. In what follows, we want to look at how these new kinds of transnational networking and mobility may now be changing the nature of migrant experience and thinking. We shall be concerned with the cultural potential that may be inherent in these transnational developments. Like Roger Rouse (1995: 370–373), we shall be attentive to the possibilities that these new connections may be creating for moving beyond identity and imagined community.

To come now to the particularities of our Turkish case study, we may say that it provides an excellent example of the new kinds of transnational connection that Portes and his colleagues are signalling. The relative proximity of Turkey to Western Europe, the availability of cheap and frequent flights and the recent proliferation of new media services and communications links are developments that are now making it possible for Turks living in Europe to achieve a new mobility across cultural spaces.

Here we shall focus on what we regard as *the* key innovation in the lives of

Turkish migrants – which is simply the ability to routinely watch television from Turkey, and to be thereby in synchronised contact with everyday life and events in Turkey (we should note here that, for the most part, Turkish satellite broadcasting provides access to services being watched in Turkey; there are very few services targeted specifically at 'Turks abroad'). What we are arguing is that the arrival of Turkish television has made a difference – a crucial difference – for Turkish-speaking immigrants living in Europe. But what precisely is the nature of that difference? If we were to put it in the terms of diasporic cultural theory, we might say that transnational television has introduced completely new dynamics into the management of separation and distance.

The difference that television makes

There is a growing body of work on transnational communications within the framework of diasporic cultural studies. Here it is being argued that new media technologies are making it possible to transcend the distances that have separated 'diasporic communities' around the world from their 'communities of origin'. 'Diasporic media' are said to be providing new means to promote transnational bonding, and thereby sustain (ethnic, national or religious) identities and cultures at-a-distance. They are being thought about in terms of the possibilities they offer for dislocated belonging among migrant communities anxious to maintain their identification with the 'homeland' (and the basic premise is that this kind of belonging must be the primary aspiration of any and every such 'community').

Now, of course we can recognise a certain kind of truth in this argument. From our own work on Turkish migrants in London, it is clear that access to Turkish-language media can, indeed, be important for overcoming the migrant's experience of cultural separation. But if there is some kind of truth here, we would say that it is only a very meagre and partial truth. The problem with diasporic media studies is that its interests and concern generally come to an end at this point. The enquiry is brought to a premature halt, with the ready acceptance that transnational broadcasting does in fact, and quite unproblematically, support the long-distance cohesion of transnational 'imagined communities' – and without ever confronting what it is that might be new and different about the experience of transnational broadcasting. Because it has been principally concerned with acts of bonding and belonging, the diasporic agenda has generally been blind to what else might be happening when migrants are, apparently, connecting in to the 'homeland' culture. The limits of diasporic media studies come from the readiness to believe and accept that migrant audiences are all behaving as the conventional and conforming members of 'diasporic communities'.

The problem is simply that the theoretical categories available to diasporic media and cultural studies make it difficult to see anything other than diasporic forms of behaviour. Individuals are derived from the social orders to which they 'belong'; they amount to little more than their membership of, and participation in, any particular 'imagined community'. This is clearly an example of the kind of social theory that is powerfully criticised by Anthony Cohen, an approach that treats society as an ontology 'which somehow becomes independent of its own members, and assumes that the self is required continuously to adjust to it' (1994: 21). In this kind of approach there is no place for self-awareness and self-consciousness – and, as Cohen argues, by neglecting self-consciousness, we inevitably perpetuate fictions in our descriptions of other people' (ibid.: 191). To see anything more than diasporic behaviour in migrant audiences, it is necessary to introduce the category of the self-conscious individual, who is 'someone who can reflect on her or his experience of and position in society, of "being oneself"' (ibid.: 65). As Cohen says, the imperative should be 'to elicit and describe the thoughts and senti-ments of individuals which we otherwise gloss over in the generalisations we derive from collective social categories' (ibid.: 4). The crucial point is that indi-viduals are endowed with the capacity for both emotion (feelings, moods) and thought (reflecting, comparing, interpreting, judging and so on). We should be concerned, then, with their minds and sensibilities, and not their cultures or identities – with how they think, rather than how they belong.

It is in such terms as these that we now want to think about the experi-ences of Turkish migrants living in London. What do they think and feel about Turkish channels and programming? What is the difference that transnational television has made for London Turks? We will start from the crucial question of distance – from the idea that the new media systems can now work to bridge global distances. And we will do so by reflecting on what this seemingly straightforward idea might actually mean. In the frame of dias-poric cultural studies, we suggest, it is about the maintenance of at-a-distance ties; about the supposed capacity of transnational media to connect migrant communities back to the cultural space of their distant 'homeland'. On the basis of our own research, we would characterise what is happening somewhat differently: in terms of how – in the case of our informants – transnational media can now bring Turkish cultural products and services to them in London, and of how 'Turkey' is consequently brought closer to them. As one focus group participant puts it, '[I]t gives you more freedom, because you don't feel so far away, because it's only six foot away from you, you don't feel so far away from it. Cyprus is like one switch of a button away, or Turkey even, mainland Turkey, you are there, aren't you?' (Focus group, Enfield, 21 April 2000). Even a young woman who migrated when she was quite young, and who is therefore not really familiar with the country, has this sense of greater proximity to the actuality of Turkey. She thinks that it is very good to be able to watch satellite television 'because you too can see what's been going on in Turkey, the news . . . I used to think that Turkey was a different kind of place [*başka bir yer*]. It's bringing it [Turkey] closer [*yakınlaştırıyor*]' (Focus group, Islington, London, 29 March 1999). Television makes a difference because it is in its nature – in the nature of television as a medium – to bring things closer to its viewers.

In one of our group discussions, two women tell us of how satellite television now allows them to be synchronised with Turkish realities. 'Most certainly [Turkish] television is useful for us,' says one. 'It's almost as if we're living in Turkey, as if nothing has really changed for us.' The other confirmed this, saying, 'When you're home, you feel as if you are in Turkey. Our homes are already decorated Turkish style, everything about me is Turkish, and when I'm watching television too' (Focus group, Hackney, London, 7 December 1999). The key issue here is to do with the meaning of this feeling of 'as if nothing has really changed for us'. In the context of the diasporic agenda, this feeling of synchronisation would be thought of in terms of long-distance bonding with the 'homeland', the maintenance of at-a-distance links with a faraway 'somewhere else'. For us, in contrast, it is simply about the availability in London of imported things from Turkey – where we might regard the availability of television programmes as being on a continuum with the (equally common) availability of food, clothes or furnishings from Turkey. 'Nothing has really changed' does not refer to ethno-cultural re-connection to some imagined 'homeland', but simply to the possibility of having access in London now to Turkish consumer goods and the world of Turkish consumer culture. It is 'almost as if we're living in Turkey' in that sense, being Turkish in London, that is to say, and not at all in the sense of 'being taken back home'.

Television brings the ordinary, banal reality of Turkish life to the migrants living in London. The key to understanding transnational Turkish television is its relation to banality. Jankélévitch notes how people who are in exile can imagine they are living double lives, carrying around within them 'inner voices . . . the voices of the past and of the distant city', while at the same time submitting to 'the banal and turbulent life of everyday action' (1974: 346). This is precisely the mechanism of splitting – where the banality of the 'here and now' provides the stimulus for nostalgic dreams and fantasies about the 'there and then'. Now, what we regard as significant about transnational television is that, as a consequence of bringing the mundane, everyday reality of Turkey 'closer', it is undermining this false polarising logic. The 'here and now' reality of Turkish media culture disturbs the imagination of a 'there and then' Turkey – thereby working against the romance of diaspora-as-exile, against the tendency to false idealisation of the 'homeland'. We might say, then, that transnational Turkish television is an agent of cultural de-mythologisation.

This process of de-mythologisation can work in different ways. Here we will give two examples of how television can be used as a kind of reality-testing device. The first comes from an interview with an active member of London's Turkish-Cypriot population, a man in his forties who has been settled in Britain for many years. We find ourselves discussing the question of young people, relationships and the family, and he expresses quite critical opinions about what he clearly regards as the out-of-date morality of the Turkish-Cypriot community. 'In many ways,' he says,

you become almost frozen in your understanding of where your community is. The longer you are here the more you are likely to have views
and attitudes that are more conservative and out of date. I've seen people
my age and even younger, expecting things of their children that they
have rebelled against.

He then moves on to suggest that transnational television could actually play a
positive role in countering this migrant conservatism. 'In many ways,' he
comments,

> I wish they would watch more Turkish television. Some of their attitudes
> are far behind what the messages are. You turn on the Turkish television,
> and some of it is refreshingly modern. It's quite normal to watch people
> having affairs, or who are having relationships, who aren't married, on
> Turkish television. You would never have had that twenty years ago. But
> some of the mindset is relating to that. The first time a girl is having a rela-
> tionship is when they get married – you see that with second-generation
> people. They don't get that from satellite. They get it from their parents.
>
> (interview, London, 20 April 2000)

What he is arguing is that television programmes and images that show how
life and morals are in Turkey now can serve as a valuable corrective to
migrant attitudes that, he believes, have become stuck in some ideal and timeless image of Turkish-Cypriotness.

Our second example comes from a young woman of eighteen, we shall call
her Hülya, who migrated to Britain from eastern Turkey when she was seven
years old. At one point, towards the end of our discussion, she tells us how
much she likes watching old Turkish films on television, 'especially the love
films', which she likes to watch 'to see the old Turkey . . . [ ] It gives you a
very sweet sense'. But earlier she had spoken about a very different experience
of watching Turkish television:

> We have one TV set, and this is why we have arguments, because I'm irri-
> tated by the news. I find it bad for my health. You might find it funny but,
> really, you sit in front of the television, you are going to watch the news,
> you are relaxed, everybody is curious about what's happening in Turkey;
> and then it says, 'Good evening viewers, today four cars crashed into each
> other'. God bless them. They show these things, people covered in blood.
> People who know nothing about rescuing, trying to drag these people out,
> they pull them, and in front of your eyes people die. I am a very sensitive
> person. Somebody dies in front of you, and they show this, and they don't
> do anything. For me, this is like torture. For them maybe it is not like
> torture, but for me it is. Two or three years ago, I was *very* upset, when this
> guy was killed because he had a tattoo saying 'Allah' on his back. Then, I
> don't know this person, but I was so touched that I cried. And I called

Ahmet Taner Kışlalı [a famous journalist]. These kinds of events make me very sad, because I'm delicate, and they wear me out, so for that reason I don't watch.

(Focus group, Hackney, London, 3 November 1999)

What is made apparent here is television's great capacity for conveying harsh and cruel aspects of the Turkish reality – Turkish news programmes are far more explicit than British ones in showing scenes of violence and bloodshed. For a great many Turkish viewers, news programmes are very disturbing – the often intense discomfort of watching the news was an issue that ran through practically all of our focus groups. In some parts of its schedules, then, television may nourish warm and nostalgic feelings. But at news time, especially, the principle of reality will always return, through images of Turkey that frequently provoke and shock. The news can be profoundly unsettling for migrant viewers. As Hülya says of her own experience, it 'creates a psychological disorder' [*psikolojik durum yaratıyor*].

What is important is the evidential nature of television (which may be constructive, as in our first example, but also disturbing, as our second example makes clear). What we want to emphasise here is the capacity of the reality dimension of television to undercut the abstract nostalgia of the diasporic imagination. Turkish viewers come to participate in the mundane and banal world of everyday television. It is this aspect of television culture that goes against the idea that the proliferation of Turkish transnational media is now associated with an ethnicisation of media cultures and markets in western Europe (for such an argument, see Becker 2001). In our own work, we have not found this to be the case. We are inclined to agree with Marisca Milikowski when she argues that it is, on the contrary, associated with a process of *de-ethnicisation*. As she says, Turkish satellite television 'helps Turkish migrants, and in particular their children, to liberate themselves from certain outdated and culturally imprisoning notions of Turkishness, which had survived in the isolation of migration' (Milikowski 2000: 444). The world of Turkish television is an ordinary world, and its significance resides, we suggest, in its ordinary, banal and everyday qualities – which are qualities it has in common with countless other television worlds.

Turkish audiences look to the ordinariness of Turkish television. Like any other viewers of broadcast television, they want 'the familiar – familiar sights, familiar faces, familiar voices', as Thomas Elsaesser (1994: 7) puts it, 'television that respects and knows who they are, where they are, and what time it is'. And, to a large extent, we may say that they are able to find what they are looking for. And yet, at the same time, there is still something that is wrong, something that does not quite work properly with transnational Turkish television. At the same time as they can enjoy them, migrants can also find Turkish channels disturbing, unsettling, frustrating. This is apparent in a very dramatic fashion in Hülya's abrupt shift from feeling relaxed in front of the television to feeling worn out by what she saw on it. Many, many other people expressed these kinds of affronted and disgruntled feelings about the programmes they were watching. In one group, a woman objects to the production standards of Turkish television. 'We perceive Turkish television as being of poor quality', she says, 'and rather sensationalist, and unedited, so it's a bit crude . . . I mean, it will show you things in an unedited way, whether it's blood and guts, or violence or whatever'. And she adds, in a joking tone, 'I can't take it seriously if it's Burt Lancaster with a Turkish accent – does not really appeal' (Focus group, Haringey, London, 22 November 1999). There is something about Turkish television that presents itself as in some way inadequate, deficient, unacceptable. The experience of watching transnational television is ordinary, but never straightforwardly.

When Turkish people talk about what frustrates them, they point to the images, the programmes, the scheduling, or the nature of particular channels. But, somehow, it seems to us, this does not really get at what is 'wrong' with watching television from Turkey. There is something more that is disconcerting about watching transnational television, an elusive something else. We can perhaps get at what this something might be from a passing observation that was made by Hülya. We were talking about Muslim festivals, and about the sense that she and her friends had that the significance of religious holidays was diminishing in the London context. We asked whether Turkish television helped to remind people of the traditional holidays, and to create the festival atmosphere that seemed to have been lost. 'How could that help?', says one young woman sceptically. And Hülya says, 'It's coming from a distance . . . It's coming from too far. It loses its significance. I mean, it could have significance, but it's coming from too far.' Later, when asked whether the availability of satellite television had implications for her identity and her relation to Turkish culture, she picks up on the same idea. 'No', she says, 'it can't, because it's too distant. Imagine that you were talking to me from I don't know how many thousand miles away. How much would this affect me?' (Focus group, Hackney, London, 3 November 1999). Perhaps we can make sense of this by referring back to Thomas Elsaesser's observation that the audiences of broadcast television want television programmes that know who they are, where they are, and what time it is. Is it that television from Turkey does not seem to know its transnational audiences in this way? Is Hülya pointing to something that is new or different about the working of transnational television? Is she signalling something that might actually make transnational cultural interactions distinctive?

Migrant experience and television theory

Turkish migrants clearly have quite complex thoughts and sentiments about the television channels and programmes that they are watching. And what is also clear is that they have a *critical* engagement with the new transnational television culture.

What they say demonstrates considerable awareness and thoughtfulness about different aspects of this culture, from the aesthetic and production values of particular programmes, through to the overall impact of the new services on the quality of their lives in Britain. What we now want to do is to go on and reflect on these complex attitudes and relations of Turkish migrants towards transnational television. We want to try to make sense of what Turkish people are telling us in the context of more general ideas about the role and significance of broadcasting in modern life (which Turks are as much a part of as any other group).

For the most part, as we have suggested above, transnational media of the kind we are concerned with here have been considered in the special context of 'diasporic culture' and identity politics. Migrant audiences have been seen as, in some way, different; and the study of their supposedly different dispositions and preoccupations has seemed to belong to the specialised domain of ethnic and migration research. We ourselves believe that their media activities should be looked at with the very same media theories that have been applied to 'ordinary' (i.e. national, sedentary) audiences. Marisca Milikowski (2000: 460) is quite right to insist that we should look at migrant viewing from the point of view of 'ordinary uses and gratifications' – for, as she observes, 'non-ideological and non-political gratifications usually go a long way to explain a certain popular interest'. This we regard as an important principle of methodological democracy and justice. We should reflect on what is happening through transnationalisation of Turkish media culture in the light of media theory concerned with ordinary uses of, and gratifications from, everyday television.

Here, we think that the work of Paddy Scannell (1996, 2000) can serve as a particularly useful and productive point of reference. We have reservations, we must say, about certain aspects of Scannell's overall project – it is very national in its orientation, and often seems to be treating British broadcasting as an ideal-type model (for critical observations on the politics of Scannell's agenda, see Morley 2000, chapter 5). But we do think that there is a great deal to be learned from his detailed analysis of the emergence of distinctive modes of address in broadcasting culture – how broadcasters learned to address listeners and viewers in appropriate ways (ways in which they would wish to be addressed). Scannell's work alerts us to the significance of the particular rhetorical structures that have come to mediate the relation of producers and consumers of broadcasting services. What he provides us with is a sustained account of the communicative structures and ethos that have made broadcasting culture work for its audiences. It is, moreover, a historically situated account, showing how the specific communicative forms of radio and television developed and functioned in the particular context of national broadcasting systems. Scannell's concern is with how, at a particular historical moment, broadcasting media came to develop communicative forms that functioned as arguably the primary mediation between the private domain of everyday life and the public life of the nation state.

It seems to us that these communicative and rhetorical aspects of programming and scheduling are absolutely crucial for our own exploration of transnational Turkish television and its audiences. Of course, the codes that have evolved in the Turkish context differ somewhat from those of Scannell's British case – the state broadcaster, TRT, has always had an 'official' tone, and it was only in the 1990s, through the development of private channels, that more informal modes of address came to be elaborated (Aksoy and Robins 1997). But we may say that they have functioned in the integrative way, working to mediate the relation between private and public spheres of life in Turkey. And what seems to us to be a key issue, in the context of our own present concern with Turkish satellite broadcasting in the European space, is what happens to these communicative structures in the changed circumstances of transnationalisation. The point about Scannell's analysis is that it is essentially a phenomenology of national broadcasting – or perhaps, more accurately, a national phenomenology of broadcasting. It assumes that there is something universal and timeless about the way in which national broadcasting cultures have worked. What we would suggest is that there will be difficulties when communicative structures that have worked more or less well in a national context are then made to do service in new transnational contexts. We are concerned with the communicative limits of structures that have served to mediate between the private and public lives of the nation.

There are two (closely related) arguments that we want to make here. The first is straightforward, emerging directly from our previous discussion, and can be made quite briefly. Scannell is concerned with what he calls the 'care-structures' of radio and television, by which he means the practices that 'produce and deliver an all-day everyday service that is ready-to-hand and available always anytime at the turn of a switch or the press of a button' (1996: 145–6). What this means, he says, is 'making programmes so that they "work" every time', and in such a way that viewers or listeners come to regard them as 'a natural, ordinary, unremarkable, everyday entitlement' (ibid.: 145–6). In considering these care structures, Scannell has put particular emphasis on the temporality of broadcasting, on what he calls its 'dailiness'. 'This dailiness yields', he says, 'the sense we all have of the ordinariness, the familiarity and obviousness of radio and television. It establishes their taken for granted, "seen but unnoticed" character' (2000: 19). And what Scannell wants us to recognise and acknowledge is the immense pleasure that this mundane quality of broadcasting has for viewers – the pleasure that comes from the combination of familiarity, confirmation, entitlement and effortlessness.

And what we want to emphasise is that this particular pleasure principle is not exclusive to sedentary viewers. Turkish broadcasting culture also exists as an ordinary and mundane culture. And the appeal of Turkish television, as with other broadcasting cultures, is equally the appeal of its ordinariness. Through it, Turks living in Europe have access to, or can extend their access to, what Jostein Gripsrud (1999) calls the domain of 'common knowledge'. They can be part of the great domain of 'anonymous discourse' that broadcasting has brought into existence, the banal domain of 'inattentive attention' (Brune 1993: 37). What we are arguing, then, is that migrant viewers are looking to find what the national television culture has always provided. Like any other viewers, Turkish-speaking viewers in Europe are also in search of broadcast television that is meaningfully and effortlessly available. They are also wanting – and to a quite a large extent finding – the pleasures of familiarity and confirmation. And our point is that the desire for such an engagement with Turkish television is entirely social, and not at all ethno-cultural or 'diasporic', in its motivation. Migrant viewers are in search of ordinary social gratifications, precisely the kinds of gratification that Scannell is concerned with.

Our second argument is more complex, and takes us back to what Hülya said about Turkish television seeming to come from a distance and, consequently, losing its significance. What we want to get at is the particular feeling of ambivalence that very many Turkish people have about transnational television (which is more than the routine ambivalence that we all seem to have). They enjoy and appreciate the programmes they see yet, at the same time, watching them can frequently cause frustration and provoke resentment. Sometimes, it seems, transnational engagement with Turkish television culture does not 'work'. In Scannell's terms, we may say that the care structures of television break down. And what we want to suggest, as an explanation for this, is that, while considerable gratification may be got from everyday television, there are particular difficulties with its 'sociable dimension', which Scannell regards as 'the most fundamental characteristic of broadcasting's communicative ethos' (1996: 23). Put simply, Turkish television often seems to its transnational viewers to be failing or lacking in its sociable aspect.

Scannell draws our attention to the remarkable capacity of broadcasting to generate a sense of 'we-ness', through the creation of 'a public, shared and sociable world-in-common between human beings' (2000: 12). What Scannell means when he talks about the creation of a 'world in common' is, of course, a national world in common; what is at issue is the contribution of broadcasting to the institution of the 'imagined community'. His account is extremely idealistic, but what we think Scannell usefully brings out is the way in which television and radio have worked to create a public world with 'an ordered, orderly, familiar, knowable appearance' (1996: 153). It is a world in which television and radio contribute to the shaping of our sense of days' (ibid.: 149). The dailiness of broadcast media gives rise to the sense of '*our* time – generational time – the time of *our* being with one another in the world' (ibid.: 174). The broadcasting calendar 'creates a horizon of expectations, a mood of anticipation, a directedness towards that which is to come, thereby giving substance and structure (a "texture of relevances") to everyday life' (ibid.: 155). According to this ideal-type scenario, broadcasting produces a 'common world – a shareable, accessible, available public world'; what it does is 'to create and to allow ways of being-in-public for absent listeners and viewers' (ibid.: 166, 168). It connects 'everyone's my-world' to the 'great world', which is 'a world in common, a world we share' (ibid.: 172, 174).

And what we are arguing here is that it is this sociable functioning of broadcasting that does not 'work' properly for migrants watching Turkish television in Europe. Transnational viewers are often disconcerted because, on very many occasions, they cannot relate to Turkish programmes as a natural, ordinary, unremarkable, everyday entitlement. In the case of news this is particularly apparent. If, as Scannell argues, 'the care structures of news are designed to routinise eventfulness' (ibid.: 160), then we may say that in our Turkish case, at least, these care structures do not function well across distance. In the transnational context, there is a problem with the mode of address. Broadcasting works on the basis of what Scannell calls a 'for-anyone-as-someone' structure of address: it is addressing a mass audience, and yet appears to be addressing the members of that audience personally, as individuals. 'The for-anyone-as-someone structure expresses and embodies that which is between the impersonal third person and the personal first person, namely the second person (the me-and-you)', says Scannell (2000: 9). 'The for-anyone-as-someone structure expresses "we-ness". It articulates human social sociable life.' In the Turkish case, it seems that viewers may often be made to feel like no one in particular. The conditions no longer exist for feeling at home in the 'we-ness' of Turkish broadcasting culture.

Why does the 'my world' of Turkish migrants no longer resonate properly with a Turkish world in common? Why are there problems with the mode of address in the case of transnational broadcasting? Why are the care structures of broadcasting disrupted? The reasons are to do with the context of consumption. As we have said, transnational broadcasting is not about magically transporting migrant viewers back to a distant homeland. It is about broadcasting services being delivered to them in their new locations – in the case of the Turks we have been discussing, it is in London. What this means is that the world of broadcasting is not seamlessly connected to the world of the street outside, as it would be for viewers watching in Turkey. Migrant viewers cannot move routinely between the media space and the 'outside' space of everyday Turkish reality. And since so much of what broadcasting is about has to do with connecting viewers to the life and rhythms of the real world of the nation, there are bound to be difficulties with the dislocated kind of viewing that migrancy enforces. Turkish migrants will often protest that Turkish television exaggerates. 'When you see these things you naturally believe them', one man said to us. 'But I've been back from Turkey for two weeks, and it's nothing like that really. It's nothing like how it's shown. Turkey is the same Turkey. Of course, there are scandals, and there are people who live through them. But television does not reflect things as they are' (Focus group, Hackney, London, 16 December 1999). Migrants tend to forget that exaggeration is an integral part of television rhetoric in Turkey, and it is only when they go back for a visit that they recognise the discrepancy between screen reality and street reality (whereas viewers in Turkey are checking out this discrepancy on a continuous basis). We may say that the decontextualisation of the migrant viewing situation often results in a kind of interference in the reception of cultural signals from Turkey.

A further consequence of the dislocated context of consumption is that migrant viewers can never be in a position to watch Turkish television naively or innocently. We must be aware that they actually operate in and across two cultural spaces (at least) – Turkish and British. As well as watching Turkish channels, most of them are very familiar with British television. And they will often make comparisons between the two broadcasting cultures (concerning, for example, programme quality, scheduling, bias, censorship). We may say that there is a constant implicit comparison going on, and very often the comparisons are explicit – Turkish programmes are always watched and thought about with an awareness of British television in mind. As one man put it to us, 'We have the opportunity to compare things we see with what happens here. Before, we didn't know what it was like here' (Focus group, Hackney, London, 16 December 1999). When we say that Turkish migrants cannot watch Turkish television innocently, we mean that they can no longer watch it from the inside, as it were. They cannot recover the simple perspective of monocultural (national) vision. They are compelled to think about Turkish culture in the light of other cultural experiences and possibilities.

We have said that watching transnational Turkish television can be a frustrating and often disillusioning experience. What we want to add in conclusion is that this disillusionment can also be a productive experience. Through their engagement with Turkish (alongside British) media culture, Turkish migrants develop a comparative and critical attitude, and may become more reflexively aware of the arbitrariness and provisionality of cultural orders. In the present argument, we have been principally concerned with how the ordinary world of broadcast television can work to undermine the diasporic imagination. What should also have become apparent in the course of our argument, however, is the potential that exists, too, for working against the grain of the national imagination, against the confining mentality of imagined community.

Conclusion: the minds of migrants

> It all depends on the rifts and leaps in a person, on the distance from the one to the other *within himself.*
>
> (Elias Canetti 1991: 20)

In this chapter, we have been highly critical of diasporic cultural studies and the agenda centred on 'diasporic media'. Our objection has been to what we regard as a fundamental wrong assumption made by its exponents: that the people who watch transnational satellite television do so as mere ciphers of the 'imagined communities' to which they are said to 'belong'. What we think has to be called into question is the idea that migrants function principally in terms of the categories of collective attachment and identification. As Roger Rouse observes, 'the discourse of identity suggests that social collectivities are aggregates of atomised and autonomous elements, either individuals or sub-groups, that are fundamentally equivalent by virtue of the common possession of a given social property' (1995: 358). Human individuals are reduced to the status of being the poor representatives of whatever imagined community they happen to have once been aggregated into. Rouse points to the socio-cultural efficacy of this logic of identity. We may consider it, he says, in terms of 'hegemonic efforts to make ideas about identity frame the ways in which people understand what it is to be a person, the kinds of collectivities in which they are involved, the nature of the problems that they face, and the means by which these problems can be tackled' (ibid.: 356). We have a fundamental problem with the project of diasporic cultural studies because it seems to us that it is, in the end, contributing to the extension and perpetuation of these hegemonic efforts in the context of contemporary global change. Everything, every possibility, remains predicated on the logic of identity.

In our discussion of transnational broadcasting from Turkey, we have been working actively against the diasporic imagination. We have tried to show how the rhetorical structures of Turkish television – the structures that have been mobilised to organise the experience of the national audience – are disrupted in the transnational context. In the migrant context, we think, where the ideal rhetorical situation of Turkish national television is significantly undermined, there may be possibilities for a more reflexive and critical engagement with television from the 'homeland'. What we have tried to suggest is that, in the Turkish case at least, transnational television might actually be working to subvert the diasporic imagination and its imperatives of identification and belonging. But our critique goes further than this. We have also argued that it is necessary to jettison the basic concepts of 'identity', 'imagined community' and 'diaspora'. Like Anthony Cohen, we have felt it necessary to go against the grain of the prevailing culturalism, and to take greater account of human consciousness and self-consciousness – to recognise that the minds of Turkish migrants may provide a more significant and interesting research focus than their identities. This means moving our agenda away from the 'problem' of migrant culture and identity, to consider how it is that migrants experience migration, and how they think and talk about and make sense of their experiences.

The point about identities is that they require simplicity. In the case of minds and consciousness, what is important is always their complexity. And it seems to us that transnational developments might open up new possibilities for the way we think about mental space – putting a new value on the rifts and leaps inside a person, and provoking those who are open to experience to travel the distance from the one to the other within themselves.

Note

1 This article is based on research conducted within the ESRC Transnational Communities Programme – Award L214252040, Negotiating Spaces: Media and Cultural Practices in the Turkish Diaspora in Britain, France and Germany.

8 Video and the Macedonians in Australia[1]

Dona Kolar-Panov

Historically, the media have played a central part in the imagination of national communities (Anderson 1983), but the distinguished characteristic of the past two decades is the role played by the emergence of new communication and media technologies that allowed various forms of symbolic communication to emerge linking the different parts of the world together.

When videocassette recorders (VCRs) entered the public sphere in 1965 (Marshall 1979: 109) the new technology formed a full circle with the already established medium of television. It appropriated the representational practices not only of television but also of film and photography and of the cinema. The convergence of cybernetics, communication and aesthetics into the technological interface of what is often referred to as the 'home video terminal' has turned the television screen into an all-purpose device. First of all video games were played on it, then rented or pirated cassettes of feature films or time-shifted television programmes were watched. However, the cheapness and flexibility of the portable video camera (portapac, camcorder and so on) allowed a broad cross-section of the public to produce their own programmes. This turned VCR from a reproductive technology into the first widespread postmodern communication medium.

The domestic use of the videocassette recorder signalled a shift in the control and power of the medium from the control rooms of television stations and the boardrooms of the television and movie corporations to the living rooms of audiences. The excitement that came with the ability to time-shift and record television programmes *in absentia*, as well as 'bring the movie theatre home', still lingers on, even if today with the help of the computer and modem we are able to create everything from simple video graphics to virtual realities. Accordingly, I see the VCR and the whole videographic apparatus (consisting of VCR, camera, screen, computer and modem and all additions to the reproduction and production of image; see Berko 1989), as being post-structuralist in essence since this apparatus allows for the creation of personal 'pastiche' (Jameson 1984) of images and sounds as no other medium has done so far. Furthermore, through its reproductive function, the VCR appropriates the specialised area of the existing technological parameters such as photography – VCR as a family album (visual) and VCR as phonograph – and video hits (musical), appropriating with it a certain authority, properties inherent and belonging to those media forms.

As a 'shadow system' (Hill 1988) the VCR acquires its place by becoming a cultural property capable of being translated into any of the systems it is shadowing. It even functions as a form of substitution for the traditional cultural systems and cultural forms such as storytelling, just as such storytelling has appropriated VCR to ensure the continuation of the qualities of an oral culture (cf. Ong 1982). Hidden behind the technologies of television and film and embodied in photograph and phonograph lies the entire 'shadow' form of VCR technology which has its potency expressed in every act of its use of photography or phonography, appropriating their properties and escaping at every point along the specific technology path of diffusion.

The most powerful property that video has appropriated from all visual (and other) technologies is the claim to a reality of representation, a claim to the representation of 'truth'. Videotapes, just like photographs, are visual records accepted both as legal evidence and historical record. This acceptance is based on the appropriation of 'reality effects' of photography by VCR as a 'shadow system' of photographic technology. Today video, like photography, presents a 'piece of reality' for its viewers, even though the audience often recognises the paradox inherent to photography and mirrored by television and video in which the image is both an objective rendition as well as a cultural construction of reality. Like photography, video is perceived as isolating and fixing an event in time and space, hence preserving it 'for ever' (Berger 1980: 50). As such, video functions to extend the life of a momentary event through each and every subsequent viewing. Furthermore, the 'rewind' and 'freeze-frame' functions of the VCR allow audiences to view the moving image in its static form many times, allowing for close scrutiny and analysis, and aiding in the meaning-making by virtue of repetition. Moreover, media audiences already literate in photographic, television and film discourses draw on their intertextual knowledge and are easily able to recognise – in their intertextuality – representations of persons/objects, places/events, events/objects and so on (see Fiske 1987: 108–27). In addition to this common visual literacy, the audience makes meanings according to the structure of their own referential knowledge which allows the spectator to engage in projecting as well as transforming the image into a site of meaning. Thus meaning-making (or semiosis) takes place through a subtle dialogue (Bakhtin 1981) between the viewer and the video as a cultural text.

The VCR and its ethnic audience

The high VCR penetration in Australia together with inflexible government policies (O'Regan 1993a) and its highly dispersed population, postponed the introduction of satellite television/cable television (pay television) and narrowcasting. Additionally, geography has limited the extent of transmission overspill; satellites, by and large, have to be specifically 'trained' on Australia to reach the high population centres. In the US and some European countries these new television technologies have been introduced prior to, or at the same time as, the domestic videocassette recorder. This has created a unique media environment in Australia that relied on video rental structures and, to a lesser degree, on the informal channels of distribution for viewing products alternative to broadcast television.

Many distributors and retailers claim to be reflecting the 'needs of the audience' based on the general and demographic characteristics of the populations in their video-rental area. These 'needs' in turn are based on the market research classification of the targeted audience which includes population mix, relative affluence, unemployment levels, numbers arriving during holiday periods (for resort areas), the range of other leisure options available and the number of broadcast television channels in regional Australia as well as competition from other 'local video stores' – video outlets whose main business is other than video rental, such as newsagents, pharmacies and so on. Since most of the videocassettes rented by the ethnic population surveyed in this research are not rented from the mainstream video outlets but rather from 'local video stores' and/or circulated through the community networks, these audiences are uncharted in the official records and reports on VCR use by both software or hardware manufacturers and distributors. With most of the research into VCR use being industry-driven, the dynamics of ethnic video remain largely invisible.

This invisibility of ethnic video markets in Australia is even more marked than in the US and the UK, where some statistical data, however limited, is available – in the US on Hispanic audiences (Meyrowitz and Maguire 1993) and in the UK on Indian audiences (Gillespie 1989). This is mainly due to the fact that both markets are covered by official rental structures owing to the size of the ethnic group concerned and the fact that the Spanish-language and Indian audio-visual productions are large and sophisticated industries. The semi-legal structure of ethnic, mainly Greek, Italian, Chinese, Vietnamese and Indian distribution channels in Australia is in part a consequence of an absence of economies of scale and ethnic dispersal. Consequently the ethnic video depends on the distribution by 'ethnic' outlets and small businesses in Australia – making neighbourhood video less available as an option.

The VCR has changed the relationship between the marginal and the mainstream in Australia, offering an alternative to the mainstream media and allowing the marginal audience to deal with the mainstream culture on its own terms. The desire of the permanent migrants to fit into the host culture and eventually become Australians does not these days have to clash with their desire to maintain a separate cultural identity based on the homeland culture. Moreover, my own research into Croatian-in-Australia audiences has shown that the fragments of the homeland which have maintained a separate cultural identity are easily called upon by the homelands in the time of ethnic revival in that homeland (Kolar-Panov 1997). For a short time such mobilisation can cause increased antagonism between ethnic immigrant groups in the host countries such as the potentially explosive tensions in the case of Australia with Croatian-Serbian and the Greek-Macedonian. What we see here is that changes in various homelands can, and do, impact upon particular ethnic immigrant communities, often widening the gap between groups which were a part of a carefully constructed multicultural identity or 'standardised diversity' (see Meyrowitz and Maguire 1993).

Conceptualising the ethnic minority audience

Ethnic minority audiences are usually but not exclusively defined in terms of their difference to the mainstream, and always inside the boundaries of a certain nation state. Under certain conditions this relation can change and the minority can define itself in opposition to other minorities which are seen as antagonistic and in relation to other nation states or would-be nation states. Most nation states have within their administrative boundaries more than one people or ethnic group. The multiethnic composition of nation states as they are today is a product of either annexation or the unification of different territories occupied by different ethnic groups, or the result either of large immigration programmes such as is the case with the US, the UK, Canada and Australia, or through the accommodation of immigrant labour from less developed countries. Australia's Macedonian ethnic community has been formed principally through immigration. In fact most of the present-day Australian ethnic groups are the product of voluntary immigration, but at times they carry the stigma of enforced exodus, as with the Macedonians from Greece in 1949 (Stardelov *et al.* 1993) or, more recently, refugees from the former Yugoslavia. Immigration to Australia typically means entering a polyethnic society with a culture that differs in varying degrees from the homeland left behind. Australian immigration policies ensure that ethnic communities are from the moment of their arrival in Australia oriented towards the host culture, because of its critical importance to the resources available to the family, community and the individual. As a result of these policies, there is a typical dual orientation among the ethnic communities towards the homeland and the host culture, leading to varying degrees of participation in both. Thus for the ethnic groups like the Macedonians in Australia a 'dual' attachment was formed through loyalty to the host political unit as citizens of the Australian state, with its 'rights and obligations', and 'a sense of affiliation and solidarity with the ethnic community into which one's family was born and socialized' (Smith 1988: 151).

The ethnic audience from Macedonia builds and seeks its dual cultural identity within the Australian national ideological configurations and processes of cultural production, and it is often assumed that the ethnic identity of its members is finally constituted and legitimated from wider domestic multicultural politics (Bottomley 1992). However, my research indicates a more complex interaction where ethnic identities are as much constituted actively through the diaspora–homeland relation as they are in reaction to exclusion or marginalisation by the host culture (Kolar-Panov 1997). This is because the positioning of the audience as well as of the individual viewer towards the cultural texts, in this case videotapes, depends on the viewers' 'cultural competence' (Fiske 1987: 19; Bourdieu 1980, 1984). The cultural competence of the Macedonian audience is constructed and informed by their collective and personal histories and cross-cut by their class or social status, gender and other differences such as their political and religious affiliations.

Cultural competence and the ethnic video

Because the ethnic fragments of the Macedonian community are dispersed across Australia, their need for 'ethnic solidarity' and ethno-specific information as well as entertainment have only partially been met by the development of Australia-wide distribution and information networks such as the ethnic press, ethnic radio and Special Broadcasting Service Television (SBS-TV). SBS is a unique broadcast television service by world standards that has provided alternative programming to the ethnic, marginal and cosmopolitan audiences, thus fulfilling needs left unaddressed by both state television (ABC) and the commercial stations (see O'Regan and Kolar-Panov 1993a, 1993b). Before the disintegration of Yugoslavia, the Yugoslav diplomatic missions and the Yugoslav-based migrant associations were other available sources. Thus the Yugoslav diplomatic missions and the various migrant organisations attached to the Multicultural Commission of Western Australia functioned as official information networks which provided both Australian and homeland information, political viewpoints and entertainment products not available in the mainstream media or not readily available to the ethnic fragments due to their lack of English-language competence. The other sources – and the more important ones for this argument – were the ethnic clubs and the web of information networks developed around them, often based on local, familial and regional affiliation.

Such organised ethnic networks extended the community through time and space in a new location, and served to repair, but also to maintain, the boundaries of the ethnic group and culture in the Australian context. They also helped to govern the nature and the extent of acculturation by helping to negotiate publicly the selection of characteristics and behaviours that are appropriate to the definition of their ethnicity.

Ethnic communities are inevitably weakened by the very process of immigration and by their geographical dispersal, their time of arrival in Australia and their diverse levels of knowledge of the English language at the time of their arrival. Obviously the higher the language competence is at the time of arrival, the higher is the level of participation in Australian social and cultural life. This leads to various degrees of adoption of many ways and styles of living, including the use of Australian symbolic goods and benefits. (At the same time, of course, these all contribute to a necessary and barely recognised divergence between the homeland and the immigrant 'fragment' over time.)

These engagements in turn ensure that the ethnic group soon becomes a 'cultural hybrid' (Hall 1993: 362; Lotman, 1990). These are made up in varying degrees of elements of the host-Australian and homeland-culture-Macedonian. What is created in this process is a new culture which is neither authentically host (Australian) nor homeland (Macedonian).

This process not only makes it increasingly difficult for any kind of ethno-separate politics and ethno-specific culture of the homeland to be sustained continuously across generations, but also ensures that the 'cultural hybrid' (or creolised culture) that develops will retain its ethnic dimensions – but in a form of symbolic ethnicity, accepted and favoured as a form of ethnicity by the host culture. Finally in this levelling process, the 'homeland' and the language of thatthe homeland often lose the importance they had for the first- and second-generation migrants (and less often the third generation) and are replaced by an identity within Australian culture and English language, but still more often than not remain marginalised. Thus, under these conditions, ethnic communities have permeable cultural boundaries (Lotman 1990), with their shape and identity changing from generation to generation and often depending on continuing immigration, if any, from the homelands. Nevertheless, the typical forms of ethno-specificity are characteristics of the first- and second-generation migrants, where the character of the cultural hybrid (or creolised culture) permits dual orientations and dual identities. In subsequent generations the cultural distance between the host ethnic cultures narrows and tends to result in a greater degree of self-identification as Australian.

Ethnic video use in the Macedonian community has a fundamentally dual character, since VCR is used for the same purposes as among mainstream audiences involving time-shifting or watching rented videos (Cubitt 1991) but is also used for viewing non-English videos of different types, some of which could be seen as ethno-specific, such as 'video letters'. On the basis of the present research I would claim that the degree of difference in VCR viewing patterns between the ethnic and mainstream audiences depends on the extent to which an ethnic minority is incorporated into the host (mainstream) culture. This is one of the most important factors in the determination of the ethnic audience's viewing patterns. The other factors which may influence the ethnic viewing patterns are the nature of the immigration (whether voluntary or enforced), the length of the residence in Australia and, of course, the class, gender and occupational base.

The ethnic video market

Ethnic video is usually, but not always, a non-English production relying as it does upon a certain knowledge of the symbolic resources shared by the community in question and not by the mainstream. However, as a result of the local nature of Australian television and the absence of cable television and satellite services at the time of this research, coupled with the predominantly anglophone cinema exhibition structures and the geographic dispersal of the

Macedonian population across Australia, the entertainment industry afforded ethnic markets and audiences only limited recognition. Since there were virtually no controls over ethnic video imports in Australia, the ethnographic research for this chapter cannot be backed up by any statistics or relevant numerical data. Consequently the account of viewership patterns is unavoidably fragmentary. Furthermore, the mainstream market is regulated through enforced copyright laws, while the ethnic market is remarkably free of such policing. The ethnic video outlets operate through different types of shop – for example, corner 'delis' (variety stores), butchers' shops, hairdressers as well as an under-the-counter service in the regular video library outlets. This makes for a semi-formal, non-transparent video market which is tightly wedded to ethnic community structures.

The development and the dynamics of ethnic video viewing in the Macedonian community have been greatly influenced by a number of factors such as the wide dispersal of ethnic audiences in Australia and the fact that the homeland of the Republic of Macedonia did not have a film or video industry oriented towards its diaspora, let alone commercially developed industries on a large scale like the Asian film industries of Mumbai (Bombay), Kolkata (Calcutta) and Hong Kong which successfully compete with the Hollywood product in East and South Asia (Alvarado 1988).

A survey carried out in February 1990 (as a part of a larger research project, see Kolar-Panov 1997) in 20 video libraries in the suburbs of Perth, Western Australia, and also in Spearwood, Hamilton Hill in the City of Fremantle area, all with a high concentration of Croatians, and in eight video libraries in Balcatta and Wanneroo (suburbs of Perth) with a high concentration of Macedonians, showed that, except for limited titles of Italian feature films in rental outlets in Fremantle and Hamilton Hill, none of the surveyed video libraries carried any material in languages other than English. However, other local shops which offered video rental as a 'side-business', such as newsagents, pharmacies and most of all, the local 'delis', offered videotapes in languages other than English. The language and the origin of such videotapes was determined by and directly linked to the ethnic background of the shop owner. Two types of videotape were available from such video outlets: Indian, Chinese, Greek and Italian tapes which were legal and available through a regular over-the-counter procedure, and others which were pirated tapes from broadcast television or professional videos mainly of music from music festivals and variety programmes taped off the air which were available under the counter.

There was a noticeable absence of videos in the Macedonian language – even though a certain interconnection exists between what is often characterised as the Mediterranean or Southern European community (O'Regan 1993a). An Italian 'deli' frequently carried tapes in Croatian and Spanish, but there was not a single shop where Macedonian videotapes were available for rent or purchase outside the strongly Yugoslav-oriented businesses with strong governmental links, or the few variety shops owned by ethnic Macedonians.

Video as cultural and linguistic maintenance

The television programmes produced in the former Yugoslavia, in this case in Skopje (the capital of the Republic of Macedonia), were at first the only programmes available in the Macedonian language. Until 1944 Macedonians did not have a separate (official) language and schools or other cultural and educational institutions were operating in languages of the current administration of the region. (Unfortunately the remaining Macedonian population in Greece and Bulgaria still does not have the right to cultural self-determination; see Danforth 1997). Thus, as a result of centuries of foreign rule, Macedonians have been denied the basic cultural technologies such as schools or even the printing press, and were often persecuted if they used their native tongue (Stardelov *et al.* 1993). Tome Sazdov (1987: 11), in *Macedonian Folk Literature*, argues that this denial of the literate use of the language led to the development of a mainly oral culture: '[U]nder such conditions of cultural and educational injustice the enslaved Macedonian could express his creative instincts and aspirations only through the medium of oral literature, in the form of folklore.' Thus traditions, folk tales, songs, aphorisms, proverbs and riddles were handed down from generation to generation preserving cultural heritage until today. Perhaps the oral basis to what today is a fully literate culture is the major reason for specific genres of ethnic videos in the Macedonian community such as tapes of short sketches, even fairy tales (watched not only by children), usually accompanied by song and dance.

The part of the Macedonian community which is formed by Macedonians from Aegean Macedonia (Greece) demonstrated a preference for watching 'historical' dramas and/or miniseries which directly dealt with their flight from Greece and/or the destiny of the Macedonian nation in general and the destiny of displaced Macedonian children during the mass exodus of 1949 in particular (Hill 1989). The videotapes that recorded the destinies of families displaced all over the world were often produced as documentaries by Television Skopje (RTV Skopje). So too there were taped (pirated) theatrical performances of modern and historical plays written by contemporary Macedonian authors dealing with the historical fight of the Macedonian nation for independence, or plays like *Pecalbari (The Migrant Workers)* by Anton Panov (1938/83) dealing with the tradition of migration and the reasons behind it. Nevertheless, the most popular genre for viewing were video versions of Macedonian popular and folk music and dance. Later, as a larger selection of tapes began to circulate in the community, information and variety programmes were increasingly favoured and sought after. The other popular genre of videotapes were the tapes of the performances of local folklore groups, popular and folk music of questionable quality, sketches and stand-up comedians. In addition everything happening in the community was taped and then circulated overseas in a Macedonia–Australia–Canada triangle.

With the re-establishment of a democratic government in Greece (1975), which saw Greek policies towards Macedonian immigrants from Aegean

Macedonia relaxed, at least in formal terms, the Aegean Macedonian migrants were for the first time since 1949 able to travel to Greece. The simultaneous advance in video technology (the camcorder) and possibility of travel to the homeland produced a new mode of communication between those abroad and those left behind, a form of video production which I have called a 'video letter'.[2]

Most of the Macedonians from Aegean Macedonia who visited their devastated villages in northern Greece had a mission other than just a visit. They had a duty to record on the videotapes those villages or what was left of them; they had to tape messages from long-lost or never-seen relations and friends. And they did this not only for their families, but more often for the Macedonian community they were coming from. The tapes were then shown at group screenings mainly in private homes with the 'hero' or 'heroines' who successfully brought the tapes back being at the centre of attention. They would tell the story of their visits and add anecdotes from the trip to their interpretations of the images on the television screen.

I have watched a tape showing the trip to what used to be one of the most prosperous villages, which was almost completely destroyed after 1949, several times with different audiences. The proud baker, turned video artist, enriched the texture of his story with each and every new viewing. The camera lingered on the piles of rocks and ruins to which the host gave meaning by identifying them as 'so-and-so's house', or the village school or shop. Only during the part where the village priest, the only remaining inhabitant (now over 90 years old), is interviewed, did the narration stop. Each time I saw this tape the audience would pay close attention to the story of how the priceless iconostasis of the once-rich Macedonian Orthodox Church were saved in the crypt of the church, which still served as living quarters for the priest. The sound was poor and the voice of the priest often interrupted by coughing, but the audience listened attentively as though they were attending a church service. All activities ceased and the children were often silenced with angry 'shushing' from their mothers.

The same tape contained footage of other villages in the vicinity, since the camcorder was bought with funds raised by several families and the 'Australian tourist' was obliged to tape as much as possible of their homeland and life in it. We were told by authors that this activity was most of the time extremely dangerous, since the Greek authorities had relaxed their policies only on the surface. The Greek government was willing to make a show of easing the visa requirements for visitors of Macedonian origin, but they were not prepared to let too much visual documentation of the effects of the civil war and what is seen by the Macedonian community as a genocide to circulate around the world, particularly not interviews with survivors of the 'genocide' like the village priest mentioned above. For this reason a lot of the taped material was confiscated (often together with the rest of the video equipment) either by the Greek police, who closely followed the movements of the 'Australian tourists', or by Greek immigration officials at the border crossings. The videotapes that have made it safely back to Australia for this reason were cherished even more, and the authors celebrated as heroes by the community.

Video letters: an ethno-specific video genre

Owing to the private nature of these particular videotapes, most of the Macedonian families purchased VCRs relatively early in the 1980s, even though market prices were still high and the massive consumption of VCR in the rest of the Australian population did not develop until somewhat later. Very often families invested in two VCRs, mainly for the purpose of retaping the most frequently borrowed tapes, and less often to overcome the non-compatibility of the VHS and Beta systems. Owning two VCRs also lessened the possibility of disagreement between parents and the younger generation who often got bored with the endless reruns of the same tapes and preferred to watch rented (mainstream) tapes or time-shifted programmes from broad-cast television. The practice of watching these ad hoc assembled ethnic videos at home is different from any other practices described in media-related research since the home atmosphere of viewing ethnic videos allowed for interruption by comments and storytelling. This was most noticeable during the viewing of the videos which I refer to as 'video letters'.

Many tears were shed when suddenly on the television screen someone recognised a relative or a friend, or when a grandmother or mother or sister appeared on the screen and filled the room with emotionally charged messages to a sister, daughter or grandmother, some of whom they had never met or had not seen for a very long time. Time and space lost their meaning and those present were transported twelve thousand kilometres into another culture, and often back in time. Families and friends were reunited in an instant, if only just for a moment or two. A number of the people interviewed commented that these tapes provided them with a strong sense of belonging and often evoked recollections of their childhood. Today, there is a well-developed and well-established communication link between families and friends via video-tapes.

There are many types of video letter that serve as a link between people, and the structure of the videotape depends to a large extent on its producer. If the video has been taken by a professional 'video agency', the tape is more or less structured and easily recognisable by its use of computer graphics in editing and titling techniques identifying the producer. There is also, more often than not, suitable music montaged to the images, music which is entirely dependent on the producer's idea of its 'suitability' for the contents of the video. For example, most of the tapes of weddings start with Mendelssohn's *Wedding March* ('Here Comes the Bride'), while tapes of funerals tend to be accompanied by appropriately sombre music, thus following the well-established musical encoding used by the film industry. I believe that most of us have by now been treated to a viewing of such videotapes, since video records of family history are not confined to ethnic video practices exclusively.

Such tapes can also come under the category which I call 'video album'. Together with the amateur videos taken by members of the family, these are used in a way similar to the way photo-family albums have been used for years, serving the purpose of sustaining private domestic lives, helping construct family biographies and, just like photo albums, they have become a part of the mass market medium of recording family history.

In the Macedonian community an ethno-specific genre of video letters was produced which contained a mixture of programmes taped off the air and family album type records of family situations such as holidays, reunions and very often 'rites of passage' occasions – such as christenings, weddings and funerals. The usual records of celebrations of birthdays, anniversaries, graduations and so on, as well as the records of such dramatic moments as the first words or first steps of a grandchild (or losing the first tooth), are mixed on these videotapes with more ordinary moments from everyday life, like showing 'why the roses got spoiled this year in grandma's garden', or 'how well the vineyard is doing'. Each of these video letters is unique and they are all very different not only because they combine the personal letter and the snapshot, but also because, besides representing the personal account of the producers, they very often contain television (broadcast and satellite) programmes pirated off the air, thus fostering an 'ad hoc' cultural exchange between Australia, Macedonia and Canada.

Some aspects of video dynamics in the ethnic Macedonian community

It is clear, then, that VCR use in the Macedonian ethnic community in Western Australia varied greatly from its use in the mainstream English-speaking population. The VCR in migrant communities performs a dual function. Besides providing a cultural link with their homeland or families and friends, VCR is also used for the same purposes as by the mainstream population – for example, for watching rented films (in English), time-shifting or watching music videos. The emphasis on music video-viewing and film renting is often a more extended practice among younger people, often second- or third-generation migrants. Nevertheless, these videos are in most cases watched habitually by other members of the household, even by the older people with negligible fluency in English.

However, the social ritual of watching videos from the 'old country' is very different from watching rental videos and time-shifted English-language programmes. Another interesting observation that I have made during hours spent watching videos with various families (and in the course of informal interviews) is that, while conversation is welcome during the viewing of videos in (their first language) Macedonian, one is often silenced if one attempts conversation during English-language programmes either on broadcast television or on video. There are probably many reasons for this, but two aspects are of special interest for this study. First, the 'ethnic' videos are usually watched over and over again, so the content is familiar, while broadcast television or rented films in English are not readily available. The other aspect might be degree of language competence: as long as English-language fluency among the majority of migrants is variable, videos in English require closer attention, whereas videos in their mother tongue are readily understood.

The interesting point here is that the same thing happens among the younger, Australian-born family members, whose fluency in English is expected to be higher than their fluency in Macedonian. My informants tell me that children of Macedonian ethnic origin most often initially reject their ethnicity and very often rebel against anything that would 'make them different', as a consequence of extreme peer pressure. Yet, once they reach young adulthood and come to terms with themselves as individuals, they very often return to seek their 'roots'. In this, they are assisted by Macedonian government policies towards the diaspora, which actively support language seminars and summer schools for migrant students. Such a tendency to maintain their culture and language is also fostered by Australian multicultural policy. This renewed interest in one's cultural roots might be one of the reasons for the considerable popularity of ethnic videotapes among second- and third-generation Australians of Macedonian origin. The viewing practices of young married Australian couples, when either one or both partners is of Macedonian origin, are also different. In the case of a marriage to a partner of the same ethnic origin (marriages inside the community are very frequent) or at least to a partner of European NESB[3] descent, the maintenance of the 'ethnic' culture is far stronger than in the case of intermarriage to a partner from an English-speaking background. The greater the propensity towards cultural maintenance, the greater the cultural practice of ethnic video viewing is favoured.

There is an interesting variation in attitude regarding language maintenance and use among the Macedonian ethnic community from Aegean Macedonia (territorially now in Greece). Many of the migrants from Aegean Macedonia speak Greek as well as a dialect (often archaic) of Macedonian. Some of them watch Greek films, mainly commercially distributed and available in local video libraries, or taped off SBS-TV. However, there is no community practice involved either in viewing or in exchanging such films except among close friends and within the family.

Some points of conclusion

In conclusion I would like to draw some pertinent comparisons and parallels between the social and cultural experiences of viewers of ethnic video. Their experiences vary from nostalgia as a key element for the older members of the ethnic community, through the function of illuminating the culture and language of their ancestors for the second and every consequent generation, to that of a shared ritual for family and friends. For the elders, videos showing the folk rituals or other aspects of the way of life in their homeland, as they remember it, appear to act as a form of collective popular memory. Also some parents are more able to convey a sense of their past to their children through video, especially if the children are not literate in Macedonian language. With the emergence of the second generation of children as parents and grandparents, the nostalgic element is usually lost and the socio-cultural use of ethnic video is primarily defined in terms of linguistic, ritual and other cultural learning.

The notion of language as a transmitter of culture is still prevalent in the community and it is a shared view among the participants involved in this research project that 'if children do not speak the language they lose their culture'. Since many second- and third-generation migrants and migrant children are illiterate in their mother tongue (as well as a number of older migrants – the Aegean Macedonians have been illiterate or partly literate in it), the role of ethnic video as a means of communication with the 'old country', together with its role in familiarising them with the culture of the parents, seem to be viewed as most important by the Macedonian migrants interviewed.

Many parents in the Macedonian community voiced their concern over what they perceive as a progressive cultural loss with each new generation of children. While young people born and raised in Australia are striving to endure not only cultural but also peer group pressure and desperately want to fit in with what for their parents or grandparents is an alien culture, their parents are still attempting to recreate the traditional culture of their past. The influences of ethnic video on the process of striving after cultural continuity and holding on to the ethnic cultural identity is specific to each generation of migrants. Nevertheless, the impact of the VCR on the very process of negotiation of the cultural identity of every individual is far-reaching and overshadows the 'fun' aspect of the entertainment value of the VCR. Because of its family and community base (rather than commercial base), ethnic video tends to be invisible outside its use in the respective community. There are also connections between the ethnic video viewing practices and cultural reproduction of ethnic identity, which not only makes such videos into a powerful medium of communication but also brands them as markers of 'otherness' or 'difference'.

The capacity of media technology (radio, television, VCR, satellite and so on), to join the private world sphere of home and family with the larger public realm beyond the boundary of the front door, has enabled video audiences in general and the Macedonian audience in particular to be in touch with places that are distant in time and space, creating symbolic communities which in turn have offered identification points often of a transnational character to audience members. The migrant communities, although not created by the viewing of ethnic videos, use VCR as a link across the world. The Macedonian community, even though it has emerged from common origins, has different experiences in the different countries, and is not re-creating but rather creating the Macedonian culture out of the shared heritage, because culture is a dynamic process and no culture stays the same but rather develops and combines old and new cultural practices (Lotman 1990). For Macedonian communities in Australia, video technology did not mean bringing the cinema into their home, rather it meant bringing their roots, their heritage, their culture, squeezing their nostalgia into the format of a videocassette and letting it flow from the television screen any time they desired it.

Notes

1   This is a shorter and revised version of the paper published as 'Video as a Cultural Technology: The Macedonian Experience in Australia', *Macedonian Review*, 24(2): 147–73 (1994).
2   The term video-letter has been utilised by others. However, it has not been defined. 'Video letter' as used here signifies a videotape which is a mixture of a personal letter and snapshots with the added effect of an oral communication. This form of personal communication is partly comparable to the videophone with the exception that the immediacy of the telephone is not present. Science fiction (novels and films) has utilised this form, first by description of either video letters left by the deceased as messages to friends and family or as audio-visual history of whole civilisations. Whichever is the case, the fascination with audio-visual communication remains as shown by film and television productions which inevitably include nowadays some form of reference to video.
3   Non-English-speaking background.

9 Actually existing hybridity

Vietnamese diasporic music video

Stuart Cunningham and Tina Nguyen

Being originally refugees and only lately immigrants makes the Vietnamese peoples in the Western world very aware of the pull between maintaining their original cultures and adapting to their new host cultures. For most, 'home' is an officially denied category while the communist regime continues in power, and so media networks, especially music video, operate to connect the dispersed Vietnamese communities. Small business entrepreneurs produce low-budget music video, mostly out of southern California, which is taken up within the fan circuits of America, Australia, Canada, France and elsewhere. The internal cultural conflicts within the communities centre on the felt need to maintain pre-revolutionary Vietnamese heritage and traditions, find a negotiated place within a more mainstreamed culture or engage in the formation of distinct hybrid identities around the appropriation of dominant Western popular cultural forms. These three cultural positions or stances are dynamic and mutable, but the main cultural and social debates are constructed around them – they are therefore a useful heuristic which can be used to organise analysis.

The Vietnamese have had a long history of migration within their immediate region but a very limited history of migration outside of Vietnam. By 1975 only about a hundred thousand Vietnamese were living outside Vietnam. However, from 1965 to 1975, during the height of the Vietnam (or 'American') War, over half of Vietnam's population were displaced internally, and now the Vietnamese diaspora numbers something over two million Vietnam-born throughout the world. (The current population in Vietnam is 76 million.) To this of course should be added a substantial second (and emergent third generation), those born to Vietnamese parents in the host countries, whose numbers are notoriously unreliable because census data collection in several countries follow widely variant protocols, but is estimated at more than half a million. About a half of the total diaspora is domiciled in the United States, with significant population centres in Orange County, San Jose, Texas, Minneapolis, Washington and Houston. Other major host countries include France, Canada, Australia, Germany and the Netherlands. Given the fraught history of the treatment of refugees in the immediate East Asian and South-East Asian region, it is not surprising that there are very few Vietnamese resettled in the country's immediate region. Overall, there are about 70 population centres across the world with some Vietnamese presence outside the homeland.

Vietnamese diasporic music video

The live variety shows, and music video productions based on and arising from them, produced by Vietnamese-owned and operated companies based in southern California and exported to all overseas communities, are the only media form unique to the diaspora as audio-visual media made by and for the diaspora. This media form bears many similarities to the commercial and variety-based cultural production of Iranian television in Los Angles studied by Naficy (1993), not least because Vietnamese variety show and music video production is also centred in the Los Angeles conurbation. The Vietnamese grouped there are not as numerous or rich as Naficy's Iranians and so have not developed the extent of the business infrastructure to support the range and depth of media activity recounted in Naficy's *The Making of Exile Cultures*. The business infrastructure of Vietnamese audio-visual production is structured around a small number of small businesses operating on low margins. It is, as Kolar-Panov dubs ethnic minority video circuits as they are perceived from outside, a 'shadow system' (1997: 31) operating in parallel to the majoritarian system, with few industry linkages and very little cross-over of performer or audience.

To be exilic means not, or at least not 'officially', being able to draw on the contemporary cultural production of the home country. Indeed it means 'officially' denying its existence in a dialectical process of mutual disauthentification (Carruthers 2001). The Vietnam government asserts that the *Viet Kieu* (the appellation for Vietnamese overseas which carries a pejorative connotation) may be fatally Westernised, whereas the diasporic population proposes that the homeland population has been de-ethnicised through, ironically, the wholesale adoption of an alien (Western) ideology of Marxism-Leninism. The widely dispersed geography and the demography of a small series of communities frame the conditions for 'global narrowcasting', that is, ethnically specific cultural production for widely dispersed population fragments centripetally organised around an officially excluded homeland. This makes the media, and the media use, of the Vietnamese diaspora significantly different from the media consumption of large diasporas, such the Chinese or Indian diasporas, which focus on large production centres in the 'home' countries.

These conditions also determine the nature of the production companies (Thuy Nga, Asia/Dem Saigon, Mey/Hollywood Nights, Khanh Ha, Diem Xua and others). These are small businesses running at low margins and constantly undercut by copying of their video product outside the United States (particularly in Vietnam itself) where their ability to police copyright is restricted by not having the time or resources to follow up breaches. They have clustered around the only Vietnamese population base which offers critical mass and is geographically adjacent to the world-leading entertainment-communications-information (ECI) complex in southern California. There is evidence of internal migration within the diaspora from the rest of the US, Canada and France to southern California to take advantage of the largest overseas Vietnamese population concentration and the world's major ECI complex.

Thuy Nga Productions is by far the largest and most successful company. It organises major live shows in the US and franchises an appearance schedule for the high-profile performers at shows around the global diaspora, and has produced over 60, two-hour videotapes since the early 1980s as well as a constant flow of CDs, audiocassettes and karaoke discs. President and owner of Thuy Nga, To Van Lai, was a university psychology professor before establishing Thuy Nga in 1969. Named after his wife, Thuy Nga was set up as a recording and production label which actuated To's stance as a cultural intellectual bringing traditional folk and contemporary Vietnamese music traditions into contact with popular American and French music. Thuy Nga Productions' *Paris by Night* series, at start-up in the early 1980s, evoked pre-1975 Saigon through its revival of cabaret music and entertainment from previously well-established Vietnamese performers, such as Elvis Phuong, Jo Marcel and Khanh Ly. Due to the rising costs of production, more public demand for live concert performances in the US and Canada, the demand for regularisation of music video production protocols and the fact that the majority of Vietnamese performers were living in the US, To moved Thuy Nga production to Orange County in the late 1980s. The first *Paris by Night* video produced in 1983 was recorded in Paris and cost about US$19,000. It consisted of 11 performances with local Vietnamese in Paris. In comparison, in the late 1990s, Thuy Nga releases at least four videos a year, consisting usually of 24 performances from a range of international Vietnamese performers, a stage and technical crew of approximately three hundred people, often recording in front of packed audiences. Production costs per video have moved to US$500,000.

Paris by Night had the challenging task of breaking into the well-established demand for Chinese-language video in the US, which 'monopolised' the overseas Vietnamese market through the 1980s. According to To, the Vietnamese audience's 'addiction' to Hong Kong multi-tape television series had a deleterious effect on their working lives and their lifestyles.[1] Within the wider issues of dealing with the new country, the contribution of 'addiction' to Chinese videos worsened the community's social dilemmas. To Van Lai's attempt to provide an alternative to the Chinese-language material began to work after 1986 when the release of its first special documentary edition *Gia Biet Saigon* (*Farewell Saigon*), which is discussed below. The revenue and profit generated from the live performances and shows help to fund the production of music videos, CDs and karaoke discs. To claims sales figures per video of approximately forty thousand and up to eighty thousand for 'specials' in the US, but also states that overseas sales are not a significant or stable revenue source due to illegal dubbing of tapes.

The other most popular company committed to high production values is

ASIA Productions (Dem Saigon/Saigon Nights). It was established in the US in the early 1980s and, in contrast to Thuy Nga, ASIA is not a family business but is owned by shareholders and run by a manager. ASIA reaches out beyond the established community performers, focusing more than Thuy Nga on promoting new talent in the US and Canada. Through an annual 'star search' competition, Truc Ho, ASIA's music director, scouts for talent, offering contracts to perform live shows, video-taping and CD recordings for the company. It also encourages its audience to take part in the 'quest for stardom' by testing talent using its karaoke recordings, and then sending in tapes of the performances. Shortlisted singers are given the opportunity to perform in front of a live audience to get feedback on their performance. Like all other production companies, the main revenue and profit derives from the ticket sales of live shows and the domestic sale of CDs, videos and karaoke discs.

The videoscape: texts and consumption

From data supplied by the production companies and distributors, the rates of sale and rental derived from samples of video store retailers, and the scale of attendances at regular live variety performances, it can be surmised that most overseas Vietnamese households may own or rent some of this music video material.[2] A significant proportion have developed comprehensive home libraries. This material's popularity is exemplary, cutting across differences of ethnicity, age, gender, recency of arrival, refugee or immigrant status, and home region. It is also widely available in pirated form in Vietnam itself, as the economic and cultural 'thaw' that has proceeded since Doi Moi policies of greater openness have resulted in extensive penetration of the homeland by this most international form of Vietnamese expression.[3] As the only popular culture produced by and specifically for the Vietnamese diaspora, there is a deep investment in these texts by and within the overseas communities; an investment by no means homogeneous but uniformly strong. The social text which surrounds, indeed engulfs, these productions is intense, multi-layered and makes its address across differences of generation, gender, ethnicity, class and education levels and recency of arrival. 'Audiovisual images become so important for young Vietnamese as a point of reference, as a tool for validation and as a vehicle towards self identity'.[4]

The central point linking business operations, the textual dynamics of the music videos and media use within the communities is that what we have called the three cultural positions or stances in the communities, and the musical styles which give expression to them, have to be accommodated somehow within the same productions because of the marginal size of the audience base. From the point of view of business logic, each style cannot exist without the others. Thus the organisational structure of the shows and the videos, both at the level of the individual show/video and at the level of whole company outputs, particularly those of Thuy Nga and ASIA, reflect the heterogeneity required to maximise audience within a strictly narrowcast range. This is a programming philosophy congruent with broadcasting to a globally spread, narrowcast demographic. This also underscores why 'the variety show form has been a mainstay of overseas Vietnamese anti-communist culture from the mid-1970s onwards' (Carruthers 2001). In any given live show or video production, the musical styles might range from pre-colonial traditionalism, to French colonial-era high modernist classicism, to crooners adapting Vietnamese folksongs to the Sinatra era, through to bilingual cover versions of Grease or Madonna. Stringing this concatenation of taste cultures together are the compères, typically well-known political and cultural figures in their own right, who perform a rhetorical unifying function:

> Audience members are constantly recouped via the show's diegesis, and the anchoring role of the comperes and their commentaries, into an overarching conception of shared overseas Vietnamese identity. This is centred on the appeal to core cultural values, common tradition, linguistic unity and an anti-communist homeland politics.
>
> (Carruthers 2001: 124)

Within this overall political trajectory, however, there are major differences to be managed. The stances evidenced in the video and live material range on a continuum from 'pure' heritage maintenance and ideological monitoring, to mainstream cultural negotiation, through to assertive hybridity. Most performers and productions seek to situate themselves within the mainstream of cultural negotiation between Vietnamese and Western traditions. However, at one end of the continuum there are strong attempts to keep both the original folkloric music traditions alive and also the integrity of the originary anti-communist stance foundational to the diaspora through very public criticism of any lapse from that stance. At the other end, Vietnamese-American youth culture is exploring the limits of hybrid identities through 'New Wave', radical intermixing of musical styles. We shall consider some textual examples of each style and audience/readership responses to them.

Heritage maintenance

Heritage maintenance embraces a range of cultural and informational production and is closely connected to the ideological monitoring role of maintaining the salience of the anti-communist stance foundational to the diaspora. Diasporic video is one of the prime sites monitored. This is borne out spectacularly in the 'Mother' issue of *Paris by Night*. *Paris by Night* issue 40 was released in 1997 to coincide with *Vu Lan*, the Season of Filial Piety, a time for special veneration of parents. The video was particularly popular, but popularity turned to condemnation in the diaspora when it was discovered that a small segment of documentary war footage showing planes strafing and killing South Vietnamese civilians was actually of the Republic of South Vietnam (RSA) air forces. Thuy Nga asserted it was the innocent mistake of a young and inexperienced editor;

both To Van Lai and compère Nguyen Ngoc Ngan were forced to publish apologies in the main newspapers and calm very angry responses on websites, in letters to the editor, on radio and in demonstrations outside Thuy Nga's offices. Some even alleged that it was a cynical ploy by the company to establish its good name in Vietnam in advance of a greater entrepreneurial effort in the homeland.

The Mother imbroglio has been extensively analysed by Carruthers (2001). Carruthers stresses the porosity of communications flows between the diaspora and the homeland, noting that the degree of ideological border-drawing on which the identity and integrity of both the homeland regime and the diasporic community depend is increasingly difficult to sustain under the pressures of globalisation. However, it is appropriate for our themes that we stress that the Mother episode illustrates the degree of psychic and ideological investment in the music video corpus and the degree to which it, like all public cultural manifestations, is monitored for deviations from the ideological foundations of the diaspora. The social text of the corpus is subtended by strong community expectations of a proper education for the young in the reasons for cultural maintenance. While much of the dissolution of boundaries between homeland and diaspora proceeds around cultural product, entrepreneurship and travel (it was estimated that about twenty thousand Australian Vietnamese visited Vietnam annually in the mid-1990s), there continues to be organised resistance to such dissolution among the overseas populations. Examples include boycotts of restaurants run by government-aligned owners; a new shopping complex known as the 'cultural court' in the heart of Westminster on Balsa Avenue, that was part-financed by homeland sources, has been conspicuously under-patronised and for a good time virtually boycotted in the months following its opening in 1996. And international attention was drawn in 1999 to the community attacks on a shop-owner in the precinct who insisted on flying the official country flag and displaying pictures of Ho Chi Minh.

The main musical expression of heritage maintenance lies in the restoration and preservation of traditional Vietnamese music style (and the instruments on which they are played). Major cultural figures such as Pham Duy, often titled in American media coverage as the 'Woody Guthrie' of Vietnam, have devoted long careers to the maintenance of the received Vietnamese heritage in folk culture.[5] The purity is maintained through a scholarly attention to the traditions and their transmission to a younger, dispersed generation; the artisanal attention to the playing of traditional Vietnamese musical instruments; and also a preparedness to transmit this heritage by contemporary technologies such as CD and the Internet. Into this category should also be placed a considerable amount of traditional folk balladry and a residual element of traditional Vietnamese opera on the tapes. This form of 'pure' heritage maintenance is clearly mainly consumed by the older generation of the educated elite.

A small fraction of the music video corpus is given over to heritage maintenance across the entire tape. These six to eight tapes are constructed quite differently to the rest and are at the other end of the stylistic continuum from the live show formats. They are compilation documentary-style video, and have been produced typically to commemorate historical anniversaries in the overseas communities' lives. An early example of the historical compilation video is Thuy Nga 10, *Gia Biet Saigon* (*Farewell Saigon*). Made in 1986, this Thuy Nga production has none of the sophisticated production values and choreography of later productions; in fact it is organised on quite different principles to the variety show format of most of the corpus. The organisational principle is one of popular memory, bearing all the hallmarks of a very specific address to the military, educational, business and government elites of the South Vietnam regime in the period leading to the fall of Saigon.

This principle of organisation makes it a virtually unwatchable tape for all but this specific audience. The great majority of second-generation and recent arrivals who participated in our focus groups and interviews asserted that historical compilation material was 'for [their] parents' or for those who 'had been through the events' being recounted. *Farewell Saigon* is a tape of approximately 90 minutes duration, comprising historical footage of pre-1975 Saigon (together with some post-1975 footage) with studio-based musical interludes sung by profiled performers of the same or similar generation to the target audience – those performers who successfully transitioned from pre- to post-1975 as part of the diaspora. The great majority of the elapsed time on the tape is a video essay extolling the strength, social balance and harmony, and dynamism of a well-governed and stable Republic of Vietnam during the Diem and Thieu years. So much can be readily deduced from the contents and organisation of the tape. What can be *adduced* from its reception and use within the specific target audience – the original diasporic elites – is both the depth of loss and longing which the tape engenders and, on the other hand, a still-strong politics of disavowal of the regime's complicity in its own downfall and the continued placing of blame on America as a 'great and powerful friend' which withdrew its support unilaterally, rendering the defence of the republic impossible. The vertiginous shifts from triumphalism to abjection, from very long static camera angles on impeccably suited parades of military to the hand-held chaos of the end-time of 1975 has strong parallels with the abrupt changes of tempo and testamental nature of the Croatian video analysed by Kolar-Panov (1997: 153). The footage combines travelogue-style panoramas of market scenes, major downtown buildings, the Presidential Palace, main girls' and boys' schools, and a compendium of religious buildings. The second set of visual materials include a highly structured, syncopated visual hymn to the women of the republic, cut to complement the ballad 'Co gai Viet' (The Vietnamese Lady) in a studio setting by three women performers wearing signifiers of north, centre and south regions of a pre-communist unified country. The third type is very extensive footage of a military parade on the National Day that was held on 26 October each year. Voice-over commentary details the different regiments in careful detail and occupies almost half an hour of the tape.

What is readable as flat 'propaganda' and inexcusably tedious editing by its non-intended audience is received very differently by its primary audience, the original diasporic elites. For them, *Farewell Saigon* is like a home movie. There are no specific time references to anchor the footage at a particular date apart from its ambience in the later 1960s or early 1970s; it inhabits a modality of popular memory, with very specific anchors of place but not of time. In one family with whom researchers were invited to watch the video, the father had been an RSA fighter pilot and had been interned in a re-education camp for 11 years before being allowed to come to Australia under the family reunion programme. *Farewell Saigon* has footage of his military unit which he finds impossible to watch. The mother can point out the school she went to as a girl – the images of a sea of white *ao dai* (traditional dress worn by Vietnamese women) spreading gaily from the gates of the school are images of Confucian educational rectitude and the innocence of youth that are almost equally impossible to watch.

There are also those for whom the politics of this tape are to be fore-grounded: 'The video brings back emotional memories of how proud and honoured Vietnamese should be with their country and not believe false propaganda and damaging accusations by foreign political analysts and the Vietcong' and 'It was produced to remind the Vietnamese and the rest of the world that Vietnam was once an independent nation until it was betrayed in the war by its American allies' are representative of the public construction that can be placed on this material by its intended audience. It is important to note that there is nothing in the tape commentary or visuals that directly attacks the USA – but there is a studied absence of virtually any signifier of what was by the time of the footage an overwhelming American presence in Saigon. There is also a very direct political sense in which *Farewell Saigon* is like a home movie. Most of the documentary footage used in the video was smuggled out of the country just before the fall of Saigon by the Vietnamese Student Association in Paris. It was then handed over to a senior military figure who gave To Van Lai copyright clearance to use the footage in his assembly for *Gai Biet Saigon*. The footage is a virtual palimpsest of the violence of exile – such media, left behind after the fall of Saigon, would have had prime value in targeting elite members of the fallen regime.

Cultural negotiation

The auspicers of the inevitable and widespread negotiation between Vietnamese and Western cultural forms are predominantly the owners of the small business music video production houses and the principal well-established performers. Many of these figures were prominent in South Vietnamese cultural production before 1975 and have maintained that position in the ensuing decades. They are educated in the heritage and have maintained the popular memory as they simultaneously auspice the inevitable hybridisation of this heritage under the commercial imperative. But this is to continue a well-established historical hybridisation. For the most established, there are direct links back to pre-1975 Saigon, and the continuities of such converged music forms being developed and practiced well before 1975 need to be accounted for. The hybridity of Vietnamese music culture has its roots both fundamentally in millennial Chinese–Vietnamese interchange and more latterly with French interchange during the colonial period. In the 1960s it was the massive influence of American rock and roll during the war, especially in Saigon, which provided the most recent pre-exile infusion of hybrid elements. Pham's historical treatise *Musics of Vietnam* (1973), even as it is committed to the identification and preservation of the country's folk traditions, shows that the south's major styles of theatrical romanticism in performance, while influenced by French and latterly American traditions, was originally a Chinese influence (ibid.: 118). Vietnamese arca studies could benefit significantly from a greater sense of the mutability and adaptability of its object of study, and this is nowhere clearer than in the area of popular culture. Terry Rambo, arguing this case, shows that even such an exemplary symbol of Vietnamese authenticity, the *aodai*, is a borrowing from Chinese culture (Rambo 1987).

Of the cultural positions available to the communities, that which accepts the inevitability of cultural negotiation and adaptation and fashions musical styles around that position seeks to minimise the more liminal postures of heritage maintenance or assertive hybridity. The musical styles are mainstreamed and stable in style, based on established patterns of intermixing Chinese, French and US inputs from before 1975. A major figure, Elvis Phoung – an Elvis cover singer before it became a global industry! – was an established performer in Saigon before 1975 whose career has continued unabated throughout the exile. Other major performers include Luu Bich, Tuan Ngoc and Khanh Ha. Befitting its mainstream status, probably two-thirds of the corpus is of this type, as it is predominantly easy listening or middle-of-the-road 'crooner' presentational styles that are the least confronting and of potentially broadest address across audience interests. The style of music renews audience connections to the soft melodic music and sentimental ballads often performed in bars and cabarets of the pre-1975 period. Visually, this style of presentation rarely employs documentary footage characteristic of the first style, nor does it involve the elaborate postmodern-pastiche stage settings and 'excessive' costuming of the third style. All the companies aim for this type of predominant content, as it will maximise its target audience. The other two categories occupy together roughly the other third of output.

'Hat Cho Ngay Hom Qua' ('Song of Yesterday') (in *Paris by Night* issue 20, 1993), a 'lien khuc' (medley) with performers Elvis Phuong, Duy Quang, Anh Khoa and Tuan Ngoc, is a good example. Performed bilingually, the medley comprises popular Western songs of Elvis Presley and John Lennon, and music from the era of the Vietnam War ('Yesterday', 'Stand by me', and so on). The performance draws upon the memories of the mature audience who lived in Saigon throughout the 1950s to 1970s; hence the title: 'Hat Cho Ngay Hom Qua'. That audience's memories of an era of continual war, struggle and devastation are mapped gently onto the 'hardships' which are the thematic substance of the original Western songs (lost and unrequited love and so on) and the massive disjunction is managed in the ambience of nostalgia and tasteful dinner jackets on the set.

Innovation within this style is centred on harmonious both-ways adaptation; Vietnamese interpretation of foreign music or traditional Vietnamese lyrics with the influence of contemporary Western music. New songwriters like Nhat Ngan and Khuc Lan specialise in translating and interpreting Chinese and French songs into Vietnamese new wave music. Luu Bich is often linked with the latter, performing a wide range of Chinese ballads translated into Vietnamese with one of the most popular songs being 'Chiec La Mua Dong' (The Leaf of Winter). Composers like Van Phung and Ngo Thuy Mien, for example, are strongly influenced by jazz and rhythm and blues. In 'Noi Long' (Feelings) (*Paris by Night* issue 39, 1997), Bich Chieu's performance of lyrics which are purely Vietnamese is revamped with a Western influence of jazz and blues. The initial reaction from one focus group of young, recently arrived school students watching this was that it was 'weird' and 'un-Vietnamese'. However, after discussion and reflection they were able to appreciate the new version of the song.

The most productive means of grasping the cultural work audiences are performing with this music is to see it as positively modelling identity transition. The simple lyrics, well known to the point of cliché ('easy listening') in Vietnamese, English or French, provide a reassuring point of recognition for those (mostly the older, more recently arrived) who find themselves displaced in an overseas community where language is the main cultural barrier, while others (mostly the young) are provided an easier way into understanding their own family's cultural environment. ASIA Productions specialise in this approach. Thanh and Jasmine, a well-educated brother and sister who are dedicated fans of the music, reflected that they were initially attracted to their own heritage by their interest in the remixing of traditional folklore music through the music videos of ASIA Productions.

The cultural negotiation position can also be distinguished politically from heritage maintenance insofar as it is prepared to negotiate certain emergent relationships with the homeland, a stance unthinkable within the first category. As Carruthers (2001) points out, the revered composer Trinh Cong Son, who actually lives in Vietnam but enjoys equal popularity both at home and abroad, has had a long collaboration with popular diaspora singer Khanh Ly. Also, diaspora artists are now beginning to test the home market with some live performances, such as at the major Tet celebrations since 1996. Indeed, there is greater reciprocity to this emergent and problematic rapprochement than might at first appear:

> The homeland pirate culture industry has been able to take advantage of lax copyright and censorship laws to enjoy the fruits of overseas Vietnamese media companies' labours without contributing to their revenues, while

overseas companies have been able to exploit the first world/third world divide by going to Vietnam to record the voices of local singers, mastering them in studios back in France and the US, and releasing the CDs at a significantly lower price than those produced entirely overseas.

(Carruthers 2001: 140–4)

'New wave' assertive hybridity

While the hybrid retains its links to and identification with its origins, it is also shaped and transformed by (and in turn, shapes and transforms) its location in the present. Belonging at the same time to several 'homes', it cannot simply dissolve into a culturally unified form. The complex achievement of the hybrid is a product of [the] obligation to 'come to terms with and to make something new of the cultures they inhabit, without simply assimilating to them'. The result . . . is a celebration of cultural impurity, a 'love-song to our mongrel selves'.

(Turner 1994: 124–5, internal quotes Hall 1993: 362)

The reception for performers who assertively seek to fully appropriate Western rock and pop (in a style that is dubbed 'New Wave') can be as intense as the political controversies around incidents such as the Mother episode. This 'assertive hybridity' is exclusively a phenomenon of youth culture, and centres on its very specific formation at 'ground zero' in southern California. The 'excesses' of controversial performers such as Lynda Trang Dai, Nhu Mai, The Magic or Don Ho have some precedent within the context of Californian Vietnamese-American youth culture (as evidenced by the specialist lifestyle magazines for Vietnamese-American young people such as *Viet Now*). However, the economics of live performance and music video production necessitates a much broader audience and thus a context beyond its niche age and style demographic. New Wave, at its most basic, refers to bilingual – English and Vietnamese – song lyrics. But it is also about playful, political and increasingly ambitious appropriations or pastiches of mostly American rock and pop rendered into Vietnamese – with some examples being 'Black Magic Woman', 'Hotel California' and 'Fernando'. But innovative performers like Don Ho have ranged much wider – for example, in *Paris by Night: Las Vegas* (issue 29, 1995), Don Ho's 'Caravan of Life' performance was based on a well-known Chinese song, translated into Vietnamese and performed in the setting which highlighted the oppression of the Nepalese.

Lynda Trang Dai is prototypical of this stance, and is a well-established but very controversial figure in Vietnamese music performance. She has established a profile since the mid-1980s modelling herself on Madonna, reprising most of Madonna's personae from the fishnet stockings-crucifix-white trash-material girl to the toned gym junkie to the feminine-*Vogue* look. It is entirely possible to see Lynda's confrontational personae as doubly mapped onto the provocations Madonna posed to sexual/musical/religious representations over this period, given that her career has been entirely played out within the Vietnamese community. Her influence can be measured by her pioneering 'assertive hybridity' and by the strength of audience response, which in its extremes is *sui generis* in the Vietnamese music industry. It is not only in sexual Westernisms that this occurs; there is much more stress in this style of music on the dramatic/excessive surfaces of performance, costume and reprising contemporary Western rock, pop and rap than on traditional Vietnamese music's emphasis on subtly coded variations of voice and face. Thanh, a young proprietor of a karaoke coffee shop who is extremely knowledgeable about all aspects of the Vietnamese music scene, offered this analysis:

> Linda is the first Vietnamese to do that [fashion a form of extreme hybridity] when she came out. It was a clash of cultures especially with the older generation. They were giving her a bad name. But guys like her performances. Now everyone [that is, Vietnamese performers] just copies Linda while she continues to copy Madonna. Linda was daring to do that because Vietnamese performers at that time were more traditional and very influenced by the Vietnamese culture.

Over time, she has – and very importantly in the Vietnamese community – officially 'earned respect' in terms of her longevity and solid track record of performance, and a typical introduction to a Lynda performance by a compère might now be the respectful coding 'a Vietnamese woman with a Western style of performance', or this saying quoted by one of the MCs linking the performances on *Paris by Night* issue 36, 'khau za ma tam phat/although the mouth speaks badly, the heart speaks of goodness'. Nevertheless, at the level of gossip and rumour in the unofficial culture, a figure like Lynda is the occasion for much boundary-marking. On the one hand, it is very difficult for the young, particularly those without Vietnamese language skills and/or sufficient background in the formal poetic rhetoric of much of the music embodying the heritage maintenance and cultural negotiation positions, to be able to appreciate them – the Westernised/Americanised posture of a Lynda offers some purchase into Vietnamese culture. For Thanh and Jasmine (Thanh's sister, who runs the grocery store adjacent to Thanh's coffee shop), the single most crucial factor in excluding potential fans of this music video is high-enough levels of language competence. On the other hand, Lynda will often bring out an 'ultra-Vietnamese' reaction, with gossip about face lifts, corruption of the language through sloppy lyrics and 'inability to sing rather than just perform', and dismissal of her claims to feminist credentials on the basis that 'women's rights are a Western issue' – precisely why, for the New Wave youth following, it should be foregrounded! 'Cyber Queen' (*Paris by Night* issue 32, 1995) is Lynda's reprise of Madonna in her Gaultier cyborg phase. Lynda and her backing singers and dancers are costumed as steely cyborgs, the women sporting conical bras. The English lyrics are consistent with the choreography of the piece, but there is a complete disjunction with the Vietnamese lyrics, which speak in traditional coding of 'winds and waterfalls'. There is also a disjunctive gesture midway through the song when Lynda unveils the Republic of Vietnam flag under one arm and the United States flag under the other. This nationalistic gesture would be characteristic of a heritage maintenance performance but is received with some bewilderment as part of this style.

Don Ho is one of the most popular performers for younger Vietnamese. His performances are noted for their elaborate choreography, set design, costuming and innovation, along with sophisticated cover versions of a wide range of exclusively Western songs. 'I Just Died in Your Arms' (*Paris by Night* issue 36, 1996) was a Western hit song in the late 1980s and, in this instance and compared to 'Cyber Queen', there is a close conjunction between the English and the Vietnamese 'translation' from the English. The Vietnamese lyrics, being a translation and not a lyrical sequence or song in its own right in the language, is, for some, a stronger provocation to Vietnamese lyrical traditions and to traditional models of romance and sexual relations. The song embraces without reservation the iconic degeneracy, the female sexual predation, the sex and death equivalences and the eviscerated manhood that are at the centre of the European vampire mythologies. And, by and large, the Vietnamese lyrical component is drawn directly into this field of meaning. There is nothing that compels identification as Vietnamese in either the staging or referencing in the lyrics. One focus group of young school-aged, recently arrived migrants were generally consensual about Don Ho being 'American' rather than 'Vietnamese' because the mannerisms in which he performs are 'foreign'. Such as his dress, the Western songs he sings, the way he dances, the fact that there are back-up dancers performing with him and particularly in this performance, the stage design being European Gothic (coffins, chandeliers, the crepuscular smoke, female vampires with extended canines, black capes and ghostly make-up). Others in the group commented that he is a 'lai', a 'half-breed', as a performer.

In 'going too far', the assertive hybridity position provokes criticism and risks losing at least part of its intended audience. A music store owner catering primarily to Vietnamese youth argues that the young listen primarily to Western techno and house music and may regard the more radical performers and styles as in fact assimilationist as they are 'cheap imitations' of dominant Western styles. If they want to 'be' Vietnamese in their music tastes, they will turn to the more middle-of-the-road material of cultural negotiation which engages identifiably distinct Vietnamese traditions.

Conclusion

Each time I view these videos, the feeling I am left with afterwards is one of complete exhilaration or of absolute sadness. There is no in between. It is either one extreme or the other. Having left Vietnam as a child of 7 years of age in 1976, I do not have strong recollection of the physical landscape of Vietnam, of the traditions, the tastes, the smell, the sights, the sounds of this 'homeland'. Every image that comes on screen builds for me the 'reality' of what Vietnam is and was. And it is these images that I collect and refer to when I speak of Vietnam. It is not the Vietnam that once existed or the country as it is now that swims in my head. Vietnam becomes for me a collection of images I have been immersed in through media.[6]

The rate of emigration from Vietnam slowed appreciably over the latter 1990s; the proportion of those who were originally refugees also diminished appreciably, while the numbers of those visiting Vietnam for business or family purposes rose. Whereas the official culture of the diaspora continues to remain strongly anti-communist and anti-homeland government, growing numbers of particularly the young are forging 'hyphenated' ('Asian-American', 'Asian-Australian') identities which owe less to the past and more to a globalising present. For such small communities, there is a remarkable diversity both of the population and their economic, social and cultural circumstances. It is arguable that diaspora communities provide examples of cultural formations at their most mutable, with political change both in the homelands and the host countries, intergenerational tension a key given the recency of departures from the homeland, and very sharp socio-economic differences between the successful and the struggling. The media consumed by overseas Vietnamese people, rather than resolving the conflicts thrown up by such mutability, as a functionalist model of media-social relations would have it, tend rather to 'stage' them, give them voice and manage them in a productive tension. Western claims to cultural pluralism would be more plausible if the 'shadow system' of diasporic video, music and popular culture was to come into a fuller light.

Notes

1 To Van Lai, interview conducted by Tina Nguyen and Stuart Cunningham, Westminster, CA, May 1996.
2 The industry does not have resources for large-scale tracking surveys.
3 Carruthers (2001) points to data from 1996 which estimates that 85 to 90 per cent of stock in Saigon's unlicensed video stores was foreign.
4 Trang Nguyen, personal communications and research notes, June 1997.
5 He wrote a historical treatise, *Musics of Vietnam* (1973), has had several special issue videos dedicated to his corpus and has recreated *Truyen a Kieu*/The Tale of Kieu as a folk opera dubbed the 'Iliad of Vietnam'.
6 Trang Nguyen, June 1997.

Part 2

Computer-mediated communication

10 Communication and diasporic Islam

A virtual ummah?

Peter Mandaville

This chapter focuses not on the diaspora of a particular ethno-national group or geographic region, but rather on a transnational community that transcends the boundaries of territory: Islam. Muslims living in diaspora – particularly in the West – are of varied and diverse ethnic origins.[1] What links them together, however, is a shared sense of identity within their religion, an idea most clearly located within the concept of the *ummah*, or world community of believers. Islam is, however, also host to a great deal of internal diversity. Invariably, different understandings and interpretations of the religion map onto particular ethnic and communal affiliations – many of which encounter each other within Western diasporas. Inevitably, then, one of the key questions that arises in the Muslim diaspora is 'what is Islam?' My aim in this contribution is to demonstrate that diasporic media can and should be understood as much more than simply a means by which information of interest to a given community can be exchanged, or a means for communicating images of that community to wider society. Indeed, the approach advocated here is distinctly suspicious of the very notion of 'given community'. The line of argument taken suggests that we need to understand these media as spaces of communication in which the identity, meaning and boundaries of diasporic community are continually constructed, debated and reimagined.[2] In this article I will explore the discursive politics that surrounds the articulation of Islam within Muslim communities in Western Europe and North America. Through a discussion of various forms of media – and the Internet in particular – I will demonstrate the mechanisms through which dominant discourses of Islam emerge within communities and are then, in turn, challenged by dissenting voices which increasingly turn to the spaces engendered by new information and communication technologies (ICTs) in order to speak their alternatives. These new media are likely to play an increasingly important role among young Muslims born and raised in the West as they search for spaces and languages in which to shape an Islam that is both relevant to their socio-cultural situatedness and free from the hegemony of traditional sources of interpretation and authority. To what extent do ICTs allow for the meaning of diasporic Muslim identities to be contested, negotiated and reformulated? How are new media affecting debates between Muslims about what Islam means today and – more importantly in the context of politics – about who possesses the authority to speak on its behalf?.

I will begin by identifying several recent transformations in Muslim diasporic discourse and explain how ICTs can be understood as important enabling agents in these changes. This section will place particular emphasis on the ways in which the younger generation of Muslims living in the West are using new media to communicate interpretations of Islam suited to the demands and concerns of their particular circumstances. The second part of the piece will offer some reflections on how the 'politics of knowledge' engendered by these technologies is likely to influence the emergence of alternative conceptions of Muslim identity and discourse in diaspora.

Living (and revising) Islam in diaspora

Up to 40 per cent of today's Muslims live in minority situations (Dassetto 1993). In the present context, we will focus exclusively on Muslim communities in the West – that is, North America and Western Europe. Minority status, as we will see, involves a number of advantages and disadvantages. It means coming to terms with an unfamiliar set of circumstances, a requirement to engage with new cultures and an ability to adjust to inevitable changes in one's own tradition. 'We cannot assume', argues Barbara Metcalf, however, 'that the old and new cultures are fixed, and that change results from pieces being added and subtracted. Instead, new cultural and institutional expressions are being created using the symbols and institutions of the received tradition' (Metcalf 1996: 7). We are therefore not talking about cases of loss and gain, or of aspects of Islam simply 'disappearing' in diaspora. What we see is a far more complex hybrid condition, one in which Islamic meanings shift, change and transmutate, where things become something else. Likewise Islam becomes represented in new forms and via new media – a phenomenon which will be explored in depth in a subsequent section. Much of this involves bringing Islam into the forums of popular culture and making it available via a wide variety of media. Television, the Internet and 'secular' literature now suddenly all become sources of Islamic knowledge.

Muslim communities are also embroiled today in complex debates about the very nature and boundaries of their religion. What does Islam mean to Muslims living in the West? From whom can reliable knowledge about Islam be gained? How can one differentiate reliably between 'good' and 'bad' interpretations of Islam? Such conversations are intensified in Western diasporic contexts due to the sheer volume of human traffic that flows through them. Muslims in diaspora come face to face with the myriad shapes and colours of global Islam, forcing their religion to hold a mirror up to its own diversity. These encounters often play an important role in processes of identity formation, prompting Muslims to relativise and compare their self-understandings of Islam. Another phenomenon closely related to life in diaspora is the way in which the traditional *ulama* ('religious scholars') are increasingly finding themselves bypassed in favour of, for instance, Muslim youth workers, in the search for religious knowledge. Young Muslims in the West often meet informally to discuss the Qur'an and other textual sources, attempting to read them anew and 'without the intervention of centuries of Islamic scholarship'. Schooled in a tradition that teaches them not just to blindly accept but to ask questions, young Muslims are deploying this inquisitiveness on the early texts in order to find in them the contours of an Islam for the here and now (Nielsen 1995: 115). There is hence no reluctance to delve into the *usul al-fiqh* (a term that refers to the core texts of Islamic jurisprudence), but there has been a shift as to what Muslims are hoping to find there. Gone is the exclusive obsession with the somatics of prayer and correct bodily practice. The emphasis now is on wider questions concerning Muslim identity and relations between Muslims and non-Muslims. One only needs to quickly peruse the discussion boards of various Islamic websites – IslamiCity, for example www.islamicity.com – to witness the new diversity of Muslim diasporic discourse.

We see, then, the importance that Muslims today are laying on rereading and reassessing the textual sources of Islam in new contexts. Media technologies, I will argue later, are playing a key role in making these texts available to a wider constituency. There is also a particular imperative here in the realm of identity and community. Plurality is of the essence, according to many Muslim thinkers today. They highlight the need for Muslims to increase their '*ummah* consciousness', and are developing 'a more open understanding of the notion of the global community of Muslims than many commentators – Muslim and non-Muslim alike – have heretofore proposed' (Vertovec and Peach 1997: 41). In this regard there would appear to be some degree of discursive overlap between a new *ummah* consciousness and recent thinking in Western critical theory. The notion of dialogue and some form of 'communicative action' (informed by tradition) within a 'public sphere' seem to be intrinsic to both (Habermas 1990, 1992). The advent of ICTs – particularly in the spaces of diasporic Islam – has been crucial in creating these public spheres. In the following two sections I want to look more closely at the relationship between various media technologies and some of the transformations in diasporic Islam outlined above. I will begin with a brief outline of the historical background in which these changes have taken place within the wider Muslim world and examine some of the technologies involved in the fragmentation of traditional sources of religious authority. I will then go on to look more specifically at the development and emergence of ICTs in Muslim diaspora communities.

'Media Islam': subverting genealogies of religious knowledge?

The salience of technology in bringing about religious change in Islam has been well documented (Robinson 1993; Atiyeh 1995; Eickelman and Piscatori 1996). In early Islam, oral transmission was the preferred mode for disseminating religious knowledge with each scholar granting his student an *ijaza* ('licence') which permitted him to pass on the texts of his teacher. Literacy among wider populations, even in urban centres, was very low. This state of affairs allowed the *ulama* and their associates (scribes, calligraphers and so on) to maintain a virtual monopoly over the production of authoritative religious knowledge. We should note here that in a sense it is almost mistaken to speak of Islam's holy book as a form of 'scripture'. The Qur'an is, quite literally, a recitation – the literal word of God as revealed to Muhammad via the archangel Gabriel.[3] It is a collection of words whose message resonates most strongly when read aloud or given voice. Even to this day, the process of learning the Qur'an is first and foremost an exercise in memorisation and oral repetition.

This goes some way to explaining why the Muslim world hesitated to embrace the technologies of 'print-capitalism' for almost three centuries. It was the experience of European colonialism and the concomitant perceived decline in Muslim civilisation which paved the way for the rise of print technology in the nineteenth century. The book, pamphlet and newsletter were taken up with urgency in order to counter the threat which Europe was posing to the Muslim *ummah*. This process heralded the final stage in the transition from an oral to a print-based culture in the context of religious knowledge (Messick 1993). The *ulama* were initially at the forefront of this revolution, using a newly expanded and more widely distributed literature base to create a much broader constituency. An inevitable side-effect of this phenomenon, however, was that the religious scholars' stranglehold over religious knowledge was broken. Gradually Muslims found it easier and easier to bypass the *ulama* in the search for authentic Islam and for new ways of thinking about their religion. As Eickelman notes, '[e]ven when persons in authority [e.g. the *ulama*] thought they were using new technologies to preserve the old, new elements and patterns of thought were introduced with the telegraph, newspapers, magazines and an expanded (even if not mass) educational system' (Eickelman 1982: 10). The texts were in principle now available to anyone who could read them, and to read is, of course, to interpret.

> Books . . . could now be consulted by any Ahmad, Mahmud or Muhammad, who could make what they [would] of them. Increasingly from now on any Ahmad, Mahmud or Muhammad could claim to speak for Islam. No longer was a sheaf of impeccable *ijazas* the buttress of authority; strong Islamic commitment would be enough.
>
> (Robinson 1993: 245)

The new media opened up new spaces of religious contestation where traditional sources of authority could be challenged by the wider public. As literacy rates began to climb almost exponentially in the twentieth century, this effect was amplified even further. The move to print technology meant not only a new method for transmitting texts, but also a new idiom of selecting, writing and presenting works to cater for new kind of reader (Roper 1995: 210).

We can understand these developments as part of a process through which religious knowledge becomes 'objectified'; that is, open to debate within the public sphere. Islam became something which could be represented, its identity now open to negotiation by a constituency previously prohibited from speaking on its behalf (Eickelman 1989). The fragmentation of traditional sources of authority is hence a key theme with regard to the nexus of Islam and new media. More particularly, these transformations in the status and provenance of religious knowledge have, in the contemporary era, helped to give rise to what Olivier Roy has termed the 'Islamist new intellectuals' (Roy 1994).

> The new intellectual has an autodidactic relationship to knowledge. Knowledge is acquired in a fragmented (manuals, excerpts, popular brochures), encyclopedic, and immediate manner: everything is discussed without the mediation of an apprenticeship, a method, or a professor . . . The new media, such as radio, television, cassettes, and inexpensive offset brochures, make snatches of this content available. The new intellectual is a tinkerer; he creates a montage, as his personal itinerary guides him, of segments of knowledge, using methods that come from a different conceptual universe than the segments he recombines, creating a totality that is more imaginary then theoretical.
>
> (ibid.: 96–7)

The rise of what we might call 'media Islam' or 'soundbite Islam' has thus been a major by-product of information technology. A new class of 'hybrid' Muslim intellectual (e.g. 'using methods that come from a different conceptual universe than the segments he recombines') has been the chief agent of dissemination for mediatised Islam. With the current world communications infrastructure, ideas and messages now possess the capability to bridge time and space almost effortlessly, and the political implications of this new capacity are not easily overestimated. 'Modern Muslim revitalization movements have been linked with an early stage of global modernisation', writes Serif Mardin, 'and one can follow this link through the effect on the revitalization of modern communications' (1989: 24).

What does this mean for the status of Islamic knowledge in the present era? How are these technologies being used by diasporic Muslims today? Let us approach these questions by looking at some of the Islamic software packages currently available. Given the size of most Islamic texts, a technology such as the CD-ROM has provided a medium which can contain the full text of several works. This means that the entire Qur'an, several collections of *hadith* (traditions of the Prophet Muhammad), *tafsir* (Quranic commentaries) and various *fiqhi* (jurisprudence) works can easily fit on a single disc. The director of the Islamic Computing Centre in London, Abdul Kadir Barkatulla, sees this development as having the greatest relevance for those Muslims who live in circumstances where access to religious scholars is limited, such as in the West.

For him, such CD-ROM selections offer a useful alternative. 'IT doesn't change the individual's relationship with his religion', he says, 'but rather it provides knowledge supplements and clarifies the sources of information such that Muslims can verify the things they hear for themselves'.[4] Barkatulla sees IT as a useful tool for systematising religious knowledge, but only those juridical opinions which have already been reached. In his terms, IT is only for working with knowledge that has already been 'cooked', not for making new judgements. To engage in the latter, he believes, one requires certain formal training and knowledge of specific methodologies:

> These resources are not intended to replace the religious scholars or commentators, but it means that they will not be able to get away with saying just anything. They will be held to account. They will have to check their sources twice because people will be able to go to the sources themselves and check to see if what was said in the pulpit corresponds with what is in the books . . . but IT is not for generating one's own *fatwas* [legal opinions].[5]

There are, however, those who disagree with Barkatulla. Sa'ad al-Faqih, for example, the leader of the Movement for Islamic Reform in Arabia and another keen advocate of information technology, believes that the average Muslim *can* now revolutionalise Islam with just a basic understanding of Islamic methodology and a CD-ROM. In his view, the technology goes a long way to bridging the 'knowledge gap' between a classically-trained religious scholar (*'alim*) and a lay Muslim by placing all of the relevant texts at the fingertips of the latter. 'I am not an 'alim,' he says, 'but with these tools I can put together something very close to what they would produce when asked for a fatwa'.[6]

The availability of such CD-ROM collections, all hyper-linked and cross-referenced, has created a new constituency for religious texts. Where Muslims would have previously had to rely on the expertise of the *ulama* when dealing with these books, they are now all available in a single medium which can easily be searched by any computer user. According to Ziauddin Sardar:

> Instead of ploughing through bulky texts, that require a certain expertise to read, a plethora of databases on the *Qur'an* and *hadith* now open up these texts and make them accessible to average, non-expert, users. Increasingly, the *ulama* are being confronted by non-professional theologians who can cite chapter and verse from the fundamental sources, undermining not just their arguments but also the very basis of their authority.
>
> (1993: 55–6)

Sardar then goes on to speculate about how all the *usul al-fiqh* (sources of Muslim jurisprudence) might be placed on a single compact disc, along with an 'expert-system'[7] that would guide the user through the literature and, in effect, allow him to generate his own fatwas (ibid.: 56). This sort of *ijtihad* ('free interpretation') toolkit would pose a further challenge to the authority of the traditional religious scholars. 'With this technology I think we are beginning to see a breaking of the monopoly over religious knowledge', says Sa'ad al-Faqih.[8] It is unlikely, however, that such a system will replace the *ulama* any time soon. They still command enormous respect in many communities and would, in any case, surely challenge the claim that their methodologies – the product of centuries of study and exhaustive research – can be reduced to a set of coded computer instructions. According to Barkatulla, a religious scholar himself, many *ulama* see the utility of information technology for the organisation of religious knowledge but believe that by becoming over-dependent on such 'gadgets', the capacity to internalise and think for oneself decreases.[9] At the same time, however, there is still an important sense in which the availability of religious texts on CD-ROM actually increases one's capacity to think for oneself.

The existence of such collections on CD-ROM has quickly become a reality in the past few years. The Islamic Computing Centre in London has been at the forefront of producing and distributing Arabic and Islamic materials in electronic format, and one only needs to glance at their product catalogue to confirm the enthusiasm with which Muslims have taken up this technology. In addition to several electronic Qur'ans (with full Arabic text, several English translations and complete oral recitation on a single disc) the Centre also sells titles such as WinHadith, WinBukhari, and WinSeera – electronic versions of, respectively, the traditions of the Prophet and his biographies. Also available are several products which begin to approach the system which Sardar first envisaged. The Islamic Law Base, Islamic Scholar, and 'Alim Multimedia 6.0 are all vast collections of religious texts such as the Qur'an, *hadith* (traditions of the Prophet, second only to the Qur'an as sources of religious authority), several volumes of *fiqh* (legal literature) covering all four schools of Sunni jurisprudence, biographies of the Prophet and his Companions, and more recent writing by figures such as Abu Ala Mawdudi. All of these databases can be kept open simultaneously and material between them is cross-referenced and fully searchable. In the United States, the Aramedia Group offers a library of Islamic CD-ROM resources with a choice of Arabic, English or Malay interface. Also available are software packages such as SalatBase, a multimedia guide to prayer which covers proper bodily practices, ritual somatics and the particular problems associated with, for example, prayer during travel. Barkatulla also mentions an expert system under development in Kuwait called al-Mawarith. This package enables a user to determine how the assets of a deceased relative should be allocated to his or her heirs according to Islamic law. It can be adjusted to reflect the opinions of the various Sunni legal schools, and will also provide textual evidence from the Qur'an and *hadith* in order to 'authorise' its output (Barkatulla 1992). Also widely available on the Internet are utilities for calculating prayer times, the beginning and ending of the fasting day during Ramadhan at any geographic point in the world and for converting dates between the Hijri and other calendar systems.

Diasporic Muslims and IT: new translocal communities?

'Academically, media studies and migration studies tend to function as separate fields', Ulf Hannerz writes, '[y]et in real life migration and mediatization run parallel, not to say that they are continuously intertwined' (1996: 101). His observation holds particularly true for diasporic Muslims, as they are currently both the subject and the object of considerable mediatisation. In what follows, I will be mainly concerned with the ways in which Islam makes use of or is rendered in various media for the consumption of other Muslims; in other words, I am interested in how Muslims use ICTs to talk to other Muslims.

Many young Muslims, as has been noted in a previous section, are bypassing traditional *ulama* and *imams* in order to learn their Islam from pamphlets and books published in English. Diasporic magazines such as the *Muslim News* and *Q-News* are also important in this regard (Lewis 1994: 206–7). Beyond the various printed literatures, we also find a variety of audiovisual and multimedia material which cater for the specific needs of diasporic Muslims. Many of these are aimed at children, seeking to teach them Islam using imagery and language similar to the Western entertainment genres with which they are already familiar. Thus we find a Disney-style animated adventure video, *Fatih – Sultan Muhammad*, which claims to be the world's first Islamic feature animation production. 'In this inspirational adventure', the advertisement reads, 'your family will see how the Muslims used not only their faith – but also strategic and technological superiority – to be successful'. Another company offers a children's educational series with a format and style similar to the muppets of *Sesame Street*. *Adam's World* 'introduces children to Islamic morals, values, and culture in a manner that's both entertaining and educational . . . By adopting such a universal approach to video-based education, *Adam's World* has found its niche among children of over forty different ethnic backgrounds'. The various episodes have titles such as 'Happy to be a Muslim', 'Take me to the Kaba', 'Kindness in Islam', and 'Ramadan Mubarak'. A wide variety of Arabic-language learning aids and Islamic quiz games for children on both videotape and CD-ROM are also available. We have already mentioned the SalatBase prayer guide. The same company also offers a series of videotapes featuring interviews with prominent Muslims in the West such as the NBA basketball star Hakeem Olajuwon and Yusuf Islam, formerly the pop singer Cat Stevens. One title, *Holiday Myths*, offers advice on how Muslims should approach and deal with Western holidays such as Christmas, Halloween, Valentine's Day and Easter.

What about the Internet? Can we meaningfully speak today about the emergence of new forms of Islamic virtual community? Where the much-cited Benedict Anderson (1983) pointed to the pioneering efforts of New World 'creoles' in the formation of imagined communities, Jon Anderson now speaks of the 'new creoles' of the information superhighway – political actors whose strength lies in their adoption of the enabling technologies of electronic print and information transfer (1995: 13–15). We should not be too quick, though, to declare that the Internet is suddenly going to radically transform Muslim understandings of political community. We need to look realistically at the number of Muslims who actually have access to this forum, and we need to take careful note of each socio-political setting which receives information via this network:

> Transnational theories, fixated on media and forms of alienated consciousness distinctive of late modernity, tend to overlook the social organization into which new media are brought in a rush to the new in expression. Impressed by what Simmel much earlier called 'cosmopolitanism,' we overlook measures of social organization in pursuit of media effects.
>
> (Anderson 1997: 1)

In addition, we need to make sure that we have a more nuanced understanding of those Muslim identities which use the Internet. We cannot start talking about new forms of diasporic Muslim community simply because many users of the Internet happen to be Muslims. Noting that in many instances Muslim uses of the Internet seem to represent little more than the migration of existing messages and ideas into a new context, Anderson warns that '[n]ew talk has to be distinguished from new people talking about old topics in new settings' (1996: 1). Yet we also have to acknowledge the possibility that the hybrid discursive spaces of the Muslim Internet can give rise, even inadvertently, to new formulations and critical perspectives on Islam, religious knowledge and community. But in order to comprehend the processes by which community is created, we also need to understand the circumstances under which these Muslim identities became diasporic. That is, how do other aspects of identity influence the terms of religious discourse on the Internet? Issues such as culture and religion, for example, are often discussed using methods of reasoning and debate which derive from the Western natural and technical sciences, rather than using the 'traditional' terms of discourse which one might find 'back home'. This reflects the nature of the professional/student life of many diaspora Muslims who are often technicians, engineers or research scientists (ibid.).

There are also those who argue that the Internet has had a moderating effect on Islamist discourse. Sa'ad al-Faqih, for example, believes that Internet chatrooms and discussion forums devoted to the debate of Islam and politics serve to encourage greater tolerance. He believes that in these new arenas one sees a greater convergence in the centre of the Islamist political spectrum and a weakening of the extremes:

> In these forums it is very important now for the leaders of various tendencies to make strong, reasoned arguments that stand up in debate because their followers are also there and they are listening. Not only

that, but the followers are now able to go to the sources themselves in order to verify what their leaders have been saying. Sometimes you get extremists who argue only out of emotion or sensationalism, but do not present arguments with any reasonable methodology or evidence from the sources. Leaders are becoming sensitive to this need. They know that they have to conduct debate according to certain reasonable rules in order to maintain their credibility with the followers . . . Not just on the Internet, but also on satellite TV and in other media forums. The ulama come on and they take questions from people who corner them and force them to defend themselves. 'The people' force them to come up with stronger arguments . . . It's like one huge public debate that thousands of people are listening to.[10]

The phenomenal popularity of the Qatar-based satellite television station al-Jazeera is a clear case in point. It constitutes the first mass media outlet for relatively open political and religious debate in the Middle East, and has an avid following both in the region and amongst diasporic communities in the West. On popular talk shows such as *Al-Itijah al-Muw'akis* (*The Opposite Direction*), al-Jazeera viewers are treated to the spectacle of prominent religious scholars and *imams* being forced to defend their ideas in the face of a questioning and critical audience. Nico Landman has argued that such television discussion programmes are also permitting Muslim women greater access to the public sphere, noting that '[t]he visibility of headscarved and very self-confident and emancipated Muslim women in the Dutch media has been greatly increased in recent years' (Landman 1997: 238).

Thus for the overwhelming majority of Muslims in the West the Internet is mainly a forum for the conduct of politics *within* Islam. 'Internet forums permit bypassing traditional gatekeepers and adjudicators of interpretive rights, procedures and adequacy,' writes Jon Anderson (1997: 2). Because very few 'official' Muslim organs such as the Organisation of the Islamic Conference, the Muslim World League or the various eminent religious schools actually have more than an extremely superficial presence on the Internet, we can characterise many of the Muslim sites which do exist as 'alternatives' (Anderson 1996: 1). That is, in the absence of sanctioned information from recognised institutions, Muslims are increasingly taking religion into their own hands. The Internet provides them with an extremely useful medium for distributing information about Islam and about the behaviour required of a 'good Muslim'. Through various news-groups and e-mail discussion lists, Muslims – many of whom are new converts – can solicit information about what 'Islam' says about any particular problem. Responses will be received from, recalling Francis Robinson's phrase, 'any Ahmad, Mahmud or Muhammad' on the Internet and this represents a further decline in the authority of the *ulama*. Not only that, notes Sa'ad al-Faqih, 'but someone will be given information about what "Islam" says about such and such and then others will write in to correct or comment on this opinion/inter-pretation'.[11] In this sense, the Internet resembles a publishing forum far more than it does a broadcasting forum because here 'users are producers, or may be producers' (Anderson 1997: 3). Given that most of this discourse involves diaspora Muslims, much of the conversation on these information networks tends to be about how Muslims should deal with various 'cultural' phenomena which they encounter in, say, Los Angeles, Manchester or The Hague. Dozens of 'meta-sites', such as IslamiCity and the Islamic Gateway, have sprung up in recent years, offering hundreds or sometimes thousands of links to other areas of the Internet containing information and resources on Islam.[12] The Muslim Students Association (MSA) network, for example, posts daily collections of news stories on Muslims and Islamic issues from around the world.

There has also been a great effort to make the classic works of religious learning as widely available as possible. Numerous websites offer various translations of the Qur'an and the *hadith*, and also articles by prominent contemporary Muslim thinkers. Various Internet forums coordinated by the MSAs of North America allow Muslims to discuss and debate the merits of different tendencies within the modern Muslim movement. A recent example of this has been a wide-ranging debate on the merits of the Jama'at al-Tabligh movement. Just as the more marginalised sects of Islam have often found life to be easier in diaspora, so have they also found a new lease on life on the Internet. Power asymmetries are often evened out online, and the World Wide Web allows the Ahmaddiya movement to appear as 'mainstream' as any Sunni site. More traditional Islamic spaces such as the mosque have also not gone untouched by IT. In 1996, for example, the Muslim Parliament of Great Britain recommended that all mosques in the UK be wired up to the network in order to provide 'porn-free access to the Internet and establish places where Muslims can socialise in a *halal* (permissible) environment'.[13]

The Internet has also served to reinforce and reify the impact of print capitalism on traditional structures and forms of authority. Instead of having to go down to the mosque in order to elicit the advice of the local mullah, Muslims can now receive 'authoritative' religious pronouncements via the various e-mail *fatwa* services. The Sheikhs of al-Azhar are totally absent, but the enterprising young 'religious scholar' who sets himself up with a colourful website in Alabama suddenly becomes a high-profile representative of Islam for a particular, disseminated and distanciated constituency.[14] Due to the largely anonymous nature of the Internet, one can also never be sure whether the 'authoritative' advice received via these services is coming from a classically trained religious scholar or a hydraulic engineer moonlighting as an amateur imam. As we noted above, however, the authority of the traditional scholars is not easily undermined. Barkatulla points out that judgements and rulings associated with IT such as e-mail *fatwas* are not yet considered permissible evidence in Shari'a courts because no reliable system for the generation of digital signatures that can verify the identity and credentials of religious scholars as yet exists. And again, the impact of these services must be measured realistically based on the number of Muslims who actually make use of them. However, we can perhaps say that they are having a fairly significant effect with regard to those questions that concern the details of daily life for a Muslim in the West. Diaspora Muslims are likely to find it convenient to be able to turn to one of their own, someone who has also lived in Western culture, so as to receive a hearing that is more sympathetic and more in tune with local affairs. It is in this context, when responding to a diverse range of social needs, that the plurality of Islam becomes most manifest.

Conclusion

More than anything else the Internet and other information technologies provide spaces where Muslims, who often find themselves to be a marginalised or extreme minority group in many Western communities, can go in order to find others 'like them'. It is in this sense that we can speak of the Internet as allowing Muslims to create a new form of imagined community, or a re-imagined Islam: 'It is imagined because the members . . . will never know most of their fellow-members, meet them, or even hear of them, yet in the minds [and on the screens] of each lies the image of their communion' (Anderson 1991: 6) It is in this sense that the idea of media technologies as a new embodiment of the global *ummah* (Mandaville 2001) begins to take on some relevance. The various Islams of the Internet hence offer a reassuring set of symbols and terminology which attempt to reproduce familiar settings and terms of discourse in locations far remote from those in which they were originally embedded.

It is inevitable when Islam is reimagined in diasporic contexts that various processes of cultural translation are set in motion. The resulting syncretisms give rise to new religious interpretations, each of which is redrawn to suit the unique set of socio-cultural contingencies into which it enters: a continual remaking of Islam through a politics of mediated community. Yet we also need to question whether information and media technologies are the harbingers of a new *ummah* consciousness, or a force that threatens to amplify differences between Islam in the West and Islam in the wider Muslim world. There are three major factors to bear in mind here. First, the new interpretations of Islam that emerge in diasporic Islamic contexts are often rather 'local' in nature insofar as they seek to make Islam relevant to the circumstances of particular communities living in the West. This must necessarily lead us to ask questions about the relevance of such innovative formulations to Muslims in other parts of the world. Indeed, there is evidence of confusion about – or outright rejection of – what comes to be derogatorily labelled as 'Western Islam' when such new ideas reach the Middle East or Asia. Second, Muslims living in the West tend to be more affluent and hence much more easily able to afford access to expensive technologies. In many parts of the Muslim world, access to the Internet is still the reserve of a small elite. Countries such as Sudan and Bangladesh, for example, are nearly impossible to place on world estimates of Internet domains. Finally, where Internet access *is* available to Muslims outside the West, heavy-handed governments often severely limit or censor access – the situation in Saudi Arabia mentioned above is a case in point.

Yet, in the final assessment, it is difficult to ignore the potential capacity of diasporic Muslim media for developing new strains of reformist discourse. In many ways it is still too early and too difficult to establish hard and firm evidence of diasporic media creating new social realities within Muslim communities in the West. It is undoubtedly the case, however, that new conversations are beginning to unfold, new ways of understanding what Islam can mean in a global era. To a large extent, as we have seen, it is within youth culture that this kind of activity is most prevalent. We are talking, in other words, of a new generation of IT-savvy diasporic Muslims. The true impact of the Muslim public sphere will therefore be felt when this generation moves into majority, and takes its place within public society. In this regard, any new *ummah* of the global media will be the distinct creation of those raised on the cusp of the twenty-first century.

Notes

1 Obviously there is a sense in which, over the course of history, all Islam has become diasporic. Indeed, the Middle East has long played a key role in the propagation and 'diasporisation' of religious civilisation (Islamic, Judaic and Christian). In this piece, my references to diasporic Islam are hence meant to invoke the transnational communities created by recent waves of migration and global labour patterns.
2 The reader should note that I am grounding this study in the social and political theory of identity and community formation (my own 'disciplinary' background), and using media as a lens through which to view related questions in the context of diasporic Islam.
3 *Al-qur'an* = 'the recitation'.
4 Barkatulla, Abdul Kadir, personal interview, London, 6 July 1998.
5 Barkatulla, Abdul Kadir, personal interview, London, 6 July 1998.
6 Al-Faqih, Sa'ad, personal interview, London, 14 August 1998.
7 This is a programme which contains rules and guidelines which tell a computer how to process, 'think' and make decisions with particular sets of data. It is usually written in an artificial intelligence language such as PROLOG.
8 Al-Faqih, Sa'ad, personal interview, London, 14 August 1998.
9 Barkatulla, Abdul Kadir, personal interview, London, 6 July 1998.
10 Al-Faqih, Sa'ad, personal interview, London, 14 August 1998.
11 Al-Faqih, Sa'ad, personal interview, London, 14 August 1998.
12 See e.g. www.islamicity.com/ or www.ummah.net/
13 'British Mosques on the Superhighway', *Muslimedia International*, 30 June 1996, www.muslimedia.com/, accessed 23 May 1997.
14 Wax, Emily, 'The Mufti in the Chat Room', *The Washington Post*, 31 July 1999, p. C1.

11 Communication among knowledge diasporas

Online magazines of expatriate Chinese students

Hong Qiu

Emergence of knowledge diasporas

The definition and classification of the word 'diaspora' has traditionally been centred on the notion that diasporic communities were forced away from home into exile. They were poor, uneducated, oriented to physical labour and inferior to those in the mainstream of society. However, today, we can easily find diasporas that do not fit into any of the traditional classifications of diaspora.[1] Some diasporas comprise expatriate technical professionals who are well educated and possess knowledge of the latest development in such high-technology fields as computer science, telecommunications and information technologies. Depending on their brains, not physical strength for survival and success, they enjoy comparatively high social and economic status in host countries. I call this group of people 'knowledge diasporas'.

This term has a triple meaning. First, in contrast to traditional diasporas, this form is primarily distinguished by its possession of knowledge. Knowledge diasporas are not forced abroad by armies or persecution. Rather, they are pushed into exile because the absence of a high-technology environment at home deprives them of substantial opportunity and free choice for personal development. Second, it is a diaspora that is actually driven into exile by knowledge. Such a dispersal occurs because these people possess the highly marketable knowledge that enables them to study or work abroad. Without such a knowledge advantage, they would still be at home. Third, this is a diaspora of knowledge in the sense that, distinct from the actual human individuals living in 'exile', the specialised knowledge that they have gathered at home and abroad is also 'in exile' and scattered in a 'knowledge diaspora'. These technical experts go into exile with their expertise, abilities and potentials. Another characteristic that separates the new knowledge diasporas from the old ethnic groups is the shifting departure and destination patterns. While the old diasporas usually followed some traditional channels of migration, such as colonisation and linguistic connections (Cohen 1997: 162), knowledge diasporas nowadays can originate from almost any country. They are dispersed to almost all lands to accommodate the globalisation process.

Despite their differences, knowledge diasporas and their traditional predecessors have at least one thing in common – the identity desire. Ethnic identity is important to ethnic groups because it gives them power to control their destiny and to succeed in their host countries (Zou and Trueba 1998: 1). An effective way to build and maintain ethnic identity is to form a community, because a community creates 'not only individual benefits for participants but also a group strength' (Watson 1997: 102). Since communities are held together by communication, community must involve communication (Berger 1995: 10). Identities are developed through the systematic and widely shared messages of the mass media (McLuhan 1965).

Traditionally, diasporas have relied on face-to-face interaction, conventional media such as newspapers and more modern means like radio and television for communication within their communities (Spickard 1996; Soruco 1996; Root 1997). But generally speaking, these media are local and regional, targeted mainly at geographically concentrated audiences. They are also constrained by time. Today's knowledge diasporas are widely scattered across the world and they live in the age of information explosion. They need more effective and real-time alternative mass media for community construction and intra-community communication. The technical trait of this group of people has determined that they look to those non-traditional media that make use of the latest communication technologies.

An important component of knowledge diasporas is expatriate university students. They include undergraduate and graduate students. Long-term visiting Chinese scholars abroad, who are typically under two-year contracts with foreign universities and research institutes, can also be included in this category since they are similar to the students on campus. After their graduation or (original) terms of contract, the students and scholars often remain in their host countries. For instance, in Silicon Valley alone, there are over ten thousand Chinese student-turned-high-technology-employees and employers.[2] This tendency is also common among students from other places such as India, Malaysia and Eastern Europe. However, expatriate Chinese students are worth special attention. This is not only because of their large number and wide dispersal across the world, but also because they have introduced an innovative communication pattern among themselves – online magazines. A study of these 'publications' can provide us with a valuable insight into knowledge diasporas and their communication patterns.

Expatriate Chinese students: collective identity

As Bar-Haim (1992: 206) points out, the range and limits of the features in an ethnic magazine are compatible with the general collective identity of the community. This idea is also applicable to the expatriate Chinese students' online magazines. It is impossible to talk about the magazines without touching on the community out of which they are born. The experience of expatriate Chinese in the West dates back at least to the early nineteenth century. Expatriate Chinese have seen three general patterns of diaspora through history: 'coolie' labour diaspora, trade diaspora and knowledge diaspora. The labour diaspora was formed in the early 1800s and continued for almost a century (Campbell 1969). Such a large outward migration was mainly the result of famine, feuds, overpopulation, devastating economic upsets and unstable social conditions in China (Campbell 1969: p. xvii; Wong 1988: 27). The Chinese 'coolies' were exclusively engaged in physical labour in conditions that were close to those of slavery. They were typically male youth from China's southern coastal areas, forced to leave their homeland in the hope of making money through hard work and to remit it back home to support their families.

Starting from the late 1870s, the nature of expatriate Chinese communities underwent significant changes as the social and economic conditions changed in their host countries. In North America, for example, at least four reasons were seen for those changes: completion of the transcontinental railways, closing of many mining companies, a high unemployment rate, and an emergence of strong anti-Chinese feelings (Wong 1988: 78). The adaptive response of the expatriate Chinese gave birth to the formation of the trade diaspora. This group of people usually ran small businesses in non-competitive fields, such as hand laundries and Chinese restaurants. The organisation of their firms rested upon such traditional relationships as kinship, clanship, ritual brotherhood and common locality of origin (ibid.: 79, 36, 116). This pattern remained dominant among expatriate Chinese until the 1980s.

The third major wave of Chinese diaspora took place in the late 1970s and early 1980s when mainland China started to open its doors to the outside world. It is estimated that between 1978 and 1998 the Chinese government sent more than forty thousand visiting scholars abroad for further studies. They were scattered in over a hundred countries and regions – 32 per cent in the United States, Canada, and Australia, 39 per cent in Western and Northern Europe, 14 per cent in Japan and other Asian countries. At the same time, Chinese employers sent eighty thousand of their employees abroad to study, and more than 120,000 Chinese left their motherland to study at their own expense. Altogether, about 250,000 Chinese left for overseas studies in the last two decades. In 1998, it was estimated that more than 150,000 Chinese students were studying or working abroad (Yang 1998).[3]

There are both external and internal factors that have contributed to the globalisation of the expatriate Chinese students. The 'pull' from without first comes from the overall globalisation process that has affected every corner of the world. The 'push' from within comes both from China's historical tradition and contemporary development. Historically, China had an age-old tradition that associated social power with upward and outward mobility (Liu 1997: 92). For centuries, the Chinese believed that the closer they were to the top of the social hierarchy, the more powerful they would be. This traditional conception of social meanings of mobility and power has been fuelled by China's economic reforms in the past two decades. Since it opened its doors to the outside world in the late 1970s, China has been increasingly integrating itself into global capitalism. The economic reforms in China have not only brought an influx of foreign investment, but also uncontrollable flows of information and media images from the outside world. To many people, especially the young educated, to cross national boundaries means to reach the location of power and wealth. This gives rise to a nationwide 'leave-the-country-fever' (*chu guo re*) (ibid.: 114).

There are not many published sources that describe the collective identity of expatriate Chinese students. Nevertheless, some common characteristics of the group of people are noticeable. First, they are geographically dispersed. Though the United States is the first choice for many educated young people who wish to go abroad, their destinations are not limited to North America. They also migrate to other parts of the world, such as Europe, Oceania and Japan. In fact, they go to almost any place that is supposed to be more developed than their home country or has better opportunities for personal development. Second, as a whole, they have a high level of education. Most of them are in master's or doctoral programmes. They are notably concentrated in marketable fields of study such as computer science, telecommunications and business. Third, as a community of migrants, expatriate Chinese students have marginal social and cultural presence, which results from three factors: they are inadequately and ineffectively organised, the community is largely ignored by mainstream media, and the students' efforts for external communication are often constrained by their lack of fluency in languages of the host countries and unfavourable economic conditions. Consequently, the expatriate Chinese students are caught in cultural isolation, cut off from their social surroundings. The social and cultural isolation motivates the students to develop their own mass media in the 'quest for media space' (Riggins 1992).

Online expatriate Chinese student magazines: an overview

The first online expatriate Chinese student magazine in the world came out on 5 April 1991 in the United States. Edited jointly by volunteer students in the United States, Canada, and other countries, the weekly *Hua Xia Wen Zhai* (*HXWZ*) covers a wide range of topics and has regular columns. Apart from translated news stories from foreign news media, it also includes articles from Chinese newspapers and magazines, original contributions, arguments and debates, as well as entertainment materials. It is published every Friday and distributed through the Internet to subscribers around the world. In January 1992, the world's second online expatriate Chinese student magazine started in the Canadian capital city of Ottawa. *Lian Yi Tong Xun* (*LYTX*), literally meaning 'News of the Association', was a comprehensive publication run by the city's Chinese Students and Scholars Association (CSSA). It invited and published contributions from students in an attempt to reflect the lives of Chinese students living abroad. The magazine was an immediate success and gained worldwide popularity.

Following the two forerunners, online expatriate Chinese student magazines cropped up in other countries. Similar publications appeared in the United States, Canada, Germany, Britain, Sweden, Denmark, Holland, Japan and other countries. It is impossible to tell exactly how many such magazines exist in the global expatriate Chinese student community. One of the reasons is the fact that these media are in a state of constant change. One vanishes today and another will appear tomorrow. However, a rough examination shows that at least a dozen have been published regularly and are enjoying various degrees of readership and influence within the community.[4] These online magazines can be roughly divided into three types: campus and local, national and specialised. Generally speaking, campus and local magazines, such as America's *Wei Da Tong Xun* and Britain's *Leeds Tong Xun*, focus on reporting activities at universities, local CSSAs and Chinese communities. National magazines cover events that have impact on the Chinese students across the country of their residence. Successful examples include Canada's *Feng Hua Yuan* (*FHY*) and Holland's *Tulip*. Specialised magazines, as the name indicates, target readers with specific interests. These include literary magazines such as *Xin Yu Shi* and *Wei Ming*. As the online expatriate magazines rise in number, they are also improving in quality. One indicator is the fact that some of them have obtained International Standard Book Numbers (ISBNs). At the same time, they are gradually being recognised by outsiders. For instance, the USA-based Online Computer Library Centre (OCLC), the largest online computer library network in the world, included *HXWZ* and *FHY* in its categories in 1995 as serious cultural academic periodicals.[5]

It is important to note that the idea of online magazines is by no means an arbitrary decision made by a few people. It is born out of the various conditions of the community of the expatriate Chinese students as a whole. According to Reddick and King (1997: 223), online media are superior to traditional printed media in two aspects in addition to global access and speed. First, becoming a print publisher not only requires a large sum of money but also involves a high degree of risk. It is especially a challenge for small publishers, because printing and distribution systems are costly and complex. However, the Internet has completely altered the publishing equation. Even the smallest online publication can potentially reach the entire international online audience. Second, the cost of establishing and maintaining online publishing can be very low. This certainly is a piece of good news to those small communities that are financially disadvantaged but eager to promote their communication status and identity. For these reasons, small communities, especially when the community members are well educated and have easy access to the Internet, have shown a particular penchant for online media. In fact, while experimenting with online media, some expatriate Chinese students have also tried traditional media. For instance, in 1994 the Federation of Chinese Students and Scholars in Canada (FCSSC) published its own monthly newspaper *Feng Hua Bao/Canada China News*.[6] But a year later the paper ceased publication due to 'financial difficulties'.[7] Through experience, expatriate Chinese students have learned that because of their unique characteristics and special social status, they cannot rely on traditional communication media to reach and connect their scattered community members. The new online media are the only solution. While the online expatriate Chinese student magazines are scattered across the world and are published by individuals with different backgrounds, the following characteristics can be identified: they are published mainly in developed countries; they are non-profit and volunteer-based; and they have a similar publishing style and layout, a wide range of coverage, an interest in political topics and reformist political positions.

Four models of development

Since the birth of the first online publication, the expatriate Chinese student magazines have gone through a tough course of development. This course has followed four models: *China News Digest* (CND) [8], Buffalonian, Leeds and *FHY*. Each model is named after the online magazine most representative of the category. The four models represent distinct forms of development. The CND model focuses exclusively on efforts of independent individual students and student-turned-professionals scattered across the world. Their journalistic practice is entirely an autonomous activity. The Buffalonian model also stresses individual efforts, but these efforts are made by students on a particular school campus. Magazines following this model are locally run, locally oriented and locally influential. These efforts are also coupled with involvement of Chinese student organisations. In the Leeds model, the journalistic activity is organisational. The development of these publications is, therefore, closely associated with their student organisations and they are an integral part of the regional CSSAs. The *FHY* model is similar to the Leeds model except that the involvement of the student organisations is on the national, not regional, level. The choice of development is not a matter of preference for the online expatriate student magazines but reflects the complexity of the environments in which the magazines are born and exist. Factors that play critical roles include such things as the number of Chinese students, degree of community awareness, readiness of volunteer staff, effectiveness of student organisations and availability of technical support. Whether a magazine can survive and develop depends greatly on the ability of the operators of the magazine to assess accurately these factors and orient the magazine accordingly.

The Buffalonian model is the most popular among the online expatriate student magazines in terms of number, but publications in this category are short-lived. Magazines following the Leeds and *FHY* models are the second most popular with a fairly stable survivability. The CND model is rare. This conclusion is also supported by my examination of the electronic student magazines archived in *Sunrise Library*, which claims to be 'the world's most comprehensive online database in Chinese'.[9] In the library's 'Online magazines' section, a total of 23 expatriate student magazines were archived in March 1999. Eleven of them fell into the Buffalonian model and nine belonged to the Leeds and *FHY* models. The other three could be grouped with the CND category. All the Buffalonian-model magazines had ceased publication. Some of them published as few as a couple of issues. Four out of the nine Leeds and *FHY* model magazines were still in operation. CND's *HXWZ* was the only Chinese-language survivor in its category.

A couple of reasons can be explored to explain the situation. First, publishing has a lot of appeal. People like to see their names in print, either as writers or editors. The availability of desktop publishing tools and online technology gives a false impression that anyone can successfully do online publication. That explains why so many online magazines have cropped up on campuses. As with many other things, it is easy to start an online magazine, but hard to keep it going. Running an online Chinese magazine consumes substantial energy and time. The inputting of Chinese characters itself can be a daunting task. It is unrealistic to depend totally on a handful of students who themselves have busy schedules. Many publishers of magazines of the Buffalonian model are not well prepared psychologically and technically for this difficulty. Furthermore, since these magazines are privately run by individual students on a single campus, they have very limited resources of help such as information channels, volunteer staff and reader support.

The Leeds and *FHY* model magazines are popular and stable because they overcome the above-mentioned limitations of the Buffalonian and CND models. First, the publication of a magazine is no longer an isolated act. Instead, it is integrated into the overall task of a regional or national student organisation. This relationship not only gives a magazine more topics to talk about but is also a guaranteed source of support. The publication can depend on help from its regional or national supervisory organisation. This advantage helps to keep a magazine from dying young. Second, since the publishers and readers share the same geographical location, magazines of these models tend to have a well-defined readership. This makes it easy for a magazine to identify its readers' needs and orient itself to them. Third, by allowing students from various sources within the same region or country of residence to jointly run a magazine, these models distribute the work and responsibilities. Consequently, they also enable the sharing of the risks of operation and thus enhance a magazine's survivability. While changes in staff often bring a Buffalonian or CND model magazine to an unexpected end, this is not a problem with publications following the Leeds and *FHY* models. In these models, a magazine is the result of concerted regional or national contributions. On the whole, the CND model is not a fortuitous pattern among the online expatriate Chinese student magazines. Two out of the three magazines of this model archived in *Sunrise Library* no longer exist. However, *HXWZ* is a successful exception. Among other things, a major reason is the fact that CND has basically been run by a group of well-established student-turned-professionals instead of currently enrolled students on campus.[10] These professionals have an obvious economic and technical edge in running an online magazine over the students still on campus.

Building a virtual community

The greatest benefit of the online media is not that they facilitate communication among already connected individuals and groups, but rather that they provide a medium for the formation and cultivation of new relationships by providing virtually instantaneous access to thousands of potential contacts who share similar interests and experience (McLaughlin *et al.* 1995: 91). As Rheingold (1993a: 61) says, individuals and groups find shared identities online through the aggregated networks of relationships and commitments that make community possible. In this respect, mass media play a significant role because of the so-called 'mobilisation theory' in mass communication. This theory holds that if a large number of people are exposed to the same mass media, they can be mobilised to foster certain ideologies and beliefs (Berger 1995: 124). Other researchers argue that the popularity of a magazine comes from a correspondence between its contents and the collective identity of its readership. Such correspondence makes the readers receptive to familiar cultural elements as well as an elaboration of them (Bar-Haim 1992: 197). It is by mobilising such shared values as culture, national identity and community awareness that the online expatriate Chinese student magazines have built up a virtual community among the Chinese knowledge diaspora.

Mobilising culture

Bar-Haim (1992: 207) argues that there is a cultural continuity among a transplanted ethnic people before and after they leave their homeland. He assumes that most of the adult readers of ethnic magazines have been influenced by past events they experienced in their countries of origin. These events shaped their cultural interests, tastes, values and world view. When they leave their homeland, they carry many of these interests with them to the countries of their new residence. To attract readers, an ethnic magazine would invest much effort in identifying and articulating these elements of continuity. Here I need to point out that since the word 'culture' is an umbrella term that covers a wide range of things, such a cultural continuity can be demonstrated at both the macro level, such as the tradition of a nation, and the micro level, as in a common lifestyle in a particular group. To promote this cultural continuity at both levels is exactly what the online expatriate Chinese student magazines do in their efforts to build a virtual community. Specifically, efforts have been made in mobilising common experience and the Chinese culture. The theme of a common experience can be divided into two sub-themes. First, there are articles in which the authors recall their past experiences back in China. Though the stories are individual accounts about trivial things, they signify the allegiances that the students commonly encountered before their diasporic experience. Usually these articles cover things that the authors no longer have now in their new surroundings. They describe the past experiences with a reminiscent tone, suggesting a contrast between their past and their disadvantaged present.

Second, many articles express the authors' affection for family members now far away. Due to visa conditions, most of the expatriate Chinese students cannot go back home during their studies abroad. With each passing day, their feelings for their parents and family members grow. As a result, any articles that touch on the theme would remind others in the community of their own families.

A culture displays itself in many ways, but the easiest way to promote it is to promote its tangible components, such as music, history and language. They are powerful because they make a particular culture stand out easily in a foreign environment. At the same time, they provide a group of people who have grown up in the particular culture with a sense of belonging. 'These conduits of collective belonging aid in reconstructing identities and redefining agendas' (Bonus 1997: 215). Therefore the promotion of these visible cultural components has always been one of the priorities in ethnic media (Riggins 1992).

The online expatriate Chinese student magazines demonstrate this effort in three categories: Chinese cuisine; Chinese customs, such as traditional Chinese holiday celebrations; and Chinese language. The students use these features to assert cultural confidence and offset their localised inferiority, especially when they feel socially and economically disadvantaged. This shows that although many student-turned-professionals have upgraded their modes of transport and housing, Chinese culture is still superior to anything else in their mind. They are proud of having grown up in such a culture.

Mobilising national identity

'Identity is a mutable, essential idea held in common, signified by agreement' (Belden 1997: 6), and it is significant because it is always associated with power (Zou and Trueba, 1998: 1). While the formation of ethnic identity has many factors, nationality is no doubt one of the most salient elements. In the context of Chinese nationality, it is true that there are micro levels of ethnic identity and Chinese people are grouped according to their regions of birth or residence, local languages and subcultures. But at the macro level there does exist a shared overall mainland Chinese ethnic identity of common experience during the long periods of turmoil and imperial rule as well as in the People's Republic.

General tactics have been adopted by the magazines to mobilise the national identity of the students. First, the magazines have done everything they can to expose the students to the 'voice' from their homeland. Inside this category, at least three themes can be identified. The first theme is to provide them with information from and about their homeland that is specifically related to them. The second theme is to report on China's latest achievements in science and technology. The third theme is postings that call on the expatriate students for direct contributions to their homeland. Within this theme, the most frequent three topics are calls for research papers, invitations to the students to go back to China to attend academic conferences, and the soliciting of students abroad to work in China. The second tactic that the magazines use to mobilise national identity is directly to initiate or sponsor programmes that encourage the students to carry out activities to help China. In many cases, such programmes come into being out of gratitude to the motherland. One example is the 'Chinese Children Project' initiated and sponsored by *FHY* in 1996. According to the magazine, the project was to help speed up China's modernisation by aiding the education of Chinese children. Nationalism is the third tactic used by the student magazines and is particularly highlighted when clashes occur between China and other countries. On those occasions, the magazines stress the unfairness and threats that foreign nations have levelled at China. They publicise the message that Chinese interests are being infringed and it is the responsibility of every Chinese to side with their motherland in such conflicts. Despite their differences in political positions, the online expatriate Chinese student magazines tend to unite unanimously under the banner of nationalism. This tactic is usually successful among the students, and its appeal is echoed in a line of a song popular among Chinese abroad which proclaims, 'We own a common name called China'.[11] While this tactic has been applied to many Sino-foreign clashes, Japan has been the major target because of the hostilities between the two countries that spanned most of the nineteenth and twentieth centuries.

Mobilising community awareness

The expatriate Chinese students, as a whole, are loosely structured due to lack of organisation. Consequently, they have a very vague awareness of the community they comprise. In most cases, when something adverse happens, they rely on individual power rather than community influence. One of the priorities of the student magazines is to cultivate and stimulate community awareness among the students. In this effort, the magazines strive to send out a clear message to the students: a community is always more powerful than an individual. Three themes are found in the articles: communication among the widely scattered community members, the 'big family' concept and the defence of community interests.

The first theme seeks to bridge the geographically scattered students in the community. It most often appears in the form of intracommunity services. The magazines try to provide the students with services that can promote communication among them. Three features are typical in this aspect. One is the 'looking-for' messages in which one student tries to find someone he or she has known before but with whom contact has been lost due to migration. Those who place these messages expect their lost friends also to be members of the online community. They and the magazines assume that most expatriate Chinese students would read their publications and chance upon these messages and re-establish contacts with their former classmates or colleagues. This use of online media is also quite common in other expatriate ethnic communities, such as the Indian diaspora (Mitra 1997). The significance of the phenomenon is beyond just looking for a lost friend: 'These are the past identities that are brought to the network which help the users find their network identity by seeking the congruencies that existed prior to entry into the virtual space' (ibid.: 63). Finding or even attempting to find one's former community through this channel helps to foster community awareness among users.

The second feature in this 'bridging' theme is what I call the 'online matchmaking' phenomenon. Because of long years of studies, a big portion of the expatriate Chinese students have missed their prime time for dating and marriage. Cultural differences and disadvantaged economic situations have inhibited many students from establishing relationships with local members of the opposite sex in the countries of their residence and developing these relationships into love. The traditional Confucian idea that both parties in a marriage should be matched in terms of family and personal backgrounds is still quite popular in China and among the students. Consequently, they turn their eyes to other expatriate students of their own kind. 'Cyberfriends' is a regular online matchmaking column in *FHT*. In each issue, the magazine publishes a dozen 'seeking spouse' messages for both male and female students. The section instantly became popular among the students upon its appearance in the online magazine. Not only is the list in *FHT* growing, other online expatriate Chinese student media are following suit and getting an enthusiastic response from readers. The third feature of the 'bridging' theme is the postings in the magazines that announce community events. As there is a general assumption that most of the students are reading the magazines, organisations for students or student-turned-professionals make use of the far-reaching influence of the publications. They place announcements in the online media when they hold events. This in turn helps the magazines promote community awareness among the students, because if they do not read the postings in the magazines they risk missing information that may be pertinent to them.

The second theme in the magazines' efforts to mobilise community awareness is the promotion of the idea that if one member in the community runs into difficulty, the rest are ready to offer help. This theme aims to create among the students a feeling that the community is like a big family, since practically every student is far away from his or her own real extended family. The magazines suggest that their readers can always expect aid in hard times by turning to the virtual community. To build up such a big-family idea, the magazines make a point of publicising 'help' stories. One of the many examples took place in mid-1993 when an *LTTX* article reported how the expatriate Chinese student organisation in Ottawa organised a film show to raise money to help the family of a local Chinese student who died during his studies in the city. The third most frequent theme in community construction is the defence of the interests of the community. When the interests of the expatriate Chinese students are threatened, the magazines publish articles to protect them. By publicising events that are against the common interests of the community, the magazines are focusing the students and serving as the mouthpiece of the whole community. Consequently, they mobilise community awareness among the students. For instance, in late 1994 when Canadian provincial governments were considering doubling the tuition fees for international students, *Red River Valley* (*RRV*), an online expatriate Chinese student magazine based at University of Manitoba, published the news and the concerns of the expatriate Chinese student community. This role of the magazines in promoting community awareness is more obvious when the interests of the expatriate Chinese students in particular are sabotaged.

Problems, trends and future

Online expatriate Chinese student magazines have had problems of various kinds ever since their inception. These problems are most noticeable in the following aspects: working staff, information sources and operating budgets. No matter which model a student magazine follows, lack of adequate staff is a problem common to almost all the publications. Some magazines have had to delay regular issues, suspend operations or cease publication due to this problem. Even those that have survived and are operating successfully complain that their development is constrained by lack of staff. Several factors contribute to this problem. First, expatriate Chinese students are busy with their studies and work. Second, there is a lack of qualified candidates to run the magazines. Third, there is a weak awareness of voluntarism among the expatriate Chinese students as a whole. While commenting on sources of information for ethnic minority media, one researcher had the following to say:

> There is also the risk that the newness of information can be exhausted quite quickly in small communities. Much of the information presented to the public may already be known to them. Intellectual ghettoization may promote uninteresting repetition and a definite lack of motivation that in turn can encourage practices that unintentionally lead to the demise of the media.
>
> (Riggins 1992: 285)

Unfortunately, this is what has happened and is still happening to the online expatriate Chinese student magazines. A significant portion of the information in the magazines is directly taken from other publications. As the magazines develop, new sources of information have been explored, but old and published information still plays a great role in the operation of the student magazines. The magazines suffer from a lack of new information as they often find there is really not much news involving the students. As non-profit publications, these magazines are providing free services to the community of the expatriate Chinese students. They depend on volunteer work for existence. This presents the magazines with a severe budgetary reality, with every magazine complaining that it does not have money for its operation. Because of a merging of the previous small magazines into much stronger publications, there are fewer such media today than in the early 1990s. Nevertheless, online expatriate Chinese student magazines have kept developing. In fact, in recent years, some new trends have emerged in the publications. For instance, as the student organisations are offering less support, some magazines are gradually losing loyalty and struggling to break away from their parent organisations. There is also a trend for student-turned-professionals to take the place of the current students in the operation of the magazines.

Will the online expatriate student magazines keep on prospering? The answer is yes, because the factors that have contributed to the birth and development of these magazines remain unchanged. In fact, some conditions have become even more favourable. For example, the technical advances in the computer networks, especially the steady progress in the application of the Internet technologies in Chinese, have greatly facilitated the operation of online Chinese media. This, in turn, will help these media to improve in quality and consequently attract more readers. Meanwhile, the magazines have become mature as their operators and editors gain experience and lessons from their past practices. They know better now how to make their media sustain steady development by avoiding shortcomings and bringing into full play their strong points. The merging of *LYTX* and *FHY* in Canada is just one example. Nevertheless, it is naive to think that online expatriate Chinese student magazines will pop up widely across the world in the future. This is neither necessary nor possible, because the overall socio-economic conditions for expatriate Chinese students will remain basically unchanged in the near future. The realistic prospects for these student media are that they will keep evolving, but in a more controlled way. They will focus more on upgrading quality than on increasing quantity.

Notes

1 For example, in his book *Global Diasporas: An Introduction* (1997), Robin Cohen classifies diasporas into six categories: classical, victim, labour and imperial, trade, homeland-oriented, and cultural.
2 Hua Sheng Bao, 'Focus on Science and Education', 6 March 2000. Online, available at www.hsm.com.cn.
3 Figures conflict depending on sources. According to statistics released by the State Commission of Education in Beijing in January 1997, a total of 270,000 Chinese had gone abroad for studies since the beginning of the 1980s. Only 90,000 people had returned upon completion of their studies. For more information, see Yang (1998).
4 For an incomplete list of these magazines, refer to *Sunrise Library* at www.sunrise site.org.
5 Feng Hua Yuan, 'North America News', no. 75, 20 November 1995. Online, available at www.fhy.net.
6 The 16 x 11.5 inch tabloid was published in Chinese, English and French with colour printing. Each issue had 16 to 24 pages and a nationwide circulation of four to five thousand copies.
7 Feng Hua Yuan, 'News Collection,' no. 46, 1 February 1995. Online, available at www.fhy.net.

8 This organization has published several online publications including *CND Global*, *CND-US*, *CND-Canada*, *CND-EP* (serving Chinese communities in Europe and Pacific regions) and *HXWZ*.
9 Sunrise, 'Introduction to Sunrise Chinese Library'. Online at www.sunrisesite.org.
10 *CND*, 'Special Issue: China News Digest Celebrates Ninth Anniversary,' 6 March 1998. Online, available at www.cnd.org/whatiscnd.html.
11 Tong Junzi, 'We Own a Common Name Called China', no. 6, Special Edition, *FHY*, May 17 1996. Online, available at www.fhy.net.

12 Globalisation and hybridity

The construction of Greekness on
the Internet

Liza Tsaliki

This chapter will focus on a notion of 'Greekness' as it is constructed on the
Internet. The World Wide Web, also known as Κόμβος (komvos) or Διαδίκτυο
(thiadiktyo) in Greek, is a site where various 'technologies of national desire'
(Maxwell 1996) can be simultaneously at work. From the proliferation of the
webpages of various electronic and print media to the increasing popularity of
an array of Internet Relay Chat (IRC) groups, the Internet connects the homeland to the numerous Greek diasporic communities around the globe forming a
'nationally imagined community' (Anderson 1983). This computer-mediated
'imagined community' is a hybrid one as it lives in the global–local nexus that
characterises contemporary societies; it is a hybrid community because by
being as much cosmopolitan as it is Greek, it breaks away from traditional,
space-bound understandings of identity and community, and is spread across
the globe, producing a common ground and shared practices around which
Greekness can be imagined.

The reorganisation of space and time and the dissolution of boundaries that
take place on the Web mean that Greek migrant cultures can re-create and
reinvent the 'commonality and fellowship' (Carey 1989: 7) they once shared.
Homi Bhabha argues that the

> 'locality' of national culture is neither unified nor unitary in relation to
> itself, nor must it be seen simply as 'other' in relation to what is outside
> or beyond it. The boundary is Janus-faced and the problem of outside/
> inside must always itself be a process of hybridity, incorporating new
> 'people' . . . to the body politic, generating other sites of meaning and
> . . . producing . . . sites of political antagonism and . . . political
> representation.
>
> (1990b: 4)

This is where the Janus-faced modality of the cybernation lies: on the dialectic
between the outside and the inside, the global and the local, the cosmopolitan
and the national, for the modern nation is 'by nature ambivalent' (Nairn 1981:
338). It is the representation of this ambivalence and the locality of this hybrid
social identity that I want to explore in this chapter. Cyberspace becomes that

time and place when and where the scattered people gather, and narrate, by means of computer-mediated communication, their myths, fantasies and experiences; the nation fills the void created by the émigrés by turning that loss into the language of metaphor. The nation as metaphor has to be seen as a tradition of writing wherein the narrative of the imaginary of the nation-people is constructed. 'Metaphor . . . transfers the meaning of home and belonging across . . . distances and cultural differences that span the imagined community of the nation-people' (Bhabha 1990a: 291).

Within this context, hence, of addressing the nation as metaphor and as narration, the Internet provides an 'in-between space' between the nation and its diaspora from which the national narrative can be *re*-articulated.

Seeking Greece on the Internet: cyber-technologies of national desire

Communicating within IRC

Internet Relay Chat conferencing offers real-time chat to a potentially unlimited number of users. IRC gained international fame during the Gulf War, when updates from around the world came across the wire and most people on IRC gathered on a single channel to hear these reports. Topics of discussion on IRC are varied, just like the topics of Usenet newsgroups are varied. Technical and political discussions are popular, especially when world events are in progress. The majority of conversations take place in English, although there are channels in German, Japanese, French, Finnish and other languages. Its format looks like a script, as each line begins with the sender's nickname, followed by the conversation text the user wishes to broadcast. As the discussion develops, one line rolls off the top of the screen to allow for the new text, appearing at the bottom of the screen. IRC talk is both interpersonal and mass-mediated as participants can have 'private' conversation on a one-to-one (or two) basis, and 'public' discussions are broadcast to all members. Computer-mediated communication within IRC is organised around networks which accommodate numerous servers; these servers provide access to a vast array of channels. Real-time chat takes place within the channels. Each channel has a number of robots ('bots') which serve as the channel's administrators and are set up by one or more of the channel users. The administrators occupy the highest rank in the bot hierarchy and are 'omnipotent'; beneath them lie the channel operators with varying degrees of 'police jurisdiction'.

In order to compensate for the lack of the 'subtleties of speech and non-verbal cues that usually accompany it' (E. Reid cited in MacKinnon 1995: 115), IRC members make full use of netiquette (network etiquette), which stands for a cyber-analogue of the external world's mores, norms and traditions. In parallel to that, they also use the 'smiley' language. 'Smileys' or 'emoticons' are pictographs made up of keyboard symbols and provide a shorthand for the depiction of physical and emotional state. The repertoire of smileys is codified in

folk dictionaries and is circulated among users, indicating that users are conscious of their sub-cultures and group-specific expressions (Baym 1995). Action
and bodily movement is conveyed by placing a word within asterisks, as in
giggle or *sniff* as opposed to simply saying 'I giggle' or 'I sniffed'. Other
ways of expression include the use of bold characters or capital letters to convey
strong emotions, or repetitive typing as in 'hahahahahahahah' or in 'waaaaaaa
hhhhhhhh' (MacKinnon, 1995), and the abbreviation and standardisation of
phrases like LOL (laugh out loud), ROFL (roll on the floor laughing), BRB (be
right back), BBS (be back soon), L8H (later), amongst many others.

What is 'Katsika': a brief history of an IRC channel

> I should warn you that the program can be very addictive once you begin
> to make friends and contacts on IRC, especially when you learn how to
> discuss in 14 languages.
>
> (introduction to www.undernet.gr)

IRC conferencing amongst Greeks has picked up significantly since 1997 and is
accommodated by a number of networks worldwide. This case study will focus
on the trials and tribulations of Undernet's *Hellas Channel*. There are various
Greek channels under the name *Hellas* on other IRC networks, such as

*   EFnet (irc.texas.net), seen as the mother of all networks. It involves hun-
    dreds of IRC servers, is highly anarchic and accommodates approximately
    twenty thousand users online;
*   IRC-NET (irc.funet.fi), the European part of EFnet;
*   DalNET (irc.dal.net), a network with many 'goodies' and services missing
    from the other networks. It offers 10 to 15 servers with a few thousand
    users; and
*   GRNet (srv.irc.gr), a network comprising mostly Greek university servers,
    although lately some foreign ones have also joined in. This is a very
    crowded and anarchic *Hellas* channel.

Every one of these operates under a different policy, with its own channel
managers and operators.

Undernet (us.undernet.org/eu.undernet.org; www.undernet.gr) was set up in
early 1993. It is an alternative IRC network operating approximately 25 to 30
IRC servers. It asserts that things are kept under control most of the time,
accommodating about fifteen thousand users online. Undernet hosts many
other channels apart from *Hellas* which are also Greek in nature and have been
created by Greeks, for example Cyprus, Greece, Greekchat, bouzoukia, night-
life, Rhodes, Kalamata. There are sport-specific channels on Undernet as well,
such as gate7, paok, aek, and pao amongst others. These channels have their
own rules and are in no way affiliated with *Hellas* channel.

What sets Undernet's *Hellas* channel apart from the plethora of *Hellas* channels in other IRC networks is the channel's strict public ethos of law and order and its underground character. From its very start (October 1994) *Hellas* was set up with a clear vision of how it should be constituted and has remained faithful to that initial goal. The channel operators at *Hellas* are there to help and if necessary intervene to ensure proper channel operation. The same applies to the entire Undernet network which is considered as the 'strictest' Greek IRC network. Although the majority of *Hellas* users are Greek-speaking, everybody is welcome to join in as long as they are not provocative and offensive. In fact, the channel advocates a 'no discrimination' quota on the grounds of race, sex, religion, language, sexual orientation, education, political orientation, beliefs, culture, descent or origin.

Although officially known as '*Hellas*', the brain child of a 16-year-old at the time, the majority of its users prefer to refer to the channel as '*Katsika*', having appropriated the nickname of the oldest security bot – itself introduced in 1996 – and promoted it to a generic term for the chatgroup. Before the introduction of the bot, IRC conferencing on *Hellas* was taking place on an open access basis (i.e. no moderation occurred). The limited number of participants ensured self-regulation. Between 1995 and 1997, nevertheless, the population of the channel jumped from a modest 15 to 158, thus making the establishment of a security bot a necessity. By mid-2001, *Katsika* accounted for 400 'inhabitants' on average at any time. Its population approximately accounted for ten thousand people, including both men and women, although it is impossible to determine an accurate gender profile for the channel. Its male population surpasses its female counterpart, a characteristic feature of the networked society, by an approximate ratio of 10 men for every four women (Herring 1994, 1996; Ebben and Kramarae 1993; Adam and Green 1998). Participants are between 15 and 40 years of age, though the most representative group is the 20–25-year-olds. They are students, university graduates in paid employment, professionals, as well as housewives. Their geographic distribution includes Greece (Athens, Thessaloniki, Patra, Kavala, Rhodes, Crete, Halkida), Britain (most British universities), Brussels, Frankfurt, Australia and New Zealand, Canada (Vancouver, Toronto, Montreal), the United States (New York, Baltimore, Detroit, Iowa, Phoenix, Vermont, Alaska) and South Africa.

Katsika was founded with certain ideals in mind which set the guidelines for channel policy. The main goal is for everyone to have a great time. This is evident from the opening credits when someone first logs on to the network: 'Welcome to *Katsika*!!! Home of the *Hellas* residents and where things happen . . . Enjoy!!'.

In that respect, the group has a recreational and social purpose. It does not aim to attract masses of people by way of freely allocating the status of channel operator (chop) since that would also destroy the quality of the channel. Contrary to other channels where there is a plethora of operators, *Katsika* argues that 'the OP Addiction Syndrome (OAS), where a user's IRC existence is based on a power trip, is not part of this channel . . . and if you visit other channels, where OAS exists you will see why'[1]. The advisory group that runs the channel asserts that their concern for the channel is sometimes mistaken as a form of fascism, however, it is due to their vigilance that Undernet's *Hellas* channel is widely considered as 'one of the coolest places on IRC networks'. Channel policy can be summarised as follows:

- We don't care for large numbers of mindless users. Enough said.
- WYSIWYG: What You See Is What You Get. We are who you see.
- We don't owe anyone anything because we are channel operators, you pay money to connect or the channel is called *Hellas*. Being an operator is voluntary, we don't get any of your money and our name does not define us [. . .].
- To put it in another way: We do our best to live our lives in harmony – do the same and enjoy IRC.[2]

Operational practice

Hellas is run by four bots, *Katsika* (the goat), Helona (the turtle), Cheetah and X. The main bots that take care of the channel are *Katsika* and Helona. These are 'eggdrop' bots patched especially for the channel and run on Forthnet, the major Internet provider in Greece with IRC servers in many other IRC networks. Messaging *Katsika*, sometimes referred to as the 'house keeper', will almost always ensure that messages will reach an operator, and users are advised to turn to it in case of an emergency. Besides the usual features which ensure normal channel operation at all times, Helona is the bot that updates the web pages of *Hellas* with information and statistics about users, e.g. top talkers, top kickers, idlers, join/part statistics and 'other cool stuff'. Cheetah is the strictest bot within the channel, coming into use once *Katsika* or Helona have been incapacitated for some reason. X is one of the most extraordinary channel operating bots. Being a female bot, her main purpose is to ensure that the channel complies with Undernet's rules and regulations. Its operation has nothing to do with the operators, but rather with Undernet's Channel Service. It is the supreme authority in the channel and is 'deaf' to anything apart from important events that take place in the channel.

Temporal structure

IRC conferencing can take two forms, synchronistic and asynchronistic. Synchronous communication takes place when all participants are online simultaneously, read messages and respond immediately. In cases of asynchronous communication, meetings need not be happening simultaneously, but instead participants can read messages and respond at different times. Conferencing on *Katsika* can take both forms of communication. Most of the time people being in IRC do not pay attention to what is going on in the channel. They could be away cooking, surfing the net, eating or talking in private with someone else, either from *Hellas* or from another channel. Specific instructions have been set up to avoid a *faux pas*, and hence risk being banned, in cases when someone appears not to be responding to another user's messages.

Speech

The language of communication amongst Greeks on *Hellas* is a mixture of Greek delivered in Latin fonts, English and a hybrid linguistic concoction known as '*Greenglish*'. Users are specifically requested not to use Greek fonts when talking to each other since only a few are capable of displaying the Greek character set correctly, while others will probably have junk displayed on their screen. In addition, there are members, mostly from foreign universities, using Windows, who do not have Greek fonts or even if they do, they are unable to install the software. There is also the case of people who have Greek fonts, but do not like them. Therefore the standard character set for *Hellas* is the Latin/US-ASCII character set. 'There is no point in writing something that only three people can read'.[3]

More specifically, participants prove to be inventive and resourceful, and since the majority of them are or used to be students in English-speaking universities, they draw from a variety of cultural backgrounds exemplified in the use of 'Greenglish'.

Another shared way of expression within *Katsika* is the use of American streetwise spelling, found in abundance in comics and other subcultures, whereby speech follows a 'sounds like' logic rather than grammatical rules. In this sense, written speech becomes economical and simplified, losing all unnecessary adornments on its way. 'Coming' becomes 'cummin', 'she is working' becomes 'shes woorkin', 'days' become 'dayz' and so forth. To illustrate this further:

> [4: 18] <*Katsika*> <sevastios> cool me is very happy.
> [4: 18] <*Katsika*> <sevastios> just finished Da mid-terms!! Finally.
> [23:51] <*Katsika*> <gaga> hey yo!
> <aStRaLoN> gagagagagagagagaaa.
> [23:51] <*Katsika*> <MaDWolF> gagaroooooooooooooos!!!!!!!!!!!!!.
> [23:51] <*Katsika*> <araXne> gagouli mou! (*i.e. my little gaga*).
> [23:51] <*Katsika*> <gaga> ma fav petz!
> [0:48] <*Katsika*> <GaVRoS> look i was kiddin bout da bounis ('*bounis*' *is somebody's nickname on IRC*) thing ok?

Sometimes, phonetic expressions follow a more English (or even north-east English) slant as in:

> <aStRaLoN> any lad or las fancys a beer?
> <aStRaLoN> any lad or las fancys a beer?
> [4:41]<*Katsika*> <yianna> me me ;))).
> <aStRaLoN> hahha.

[4:41]]<*Katsika*> <HSOC>@ChEEtah> whiskey roXXXXXXXXXXX
XXXXXXXXXXXXXXXXXXXXXXXXXXXXXXXX.
[4:42]]<*Katsika*> <sevastios> heheehe tequila for me.
<aStRaLoN> come pretty las I go plenty of this bloody golden liquid.
<aStRaLoN> okidoki.
[0:39] <*Katsika*> <GaVRoS> hey kerasi . . . where u been hiding?
[0:40] <*Katsika*> <Kerasi> gavvy i got me a LIFE re!!!;) (*'re' = Greek slang
in the text, the closest equivalent of which would be 'man'*).
[0:40] <*Katsika*> <GaVRoS> no shit? well its about time i'd say :)).

Also common is the written representation of 'phonetic effects', usually presented as a relentless repetition of the same syllable, as in a mantra. Similarly,
the excessive use of exclamation marks and other expletives and emoticons is
also frequent amongst *Katsika* users:

[23:22] <*Katsika*> <yannakis> spera all (*'evenin' all'*).
[23:22] <*Katsika*> <Mariia> yo yannis.
[23:22] <*Katsika*> <Mariia> whats up.
[23:22] <*Katsika*> <yannakis> hi maraki :) mia xara koukla, esy? (*i.e. 'hi
Maria. I'm fine, what about yourself?'*).
[23:23] <*Katsika*> <Mariia> EXCELLENT SPLENDID GOOOOOO
OOOOOOOOOD!!!!!!!!!!!!!!!!.
[0:50] <*Katsika*> <GaVRoS> buxaxaxaxaxaxaxaxa (*i.e. loud laughter*).
<aStRaLoN> ahahahahahahahaha.
<aStRaLoN> afto to gelio sou SKOTWNEI! (*i.e. 'this laughter is a killer!'*).
<aStRaLoN> hehehehehehehehehe.
[0:51] <*Katsika*> <GaVRoS> buxaxaxaxaxaxaaxax!!!!!!!!!!!!!!!!!!!!!!!!!
<aStRaLoN> man!!!.
[0:51] <*Katsika*> <GaVRoS> de mporw na sygrati8wwwww (*i.e. 'I can't
help myselfffffff'*).
[0:51] <*Katsika*> <GaVRoS> buxxaxaxaxaxaxaxaxax!!!!!!!!!!!!!!!!!!!!!!!!!
<aStRaLoN> hahahahahahahahahaha.
[0:52] <*Katsika*> <GaVRoS> ax (*i.e. sigh*) . . . dat was gOOd.
<aStRaLoN> axxxxxx (*i.e. long sigh*).

Most often, users on *Katsika* will talk to each other without making any distinction between Greek, English or standard network expressions:

[23:04] <*Katsika*> 2. zip: **sowwwwwwwyyyyyyyy** kali moy alla den
geinotane eimastan **from dawn till dusk** sthn ek8esi kai meta vour gia
ypno ase poy telika meiname me alloys 2 pou hr8an sto asxeto . . . Tespa
otan 8a er8w panw 8a sou kanw dwrw mia **hooker** politeleias **just 4 u
ma lil one**!!! Filakia kali moy . . . (*'sorry my dear but I couldn't help it. We*

were at the exhibition from dusk till dawn and then went straight to bed, let alone the fact that two guys came up out of the blue . . . Anyway, when I come round I will give you an expensive hooker as a present, just for you my little one!!!! Kisses, my sweetie!!!!')

<aStRaLoN>ti me epiase kai milaw agglika? (*'what's the matter with me, why am I talking in English?'*)

<aStRaLoN> **smn stop me**!

[4:42] <Katsika> <sevastios> astrale exeis afomoiwsei thn aggliki coultoura? (*i.e.* 'astralon, have you adopted the English culture?')

<aStRaLoN> plirws Sev (*i.e.* 'absolutely Sev').

<aStRaLoN> avrio lew na paw kai gipedo (*i.e.* 'tomorrow, I'm thinking of going to the football ground').

<aStRaLoN> kai meta se kamia pub (*i.e.* 'and to a pub afterwards').

<aStRaLoN> na ta piw me ta **localia** (*i.e.* 'to have a drink with the locals' – 'localia' is Hellenised English).

Then again, conversation can switch to a predominantly English mode:

[23:30] <*Katsika*> <Mariia> tell me ppl is there alot of retards in greece, if i come to greece with a psychology degree will i find alot of fucked up ppl like babbos to work on or no?

[23:30] <*Katsika*> <Markious> **like babbos**?

[23:30] <*Katsika*> <Markious> **yeah. sure**!

[23:30] <*Katsika*> <Mariia> ok!

[23:30] <*Katsika*> <Markious> **MadWolf, yannakis, me**!

[23:30] <*Katsika*> <Markious> **all of us**!

[23:30] <*Katsika*> <Mariia> **cool**!

[23:30] <*Katsika*> <yannakis> **yeap, we need you mariia.**

[. . .]

[23:31] <*Katsika*> <Mariia> **good then i am comin.**

<aStRaLoN> **don't u just hate shrinks.**

<aStRaLoN> **they r nice only at the end of the session.**

<aStRaLoN> **then they forget the sympathy and comfort.**

<aStRaLoN> **disguised businessmen.**

<aStRaLoN> **u r dithpicable** [*i.e.* in a Daffy Duck voice: you are despicable].

In terms of subjects for discussion, participants on *Hellas* are inasmuch active in small talk as they can become enthralled in existential discussions or in cheeky conversations. Here are some examples:

[23: 52] <*Katsika*> <yannakis> gaga ti kaneis mikre? (*i.e.* 'gaga, what's up kiddo?')

[23: 52] <*Katsika*> <gaga> mpenw mesa avrio (*i.e.* 'I'm going in tomorrow' meaning, he's been drafted for conscription).

[23: 52] <*Katsika*> <yannakis> ooops, perastika mikre . . . kalos fantaros (*i.e* 'my condolences kiddo . . . [have a] safe military service' – a standard wish to anyone about to join the army in Greece).

<aStRaLoN> ohhhhhhhh kalo mou agori! (*i.e.* 'my good man').

<aStRaLoN> tha se steilo tin fanela pou pleko mines twra (*i.e.* 'I'll send you some underwear I've been knitting for months now', meaning: this goes back to WWI, when mothers knitted woolen underwear for their sons at war).

[23: 53] <*Katsika*> [koukZ] gaga **i wish u all the luck in the world** . . . kalos politis . . . (*i.e.* 'safe return to your civic status', a standard wish in such cases), **we will definitely miss you . hugz** and makia (*kisses*) :)))).

[23: 53] <*Katsika*> [LisaKi] **we'll miss you gagaaaaaaaaa baby! Stay safe, don't do anything naughty.**

[7:50] <yianna> den einai **weird . . .** posa krybontai **in all of us behind this screen** (*i.e.* 'isn't it weird . . . how much each one of us hides behind this screen').

[7:50] <yianna> **and behind the person we let ppl see.**

<aStRaLoN> nai (*i.e.* 'yeah') . . . **its amazin.**

[. . .].

[7:52] <yianna>3ereis otan proto mbika sto irc (*i.e.* 'you know, when I first joined the irc').

[7:52] <yianna> **everyone had a different idea of who i was.**

<aStRaLoN> heheheheee.

[7:53] <yianna> kai otan me gnwrisane . . . den mborousan na to katalaboun . . . giati blepan **what i look like in real life** . . . kai nomizan pws **i was putting on an act . . .** ('and when they got to know me . . . they couldn't figure it out . . . cause they saw what I look like in real life . . . and thought I was putting on an act').

<aStRaLoN> :))).

[. . .].

<aStRaLoN> **this is a stage for everyone to put on an act.**

<aStRaLoN> **this is a theatre.**

[7:55] <yianna> na 3eroun **over 200 ppl from all over the world** thn real yianna .kai twra na mbenoun atoma pou me gnwrizoyn **20 ys in real life** sto irc . kai na me gnorizoyn **for the first time** (*i.e.* '200 people from all over the world know the real yianna. and now people whom I've known for 20 years in real life join the irc . . . and they get to know me for the first time').

[23:35] ***personal joined the party line.

[23:35] <*Katsika*> <Mariia) persy!!!!!

[23:35] <*Katsika*> <personal> **yoz.**

[23:35] <*Katsika*> <araXne> **alo persy!**

<aStRaLoN> **ladies and gentlemen elvis has left the buildin but WHO CARES PERSONAL IS HERE!**

[23:37] <*Katsika*> <araXne> **come on barbie let's go party!**

[23:38] <*Katsika*> <Mariia> **cut the barbie song ken it is degrading and sucks!**

[23:38] <*Katsika*> <araXne> xa xa.

<aStRaLoN> **whats new M everyone knows that Barbie sux good!**

[23:39] <*Katsika*> <Mariia> **u've tried her astr?? u have a plastic inflatable one or sth?**

<aStRaLoN> **yes i have one.**

<aStRaLoN> **i just play the song and shes woorkin.**

[23:39] <*Katsika*> <Mariia> **is she good does she satisfy u**.

<aStRaLoN> **and when i am really horny.**

<aStRaLoN> **i put the song on repeat.**

Rules and regulations, dos and don'ts in Katsika

Many people confuse IRC, which is a written medium, with normal speech and replicate their offline behaviour on-screen. As with any other IRC channel, *Katsika* has devised its own rules and regulations, and has a clear and articulate policy on what is permitted and what is not. Users are advised to avoid, *inter alia*:

1   *Flooding*: this happens when a user writes a long text (more than three lines, or too long one-liners) in a very short time, causing the screen to move up too fast.
2   *Capping*: writing in capital letters in excess is equal to shouting and hence considered to be rude.
3   *Repeating*: once written, information remains on everybody's screen, so repeating the same thing in short intervals makes no sense.
4   *Advertising*: *Katsika* has a very strict policy against advertising, since it perceives itself as a strictly discursive space.
5   *Solving international differences online*: provocation on the basis of geographical, cultural, political or any other differences is not welcome.
6   *Using abusive and vulgar speech or responding to such language*: users are advised to refer to an operator in case of an argument instead of taking the situation in their hands. Feedback mechanisms are in place in case users are not satisfied by the way an argument has been adjudicated.

You are being watched: power structures within Katsika

Katsika's hierarchical structure breaks down to one owner, 12 masters, 12 co-masters and 65 channel operators. There are also plans for the introduction of 'a new breed of ops', the Sops or Strict Operators. All of them regulate the behaviour of the 'lay public', the users, and are responsible for the smooth operation and improvement of *Hellas* (although masters and co-masters have greater operating responsibilities than the 'simple' operators).

The channel owner is the individual(s) who established the IRC group and an online equivalent to a 'president of the board'. He (more probably than a 'she') is the highest authority regarding administrative and structural issues on the channel. Masters and co-masters play a role similar to an 'executive committee' and are members of the channel's board. A special discussion forum with two separate 'arenas for deliberation' has been created where decisions regarding *Hellas* are taken and aired publicly. A four-member body, the *Op-Team*, is elected from the ranks of the masters and co-masters in order to regulate promotions, demotions and appointments of new ops and sops.

In terms of the gender profile of masters and co-masters, it seems that the majority of them are men. This has to be attributed partly to the overall smaller presence of women on the Internet, and on IRC, in general and in Greece more particularly. It also has to be attributed to the extremely technical aspect of such tasks and jurisdictions which presuppose a deep and informed understanding of the channel's philosophy and operative ethos. Women users, at least so far, are not so intensively occupied in IRC, let alone in elaborating its public service principles, and spend much less time online than men. As the channel develops, new roles are created which are filled by women co-masters as, for example, in the public relations domain. Despite the stereotypical depiction of women as 'good in communication skills', such roles and responsibilities pave the way for a more sophisticated female participation in the upper echelons of IRC management.

Chat police or chat facilitators?

'A CHOP (channel operator) is NOT a cop' argues *Katsika* and should not be treated as such. Operators do not exist to kick, ban and annoy. Operators in *Katsika* have been set up in order to moderate the flow of the channel, regulate reproachable conduct and protect users from any kind of harassment from other users. At the same time, however, users have to be protected from any operator 'on an ego trip' who may abuse their power. To this effect, all ops have to abide to a sacred code of conduct, the Rules and Regulations for Channel Operators. For those ops found guilty of abusive behaviour strict procedures are in place for their removal.

Those who make it are given temporary status initially and are scrutinised by the Op-Team. If needed, they should be prepared to attend IRC training courses specific to *Katsika*. When the time comes, a master or co-master will put forward a temporary operator's name for operator status. The proposal will be taken and voted upon by the Op-Team and depending on the outcome the candidate will be promoted or demoted.

Watching the watchers: rules and regulations for channel operators

Katsika is a democratic community in the sense that its watchdogs are not left unaccountable . Instead there are strict rules regulating their behaviour and ensuring that there is no abuse of power or promotion of super-egos. Being appointed should only be seen as a chance to show and prove that newcomers are:

- capable and competent,
- patient and knowledgeable to guide other users and
- tolerant and flexible while enforcing channel rules.[4]

New operators are also urged to keep in touch with each other so that they can exchange views and extend their knowledge and expertise in moderation. Particular attention is paid to the channel's primary objective – 'to provide a room where users can meet, have fun and enjoy their free time'. CHOPs should under no circumstances forget that their task is to guarantee and safeguard that objective, hence personal feelings and moods should be left out while on duty.

A specific set of rules regulate and legitimate the new CHOPs' authority for moderation. Furthermore, *Katsika* provides a detailed outline of banning procedures (see Table 12.1). Ops are advised to be articulate as to the reason for the kick and/or kick-ban. Reasons should be preferably given in both Greek and English, so as to be clear not only to the offender but also to the rest of the channel. Passing judgement in a humorous and intelligent way is a plus. If offenders do not respond to the op's warning and/or kick, they are banned with a public requirement that they reach the op in private and account for their actions. Offenders will have to confirm that they will respect the rules in the future. The usefulness of following up a kick/ban with a private conversation with the user is that this is considered as a direct way to educate users. In addition, *Katsika* is making a point that kicking and banning is not a sport but a

Table 12.1 Kicking and banning procedures in *Katsika*

Reason and ban	Direct kick	Warning, then kick, then simple ban	Private advice	Bot function (*except if down/lagging)
Caps	No	Yes*	Yes	Yes
Repeating	No	Yes*	Yes	Yes
Colours	No	Yes*	Yes	Yes
Join/part flood/Wingates	Yes*	No	No	Yes
Text flood	Yes*	No	No	Yes
Clones	No	No	No	Yes
Invites (main and private)	Yes	No	Yes	No
Advertising/spamming	Yes	No	Yes	No
Virus infected	Yes	No	Yes	No
Port scanning	Yes	No	Yes	No
Nuking	Yes	No	No	No
Use of Greek fonts	No	Yes	Yes	No
Use of non-official foreign language	No	Yes	Yes	No
Web chat without text mode on	No	Yes	Yes	No
Swearing, bad language	No	Yes	Yes	No

way of enforcing certain rules for the common good. In this way, apart from creating a pool of users educated in civic values, CHOPs will gain respect points from people who might otherwise think that they merely enjoy kicking and banning.

Conclusion

> i feel i ve been here since it was an idea. Now it has consumed us, like a habbit. Congrats.
>
> (19 December 2000 17: 32)
> [one user's feedback comment regarding the channel]

In this chapter I have explored the construction of identity and community among Greeks on the Web. I have focused on the social dimensions of an Internet Relay Chat group, Undernet's *Hellas* channel. Through these cyber-technologies, an electronic, computer-mediated national community is constructed in the same way that Benedict Anderson's imagined community becomes a nation (Jones 1997; Mitra 1997). Migrant and homeland Greeks regain a sense of fraternity and conviviality, rooted in an original home where everyone belonged, now reconstructed in cyberspace which they inhabit at the time of the 'permanently ephemeral' (Benedikt 1991: 11). Computer-mediated communication becomes the language of the 'nation as metaphor', and cyber-space becomes the location of the national narrative, now floating within a global/local nexus where actual presence and its proxy implode.

In my discussion about the construction of a hybrid community amongst diasporic Greeks on the Web, I have, like other advocates of virtual communities (Baym 1995; MacKinnon 1995; McLaughlin *et al.* 1995; Fernback 1997; Mitra 1997), depicted various characteristics which show that these cyber-social formations share normative features with real-life formations. Online, people have access to different ways of communicating, grouping, subgrouping and regrouping, including and excluding. Participation in a virtual community means people select who to interact with on the basis of common interests, rather than by accident of birth. In this respect, virtual communities are places where people gather for conviviality and social bonding (Rheingold 1993a). In fact, in virtual communities people decide to meet someone physically *after* they get to know them (by contrast, in real life socialisation works the other way round: we meet people first and we get to know them later). In this context, diasporic Greeks use *Katsika* as a means of forming social and personal relationships. Some very good friendships have been established since it was set up, where those who know each other share all kinds of information about their personal lives. Once needed, they even 'show up' to manifest their support for their friends, as in the case of Radio Utopia, a live radio broadcast at the University of Sunderland in the United Kingdom. Radio Utopia is an annual event totally fronted and organised by students, among which there are many Greeks. *Katsika* being a community with a wide diversity of population, there were people calling from different corners in the globe to comment on the programme and report the way in which they were all logged on to the Internet for a live broadcast. A specific sense of national belonging was forged there and then among those people, loyal denizens of *Hellas*, talking to their friends across the world and listening to music, news and celebrity gossip from the distant homeland. Some of them had even organised a social gathering in order to listen to the 'Greeks' from Sunderland University. More importantly, two *Katsika* conventions have been organised, one in Athens and the other in Thessaloniki, with all the necessary paraphernalia and merchandising, such as T-shirts with *Katsika*'s logo, so that users from all over the world can get together and meet with their virtual friends in real life. Communication via IRC is also complemented with frequent phone calls between friends.

There is serious talk and idle talk in cyberspace, as much as there is in 'real' life; information about almost everything is shared among participants on a basis of reciprocity, analogous to a gift culture. It is idle talk, though, which is context-setting: fellow members get to know each other and 'size people up' on this basis (Rheingold 1993a). Similarly, *Katsika* functions like a Greek καφενείο (kafenío), a coffee house, where individuals drop in to take part in informal conversations, where small talk and idle talk is a rubric.

Like their real-life counterparts, cybercommunities have their constraints too. The tension between the individual and the collective good underlies all concepts of community, and virtual communities are no exception. Invoking Rousseau's notion of the social contract wherein part of individual freedom is relinquished for the sake of the common good, predetermined behavioural norms like the netiquette and the Frequently Asked Question files serve as the manifestation of collective life in virtual communities and as sources of acculturation for members (Fernback, 1997). Issues of power, authority, dominance, regulation and rebellion are as relevant and significant in cyberspace as they are in real life. MacKinnon (1995), motivated by his desire to look for the 'Leviathan' in cyberspace, examines indications of restraint in Usenet, such as group moderation and conformity to netiquette, as serving the common good: absolute individual freedom must be given up in order to preserve civil liberty within the computer-mediated communication environment. It is in this context that *Katsika* has introduced such a detailed and articulate policy of moderation of user behaviour. However, the state of governance in *Katsika* does not fall short of regulating even the legitimate use of authoritative violence. A variety of very explicit rules have been set out to regulate and dictate the behaviour of the watchers themselves, while steps are taken towards creating a population informed in civic values.

Advocates of the existence of Internet communities offer the development of distinctive referent language and other forms of expressive communication as an additional attribute of community. The virtual equivalent of jargon, such as 'flaming', 'emote', 'mudding' and 'chat'; graphic accents; the use of truncated speech and 'emoticons'; and other uses of ASCII text to convey effect are some of the tools invented with the sole purpose of conveying nuances of speech and emotions among the members of the network community. The users of *Katsika* employ all of them, and have in addition constructed their own hybrid *lingua franca*, *Greenglish*. This is a shared form of expression and communication that only Greeks, with an anglophone background nevertheless, can take part in and appreciate and forms a flexible linguistic embodiment of the émigré Greek community.

Population movement across borders and the subsequent emergence of diasporic immigrant communities across the globe has produced large groups of people whose places of origin are far removed from their homelands. Furthermore, the majority of those immigrants, particularly the students and the well-educated professionals, are spatially distanced from each other, something that has increased their need for alternative means of community formation. Diasporic people are using CMC technologies to re-create a sense of community through the rediscovery of their own commonality by being 'citizens of the world'. Through this process, new images of community and nation are emerging through the discursive activity of IRC. The features discussed in this chapter show that electronic communities are far from dehumanised formations; despite the absence of physical space and face-to-face 'handshakes', cyberspace is perceived and experienced as a place where people share a sense of belonging, forms of expression, meanings and emotions, language, memories and rules of conduct which are as genuine as their real-life counterparts. They also indicate that the conditions of existence of diasporic individuals and their need to form community cannot be understood in traditional terms where spatial proximity was a necessity. It is only when the discussion moves to the more abstract level of shared practices and experiences that it is possible to begin to understand how a shared system of communication such as computer-mediated communication, with its shared language and systems of meaning, can be used to produce communities beyond any geographic closeness. This is why the concept of the 'imagined community' becomes powerful in the case of communities formed in the electronic forum.

Acknowledgements

I would like to thank babbos and Astralon/Nolartsa for their help and advice on a number of issues concerning the operation, ethos and development of *Hellas/Katsika*. The author is solely responsible for her interpretation of their comments.

Notes

1 Hellas Channel (n.d.) 'Constitutive Chart of Hellas', unpublished document.
2 Ibid.
3 Ibid.
4 Hellas Channel (n.d.) 'Hellas Rules and Regulations for Operators', unpublished document.

13 Rhodesians in hyperspace

The maintenance of a national and cultural identity[1]

Tony King

Rhodesians are the second 'Jewish' race in that there is a country to which they should belong but circumstances have forced them to reside worldwide. They endeavour to instil in their children the respect, culture and attitude that man's moral fibre should attain to [*sic*] but alas all remain 'children of the universe' in a strange, perplexing, non-tangible brotherhood. Are we the lost race?

Rhodesia was a way of life rather than a country . . . That piece of land once called Rhodesia, now Zimbabwe, will be around forever but the way of life is unfortunately gone forever. I'm just glad to be one of the few who did experience it.

(W.G. Eaton 1996: 62, 80)

One of the salient themes of the Nationalism, Identity and Minority Rights conference at Bristol University in September 1999 was discussion about diasporas, migrations and relocations of various types. Most such population movements have been forced, through political persecution, armed conflict and economic necessity, and the iconic image of present-day diasporas is of nameless refugees gathered on a boat or in asylum processing centres.

The Rhodesian diaspora after the independence of Zimbabwe in 1980 is one of those diasporas which was none of the above. It was a diaspora of the privileged, and as such goes against the grain. The white diaspora from Rhodesia numbered some 150,000 between 1976, when large-scale emigration started, and 1982 when the numbers leaving tailed off. In total, over half the white population left in the space of six years, so the Rhodesian presence is much greater overseas than in Zimbabwe.

In addition, the pattern of the white population of Rhodesia was always one of migration and re-migration. Born Rhodesians never outnumbered those born elsewhere, and so white society was in fact one of sojourners, although a definite Rhodesian identity centred on the physical country itself did develop. A modern continuation to the Rhodesian tradition of migration is that thousands of white Zimbabweans are applying for new and renewed British passports because they feel threatened by the current situation in Zimbabwe.[2] As things stand, it is not unlikely that a large exodus of whites from Zimbabwe will follow in the near future, the largest for 20 years. While many of these people are legally entitled to British passports,[3] the very fact that they are taking advantage of this is an indication of the nuanced way in which their identity is constructed.

The Rhodesian diaspora has an active presence on websites and e-mail, and is an indicator of how a national and cultural identity can be preserved and developed in 'exile'. This demonstrates several things. The first is that, given that Rhodesians were usually much better off than the average refugee and although they could not export their money, they usually migrated to countries which would welcome them, like the UK, the US, South Africa and Australia. Since they often had skills that allowed them to start anew in their new host countries, leaving Rhodesia/Zimbabwe and parachuting into a new country was relatively painless. This is a group of people that was largely skilled and had access to money. And as a result they are in a position to own home computers or are likely to have Internet access at work, and therefore they have found it easy to be wired and online. Additionally, this examination of Rhodesians in cyberspace also comes at a time when the Zimbabwean government has passed a law allowing the president to authorise interception of electronic telecommunications, including e-mail,[4] something that might seem premature in a country where only some thirty thousand people are online.[5] Some of the subscribers on the Rhodesian e-mail list Indaba[6] live in Zimbabwe, and it is as yet unclear how this new law will affect their presence on the list seeing that it contains huge amounts of content which the Zimbabwean authorities would classify as defamatory to the state.

The World Wide Web acquired its current ubiquitous presence in 1995 when software packages began to include browsers, like Explorer and Netscape, thus making it very easy to surf and search for and follow links. Anyone who has used the Web will know two things: how easy it is to start up a website or e-mail discussion group, and how many such entities are dedicated to single-issue or limited-interest pursuits. Scholars of nationalism and identity will also have noticed how much material there is on the Web, in the shape of websites, e-mail discussion groups and suchlike, dedicated to discussing and proclaiming any number of national identities. This author has spent considerable time browsing through identity discussion groups on Internet service providers, and also searching for websites that support different manifestations of the huge variety of national identities that exists worldwide today. Some, like the SAE website (www.sae.gr and www.saeamerica.org) for diasporic Greeks,[7] have official approval. Many do not, and are an example of the democracy of the Web in that there is no censor to limit what one can and cannot exhibit.

However, a couple of caveats exist about using the Internet for the maintenance and development of identity. Although many national groups have a strong *presence* on the Web, it is too early to gauge the *effectiveness* of the Web in maintaining and developing national identity. There is certainly no evidence that the presence of national groups on the Web somehow adds to their strength in reclaiming or carving out a sovereign, political entity, as opposed to simply keeping in touch. Thus far, in many ways, the Web is little more than a newer, faster way of disseminating information, but the information itself is not necessarily different from what it would be in a pamphlet or newspaper. For those with access to the relevant technology, the Web can be an aid in spreading information. But precisely because it does not need large resources to use or to print information, in the way a newspaper does, it raises the issue of the development of new elites which can bypass traditional political and economic elites. This leaves the credibility of people behind the Web-based spread of information and opinion open to question.

The Web is useful in charting changes in elite structures and access to information. Some scholars of nationalism, such as Benedict Anderson (1991) and Linda Colley (1992), have analysed the fashioning of identity as an elite project to maximise the control of resources. The Internet, on the other hand, is more democratic – while governments and traditional elites are establishing websites, sundry individuals and organisations outside the establishment are also engaged in the same practice. The Internet in many ways is a 'free for all', and does not have a dominant focus or central control in the way there usually is with, say, the print or broadcasting media. Therefore this medium is ideal for individuals or small organisations, although it also raises pertinent questions for the researcher about the validity and reliability of sources on the Web. For example, the 'World Association of X' can simply be one person and a computer, and might nonetheless come near the top of a search since search engines simply match words to websites without doing the kinds of background check we take for granted in assessing other sources. Many people who are barred from more traditional media can retreat into the Internet to propagate their opinions – for instance, according to Channel 4 News on British television on 11 April 2000, the British right-wing revisionist author David Irving now has great difficulty finding a reputable publisher having recently lost a libel action, and has retreated into the Internet. Traditional national elites cannot control the Internet, at least not in the way in which they would like, although a number of countries – Singapore, China, Zimbabwe and Malaysia, for example – have taken steps to limit their citizens' freedom on the internet.

Nonetheless, even within the new type of technological democracy where individuals have the sort of access which is impossible in the traditional media, there still are elites emerging, namely those who have the resources to access and use the Web. The difference now is that many components of the new elites are non-traditional, in that they do not need to command huge resources or require the mobilisation of human and economic assets. The proliferation of websites devoted to almost every conceivable subject is evidence of this. In a lot of ways, we are not seeing a democratisation – more the dilution of the old elites, and the emergence of new ones. We are also seeing the way in which old elites adapt to this new challenge to their authority, for example by blocking access to the Internet.

However, the use of the Internet in global terms is still very limited. It is the preserve of wealthy, Western societies with not only the time and money at an individual level, but also the infrastructural development necessary to carry Internet traffic and allow reliable access to their citizens. As such, while the use of the Internet for ethnic groups in most parts of Africa is severely limited by a lack of access and resources, groups such as the Rhodesian diaspora have the resources to make good use of it. Additionally, the Web's influence cannot yet be compared to the print media for the reason that its penetration is not comparable – one cannot leave a website lying around in a café, for example, for others to pick up and peruse. In any case, simple literacy, the cornerstone of the spread of national identity through the print media, is insufficient in the case of the Web, since the latter also requires reliable access to a networked computer, something out of reach of most people with simple literacy in the world today. In addition, one cannot chance on an interesting article on the Web in the same way as in a newspaper – surfing the Web requires more deliberate effort and previous knowledge of what one is interested in reading. In some ways it is more comparable to the early days of the telephone, in the sense that it is still accessed by a minority worldwide, and it requires similar knowledge of what one is looking for, or who one is calling. So while the Web provides scores of examples of how national groups appropriate new technology to distribute their message, discussion of the power of the Web in our case is very premature.

Concerning the use of the Web for disseminating or publicising national groups and identities, a number of scholars and commentators have seized on Benedict Anderson's phrase 'imagined communities' to describe the way the Internet is used to bring people of the same national group together across the distance of a diaspora.[8] Such an approach is wrong. The entire thrust of Anderson's analysis concerns the growth of nationalism through the lens of an imagined *political* community (Anderson 1991: 6), the end point being an entity which is both limited and sovereign, something which can wield tangible power. If one removes the word 'political' from his phrase, the 'imagined community' of people of a certain national group using the Internet is limited simply to people with similar interests using the Web and e-mail for communication. By removing the political dimension of imagined communities, diasporic Rhodesians – or Greeks, Armenians, Assyrians or whoever – using the Web to maintain contact and post webpages is little different from philatelists worldwide sharing their love of stamp-collecting via the Web. The only thing Anderson's imagined political community and the dispersed users of the Web have in common is that they share an interest or an identity but do not meet face to face.

Rhodesian identity

Rhodesian identity developed as part of the British Empire, drawing strength from the Empire as a comforting umbrella where the isolated Rhodesian settlers could feel as though they were not alone in the world. Indeed, they could feel that they were an integral part of the imperial project. Rhodesian identity developed in opposition to Africans and Afrikaners. The Africans were considered to be an overwhelming, menacing majority, and Rhodesian identity was based largely on the small size of white society and the commensurately large threat of the African majority. The 'founding battles' of Rhodesian identity were the African uprisings of 1896–7.[9] The threat of physical violence by Africans served to knit together the small settler community, and magnified the hostility the settlers felt towards the African majority. Once peace was established and the polarisation of violence had abated, this animosity continued in less clearly defined ways. The overwhelming characteristic was fear. The whites rarely believed themselves to be at peace with the land and its inhabitants around them. In the 1940s Prime Minister Godfrey Huggins spoke of the whites as 'likened to an island of white in a sea of black'. This powerful image suggests that African and European society were polar opposites, and that the latter could be obliterated by the former: the complexity of white society washed away by a hostile, formless mass – a black 'sea'.

Connected to this fear was a pastoral sentiment which developed within Rhodesian identity, encompassing only the whites (Chennells 1982: 160–221). The Rhodesian self-image was one of hardy pioneers who had tamed nature and made a precarious living out of a hostile environment – ironic, given that from the late 1940s onwards a significant majority of whites had not been born in the country, were not of pioneer stock and were living in comfortable suburbs. Significantly, many – but by no means all – of the white urban elite also owned farms. Nonetheless, the Rhodesian identification with the landscape was a powerful one, and it is something which continues among the Rhodesian diaspora today. Rhodesian pastoralism stressed that the threat which this 'wild' land and its 'untrustworthy' Africans posed was contained only by the standards of 'civilisation' which the whites had introduced, and to 'weaken before its unfriendliness, to sink into its rhythms, was to invite a loss of identity, a severance from the western inheritance' (Edwards 1978: 92–4). The Rhodesian arcadia, therefore, was not a source of comfort, but a manifestation of the way in which whites had overcome adversity to subdue the land that would turn on them if their vigilance faltered.[10] Attitudes towards African rural life were very different, and African traditions were not part of the founding myths of Rhodesian nationalism. They were seen as interesting museum pieces, unsuited to modern life but nonetheless quaint. They were also part of the idea of the noble savage, the primordial African tradition against which Rhodesians identified themselves.

It was much easier to portray Afrikaners as an outside threat to Rhodesian nationhood and identity and to emphasise a physical as well as emotional division between them and the Rhodesians. This was especially pronounced after the National Party won the South African election in 1948, setting itself apart from the Empire and emphasising, by way of contrast, the depth of Rhodesian imperial loyalty. Significantly, the Rhodesians refused to attend the opening of the Voortrekker Monument outside Pretoria in 1949 because it would indicate Rhodesian approval of South Africa's growing detachment from the Commonwealth and the Empire.

The public manifestations of Rhodesian identity became increasingly more pronounced and less subtle after the Unilateral Declaration of Independence (UDI) in 1965. They were also more overtly and deliberately introduced in order to inculcate a national identity because of the Rhodesians' isolation from the metropolis and the African population. The conspicuous trappings of statehood included the new Rhodesian flag and a 'president'. The National Archives also played their part in cementing Rhodesian identity, especially from the 1960s onwards, by engaging in the proactive collection of Rhodesiana – personal papers, photographs and so forth.

However, by far the greatest marker of identity in evidence on the Rhodesian websites and Indaba is the guerrilla war of the 1970s. Just as with the African uprisings of 1896–7, the guerrilla war bonded the small white population, serving to overcome many of the class and ethnic divisions within the white population itself (see Ranger 1967 and Beach 1986). The active search for an 'other' was helped by Rhodesia's isolation, through UN-inspired sanctions, from the rest of the world, and the regime was never recognised even by South Africa. It was therefore easier to portray Rhodesians as an embattled minority alone against external enemies, be they Britain, the communist bloc or the Organisation of African Unity.

Central to the development of a Rhodesian identity, Rhodesian-style segregation had never overtly been one justified through ideological absolutes, unlike South African apartheid which was based on the Dutch Reformed Church's Calvinism for intellectual justification. Rather, it relied on the subtler, more indeterminate question of 'culture' and 'civilised standards', and by the economic boom of the 1950s on the material difference in opportunities between the races. Situating Rhodesian racism around the concept of 'culture' involved shifting the theoretical boundaries of inclusion and exclusion. But in using this concept the Rhodesians could not realistically argue that 'culture' did not evolve and that Africans could not one day advance to a point of parity with whites. On the other hand, they could usefully fudge the boundaries, and assert that there was nothing stopping African advancement while at the same time placing obstacles in its way, like an increasingly qualified franchise (King 1996).

Indaba

In November 1996 the Zimbabwean current affairs magazine *Parade* published an article about 'Indaba',[11] an e-mail discussion list for Rhodesians. The article's tone was one of intrigue and subterfuge – messages are 'intercepted', and *Parade* took the attitude that the people on the list posed some sort of threat to Zimbabwe by actively prolonging a Rhodesian identity. Given the prominence of many white citizens in Zimbabwe, white preponderance in the professions and the economy, and the anti-white backlash which started in the late 1990s and has been gathering pace, a look at white attitudes today is useful. Although Indaba is predominantly a list for diasporic Rhodesians reminiscing about the 'good old days', there are a few white Zimbabweans on the list who usually provide the most accurate descriptions of what modern Zimbabwe is like for the benefit of their fellow Indaba subscribers.

What makes a Rhodesian e-mail discussion list and website all the more interesting is that Rhodesian identity is now purely in the memory. There is no mother country for them to look to, so the Rhodesian identity is one which is preserved in a mental space, without a physical space for reference, and which now uses modern technology in the shape of e-mail and the Internet to prolong and maintain its identity. The Rhodesians have lost their 'imagined political community' of the British Empire, and Rhodesia as a physical entity, and are now a community which is 'imagined', all the more so given the component parts' scattered isolation from each other, and from the core of white settlers in Zimbabwe. The importance of Indaba as a way of binding Rhodesians together as a community was voiced by one contributor: 'I think that Indaba is about bringing us closer together so that we can share our love for our homeland, disagree about many things, and still be a community albeit split by the four oceans'.[12]

Indaba was created in May 1996, within months of the introduction of greater accessibility to the Web, and is used to maintain a Rhodesian identity through the discussion of attitudes and beliefs expressed by those Rhodesians who subscribe to it. This author joined Indaba in late May 1996, sifting through thousands of postings. Only about a fifth were considered relevant, since the subject of interest was modern Rhodesian attitudes and identity. Fruitful periods (such as the second week of September 1996) were interspersed with long barren ones where for weeks little other than trivia and the trading of insults would appear. Most postings are jokes, cricket scores, idle chat or weather reports from around the world, but there was often vitriolic debate about Rhodesia, Zimbabwe and the modern world. Perhaps significantly, impassioned debate on Rhodesia, Zimbabwe and the meaning of being 'Rhodesian' declined sharply within about six months of Indaba's establishment.

Nonetheless, Indaba was created at a propitious time for Rhodesians themselves. A new book on the Rhodesian diaspora by a Rhodesian living in northern California had renewed interest among Rhodesians about their own history, and is the only study to date of the Rhodesian diaspora.[13] Although not an academic book per se, Eaton uses respectable market research methodology to trace the changes (or not, as the case may be) in Rhodesian attitudes as affected by the experience of 'exile'. The Internet and e-mail were of limited value to him as he did not use them to track down Rhodesians and very few responses to his questionnaire came to him that way, so there is still a gap in the scholarship relating to the Rhodesian diaspora's use of e-mail and the Web. The membership of Indaba is mostly in the 35–75 age range. A few contributors are younger and older. The vast majority are men. The sample this author gleaned from Indaba is not scientifically selected. There were some 125 sub-scribers to Indaba in April 2001 (and only a handful of them lived in Zimbabwe), of whom about 20 post messages with any regularity at all, and of whom maybe a dozen could be considered constant users (www.rhode-sia.com/indaba). Membership of Indaba is limited to those who possess a computer and modem, and who also have enough interest in 'Rhodesia' to bother subscribing, and so the attitudes and debates are those of a tiny circle of people who have never met each other in person (this was established early on in Indaba's life). It would be hasty to assume that they are representative of Rhodesians worldwide, and one cannot reliably extrapolate assumptions held by Rhodesians throughout the world by reading postings on Indaba. There is a clear division between those subscribers who live in Zimbabwe and those who do not; it is at its most pronounced when the state of modern Zimbabwe is dis-cussed. Until the farm occupations in Zimbabwe started in early 2000, directly affecting many white Zimbabweans, the Zimbabwe-based subscribers found themselves having to assure Rhodesians elsewhere that Zimbabwe has not descended into chaos and anarchy and was still a pleasant place to live. Even following the farm occupations, Zimbabwe-based subscribers offer much better-informed opinions on the situation than the diasporic Rhodesians.

There is a surprisingly wide variety of attitudes on Indaba, from those who are glad to be called 'Zimbabweans' to those who describe themselves as white supremacists. Most subscribers are not white-hot racists, but rather paternalists who would flinch at being described as racists, and who regularly admonish other Rhodesians who display racist tendencies – racism, in their eyes, was simply not what Rhodesia was about.[14] There is only a handful of subscribers who insist on using racist epithets and thus disturbing the carefully selective identity, and only one describing himself as a 'white supremacist', who regu-larly got slapped down[15] – and he is almost always a lone voice. Most Rhodesians on Indaba have extremely fond memories of the Africans they knew when they lived in Rhodesia (and not only in a master–servant capacity). This is especially pronounced among subscribers who fought on the Rhodesian side in the Zimbabwean liberation war of the 1970s – after all, 80 per cent of the Rhodesian forces were black – and these Rhodesians invariably served with blacks. A few even admit to owing their lives to their black comrades.

Rhodesians Worldwide website

The Rhodesians Worldwide website is owned and updated by a Rhodesian based at Edith Cowan University, Western Australia. Rhodesians Worldwide (RW) is an organisation that keeps Rhodesians around the world in contact with one another, and is proscribed in Zimbabwe. It consists largely of personal and business contacts, and organises reunions and suchlike. In keeping with the mental time warp many Rhodesians find themselves in, this author found many advertisements in the buy/sell pages of the RW website asking for the green-and-white UDI flag which Rhodesia adopted in 1969. This suggests that

Rhodesia's illegal unilateral declaration of independence in 1965 struck a chord belatedly. At the time of the event itself, many Rhodesians were apprehensive about the prospect of an open rebellion against the British Crown. However, today many Rhodesians see it as the apex of the manifestation of a Rhodesian national identity.

As well as supplying an easily accessible forum for Rhodesians to contact each other, RW also provides links to other sites which, to be fair, are often esoteric and appeal only to those with an interest in the various facets of Rhodesiana. Some are very useful, especially when this author was looking for obscure out-of-print books. There are also sites dedicated to, for instance, paintings of southern African birds, postage stamps and Rhodesian fashions. The most useful sites for the purposes of this paper are the ones devoted to reminiscences of the Zimbabwean guerrilla war in the 1970s. In addition, there is a humorous site for the 'Rhodesian Government-in-exile', owned by the one-time *Rhodesia Herald* cartoonist Vic MacKenzie.

The Rhodesian websites and Indaba e-mail discussion group also highlight the ways in which a Rhodesian identity existed beyond the usual assumptions about racism, economic expediency and a comfortable way of life. Here we have people whose self-identity is intimately connected with the country itself, and whose perceptions of it very often do not differ greatly from those of Africans. Both can agree on the magnificence of the Vumba mountains at sunset, for instance, or on the 'mysterious beauty' of Great Zimbabwe (although the political baggage of either side is radically different). Rhodesians on the discussion list hark back to the 'good old days', but there is more to it than that. Despite majority rule, there are surprisingly few Indaba subscribers who would want Zimbabwe to revert to Rhodesia. Most of them accept that Rhodesia does not exist any longer, and are happy to reminisce about the 'good old days' of sunshine, Castle lager, large houses and a 'happy' African population. This does not necessarily blind some of them to the inequalities inherent in the Rhodesian system, nor to the fact that perhaps they should have been nicer to Africans. Many, probably most, contributors are nostalgic without being overtly racist, and a few clearly admit that it was Africans who provided the cheap labour which buttressed the Rhodesian way of life, and that the downfall of Rhodesia was its inbuilt discrimination.

Conclusion

The issue of a post-Rhodesia Rhodesian national identity was keenly debated on Indaba for a few months after its establishment, but did not draw any firm conclusions about what it means to be a Rhodesian today. Clearly, it does not matter that the country is now called Zimbabwe and has a black government. This seems to bind Rhodesians around the world closer together, as if the danger of the memory of Rhodesia fading makes the effort to keep it alive all the more urgent. There is almost universal agreement on Indaba that they are not 'ex-Rhodesians' but just 'Rhodesians'. One of the more level-headed contributors wrote, 'I am first and foremost an African. Not an ex-Rhodesian, ex-Zimbabwean or ex anything else. I've never met an ex-American, ex-Greek, ex-Yugoslav or any other nationality so why should any of us use that prefix?'[16] Interestingly, most contributors are not completely oblivious to the African society which surrounded them when they lived in Africa; they merely see it through their own idiosyncratic filter. Indeed, many boast of their proficiency in Shona or Ndebele, and some voice regret that they did not learn those languages when they had the chance. The two most racist subscribers call themselves 'tsotsi' (rascal) and 'murungu' (white man), using Shona words to demonstrate their attachment to the country, not just the white Rhodesia they grew up in, but the whole country with all its ethnic groups.

For most Indaba subscribers, 'Rhodesia' was not just a comfortable way of life. It also symbolised a certain decency and blunt honesty,[17] and most Africans would doubtless disagree with this. One subscriber wrote

> Growing up in Rhodesia, I had the wonderful privilege to live in a society where the schools were for education, the churches were places where God was worshipped, business was for making an honest profit, not at someone else's expense, you opened doors for ladies, gave up your seat to the elderly and doffed your hat. Films were for entertainment, not perversion, and music was tuneful; not a mesh-mash of disgusting lyrics and anarchistic junk. Sport was a game, not a business and if you cheeked the ref you got it in the neck. I grew up to regard society as a thing of value, worth defending, not breaking down.[18]

This view of what Rhodesian values entailed is necessarily partisan, and is hardly reflected in so much of the day-to-day racism of Rhodesian society, but there is a clear implication that for Rhodesians today, the old Rhodesia was not a nasty, brutish, racist place; rather, it embodied common decency and gentle values. It was not racist, they would argue, and indeed, the few Indaba contributors who use offensive words such as 'kaffir' or 'munt' are quickly castigated by their fellow Rhodesians for betraying those decent Rhodesian values. What *did* constitute racism was not Rhodesia, but Germany during the Nazi period, from which Rhodesians felt themselves far removed – after all, Rhodesians, Ian Smith included, had enthusiastically fought on the Allied side in the Second World War.

Given that the Rhodesia which nurtured these values is no more, and that it has been replaced, in these people's opinion, by an inferior entity, there is a certain amount of wilful ignorance. Quite often Indaba subscribers exaggerate current problems as if the tribulations of modern Zimbabwe are somehow unique, they often ignore the iniquities and injustices of the Rhodesian system – or justify discrimination because Africans were supposedly far behind the whites – and they repeat the old canard about Rhodesia's Africans being the 'happiest Africans in the world', although to assume that all Indaba subscribers are in agreement with this mindset would be hasty. The issues of tolerance and the current state of Zimbabwe have both generated impassioned debate on Indaba. However, there is broad agreement among Indaba subscribers that Rhodesia was better run than Zimbabwe, and that the lot of the people has certainly not improved in the last two decades. In particular, much is made of the ruling class's excesses, such as the amount President Robert Mugabe (or 'King Bob' to the Indaba stalwarts) spent on his wedding in 1997, the arrogance of power as demonstrated by the presidential motorcade, the rigged presidential election of 2002 and the inaccessibility of the ruling circle – although they do not seem to realise that the Rhodesian government was just as inaccessible to the average African citizen.

Therefore, on the one hand, many Rhodesians on the Internet are stuck in an idealistic time-warp about the 'old days' in the mother country. On the other, the Web is now serving to maintain and develop a sense of Rhodesian identity which has no mother country to look to. To prove the point, there are a few younger subscribers to Indaba who are under 30 and mostly resident in Zimbabwe, who say that they do not remember Rhodesia much (except for the light, the vivid colours and other childhood memories), but who nonetheless feel Rhodesian in the sense that they identify with the values of decency outlined earlier. These people are not a threat to Zimbabwe. In most cases, they have come to terms with independence, and prefer to keep Rhodesia as a memory rather than hope for its resurrection. In particular, the younger subscribers who still live in Zimbabwe see no problem in being both Zimbabwean and Rhodesian at the same time. To them, Rhodesia was about a shared sense of values that now makes them good citizens of Zimbabwe. However inaccurate their reading of these values may be, a study of Indaba and of white attitudes is a useful exercise in understanding modern Zimbabwe and some of the people who helped shape its history.

Notes

1 This paper was presented originally at the Nationalism, Identity and Minority conference at Bristol University in September 1999. My thanks are due to Karim H. Karim, Christine Jacobsen, Donal Lowry and Kate Flynn for their comments and criticisms. They bear no responsibility for any errors of fact or judgement.
2 Chris McGreal (2000) 'Zimbabwe land crisis deepens' *The Guardian* (London) 27 March 2000, p. 12. This paper was researched and written in 2001. Subsequently, events in Zimbabwe unfolded very rapidly, and specifically the ruling ZANU-PF party used extensive anti-imperialist and anti-white rhetoric to garner support for President Mugabe's election victory between 9 and 11 March 2002 thus casting doubt over a long-term white presence in Zimbabwe.
3 Before Zimbabwean independence in 1980, most whites had Rhodesian passports which, despite Rhodesian UDI in 1965, entitled them to enter the UK and allowed the almost automatic adoption of British citizenship. After 1980 most white Zimbabweans were entitled to full British passports through the above and also their family ties in the UK – unlike, for example, the Hong Kong Chinese. While it is illegal in Zimbabwe to be a dual national, in reality many whites have retained their British citizenship by simply not renouncing it.
4 Nua.com www.nua.ie/surveys.

5   Nua.com www.nua.ie/surveys. In May 1999 the number of people considered online in Zimbabwe was estimated at around thirty thousand, or about 0.2 per cent of the population.

6   To subscribe to Indaba, send the message 'subscribe indaba' to: majordomo@listserv.ecu.edu.au, or follow the links on the Rhodesians Worldwide website (www.rhodesia.com) to listserver.ecu.edu.au/mailman/listinfo/indaba. The word 'Indaba' is Ndebele for 'council' or 'meeting', and carries with it an aura of discussion and consultation. Interestingly, the discussion group aimed at expatriate black Zimbabweans is called 'Zimnet', lending it an air of technological advance.

7   SAE (Symvoulio Apodimou Ellinismou) is based in Chicago and Thessaloniki and its chair is a Greek-American named Andrew Athens. SAE's campaign to raise funds for the benefit of Pontic Greeks from the Black Sea has official approval from the Greek government.

8   In a panel of eight speakers on Internet diasporas at a conference at the University of Swansea (UK) in September 2000, all but one used the phrase 'imagined communities' to describe the concept of people with a common ethnic background dispersed throughout the world using the Internet to maintain their identities.

9   For background on these uprisings, known as the first *chimurenga*, see T.O. Ranger (1967) and David Beach (1986).

10 The Rhodesian attachment to the land was also manifested in comparisons between 'efficient' European agriculture as opposed to 'wasteful' African cultivation. In particular, whites perpetuated the myth that they knew how to conserve the land and its resources as opposed to the Africans, although in actual fact until the 1940s white agriculture was responsible for massive erosion and misuse of land. See Ian Phimister (1986).

11 'Keeping in touch via e-mail', *Parade*, November 1996, 8.

12 Indaba, 20 September 1996, Chris Whitehead, 'Memories of war'.

13 Eaton 1996; Eaton also suggested establishing a scholarship for descendants of Rhodesians 'and leaving a lasting legacy of our former country'. See Indaba, 11 September 1996, W.G. Eaton, 'Rhodie Scholarship'.

14 Indaba [no subject] Alastair Honeybun, 12 June 1996.

15 Indaba, 15 September1996, Jeremy West, 'Vaun McLaggan's contributions to Inbada'.

16 Indaba, 11 September 1996, Geoff Hill, 'Identity'.

17 Indaba, 15 September 1996, Derek Wilkins, 'Good will and better'; 16 September 1996, Harry Rose, 'Common decency'.

18 Indaba, 16 September 1996, Mike Hagemann, 'Common decency'.

14 The movement for a free Tibet

Cyberspace and the ambivalence of cultural translation

Michael Santianni

The movement for independence and an end to religious repression in Tibet must be understood as a constellation of Tibetan claims to freedom, and Western 'imaginings' of Tibet and Tibetan identity. The present chapter will show how the Tibetan freedom movement has been articulated through a strategic dialogue between the indigenous and diasporic Tibetan community and the 'West'. This dialogical construction has produced an ambivalent blend of a neo-'Orientalist' imaginary and the legitimate politico-spiritual claims of Tibetans. Most recently, the Internet and other online technologies have become an arena for a tactical reinscription of both the neo-Orientalist's Tibet and the diaspora's essentialist project of emancipation.

After a sketch of the recent history of the Tibetan situation, this chapter will trace the Western colonial imaginings of Tibet with the help of the postcolonial critique of Edward Said and Homi Bhabha, to explain how the appropriation of Eastern spirituality by the 'New Age' movement has contributed to this imaginary. I will discuss how the Tibetan diaspora in the West has worked tactically to instill the spirituality of Tibet in the Western consciousness, and legitimise the movement for freedom through the appropriation of a Western institutional discourse of universal justice. The role of computer-mediated communication (CMC) will be foregrounded, in terms of ameliorating the cultural dialogue between Tibet, the diaspora and the West, ultimately offering some new insights into the formation of identity and community, both online and 'offline'.

A history of the conflict

The victory of Mao Zedong's Communists over Chang Kai-Shek's Nationalists in 1949–50 led to the creation of the People's Republic of China (PRC), and the decades of suppression of Tibetan culture which have ensued.[1] In 1955–6, the PRC began its campaign to undermine both the spiritual and political import of the Dalai Lama in Tibet; repression at the hands of the People's Liberation Army (PLA) led to a series of violent uprisings, culminating in the crushing of the decisive revolt in Lhasa in 1958–9. Consequently, the Dalai Lama and approximately eighty thousand other Tibetans went into exile in

India, where the Dalai Lama established a government-in-exile in Dharamsala. In 1966 Mao initiated the 'Cultural Revolution', whose ramifications included the systematic eradication of traditional Tibetan values. All religious practice, public or private, was outlawed, and heavy military presence and surveillance were maintained within Tibet, leading to more violent revolt in 1969. With Mao's death and the rise of reformer Deng Xiaoping in 1978, freedom of religious practice was restored to Tibetans, and Mao's policies of collectivisation were rescinded. Failure to resolve the 'Tibetan question', however, inspired the Dalai Lama to embark on a campaign to garner support from the international community. His 'political jockeying' garnered a sympathetic response from the USA in 1987, provoking reaction from the PRC, ultimately leading to more protest, the declaration of martial law and, conversely, a worldwide resurgence of Buddhism (Goldstein 1998: 14).

Relations between the Dalai Lama and China have since remained strained, with the PRC occasionally attempting, often violently, to eliminate political dissension in Tibetan monasteries. The Dalai Lama was awarded the Nobel Peace Prize in 1989, and has stepped up his international campaign for awareness of the Tibet situation; his visit to New York City, one among a number of stops in the United States in 1999, was his thirteenth since 1979.[2] A myriad of global non-government organisations (NGOs), campaigns and monitoring networks have been working towards the cause, such as the International Campaign for Tibet. Media campaigns have been spearheaded by a variety of celebrities, including the popular singing band Beastie Boys, who have organised the yearly 'Tibetan Freedom Concert' since 1986. A recent spate of popular films about the Tibetan situation, most notably *Kundun* (1997) and *Seven Years in Tibet* (1997), have met with enough success to incur the threat of political sanctions by China. The Dalai Lama has softened his stance on independence in recent years, calling instead for a 'federated autonomy' for Tibet, citing the disadvantages of returning Tibet to its prior system of feudal government.[3].

Global media, especially the Internet, provide a particularly interesting site for the ongoing articulation of the Tibetan struggle, with the emergence of an extensive online community focused on Tibetan politics and culture. A number of recent studies have analysed the ways in which particularistic uses of media by diaspora have enabled both the creation of new types of communities and the maintenance of existing ones. As Daniel Dayan claims, '[p]articularistic media complement the role of institutions in charge of the custody and transmission of filiation and memory' (1998: 105). The value of these technologies, moreover, can far exceed particularistic communication within diasporic groups; additionally, media establish a vital connection to other individuals and communities who can fulfil a variety of support functions. Thus the Tibetan government-in-exile maintains an official website, offering regularly updated messages from the Dalai Lama, and news about the situation in Tibet. Tibet Online is responsible for establishing and maintaining the electronic network of the government in Dharamsala, providing 'the Tibetan government, as well as the international Tibet support community, with Internet resources, guidance and expertise'.[4]

The diaspora itself maintains its own online communities, providing forums for localised diasporic communication and coordination. Further, these groups can ostensibly offer members more direct participation in the efforts of a global movement for Tibetan freedom. There are a number of websites managed by diasporic Tibetan communities in the United States, including the Wisconsin Tibetan Association (WTA). The mission statement of the WTA suggests that Tibetan immigrants participating in the Tibetan USA Resettlement Project in 1989 'are also the 1,000 ambassadors for the future survival of Tibet'.[5] Additionally, the diaspora's need for 'unfiltered' news is met by the extensive Tibet Information Network (TIN), which provides information in English, Chinese and Tibetan.[6] I see here how media can become 'instruments of survival for endangered cultures; when their presence insures the maintenance of links within geographically dispersed groups' (Dayan 1998: 107). The increasing importance of communication technologies to the Tibetan diaspora is addressed further by the Tibetan Computer Training Centre, designed to improve 'work skills and serve as a nucleus for spreading technical literacy throughout the Tibetan diaspora'.[7]

My research on Internet resources relating to Tibet, however, revealed that websites devoted to diasporic communications are by far in the minority. For the most part, Tibetan culture appears to be sustained online by proxy, by Western activist organisations devoted mainly to enlightening fellow Westerners and organising protest. Nevertheless, diasporic communities have often been successful in addressing and mobilising sympathetic audiences outside of the diaspora to bolster oppositional movements. Karim cites the example of a Burmese exile who, by using an Internet website, successfully lobbied the United States Congress to address the issue of economic sanctions against the Burmese government (1998: 16). While I could find no comparable evidence linking websites devoted to Tibetan freedom and successful lobbying campaigns[8] it is clear that the objectives are similar. Websites such as those of the Milarepa Fund and Free Tibet appeal to the Internet 'community' to participate actively in the movement, through petitions, letter-writing campaigns, financial contributions and simple word-of-mouth awareness. Alongside and supporting the official presence of the Dalai Lama, NGOs utilise the Internet to mobilise resources: financial support, information pertaining to the cause, coordination of protests and other political activities, the solicitation of members and so on. Additionally, online media provide a vital monitoring apparatus to keep NGOs abreast of developments in and around Tibet.

These websites aim at fostering what Murdock terms 'cosmopolitan democracy', the utilisation of media to address diasporic concerns including development and human rights issues (cited in Karim 1998: 16). The difference, however, is that while Tibetans are not excluded from participation, the dialogue constructed around these issues is ostensibly Western, hinting at an 'imagined' cultural dialogue between the West and Tibet. Dayan addresses the emergence of 'micro public spheres' through mediated communication within diasporic groups, entailing an interaction between these 'peripheral' groups and the 'values and procedural models that prevail in the larger one'. Eventually, he claims, 'a process of homogenization might take place, affecting the internal organization of the community; leading to new sites of power, to new modes of legitimation, to new internal strategies' (Dayan 1998: 109–10). Hence the increasing use of the Internet by the Tibetan diaspora, especially the government-in-exile, for the dissemination of its message – clearly the use of new media is in part a product of and an opening for the dialogue between the Tibetan diaspora and Western voices. As I will argue, the dynamic and mediated interpenetration of cultural values has indeed meant a certain 'Westernisation' of the Tibetan movement. The homogenisation which Dayan posits, however, need not be equated with outright assimilation, for the tactical struggles of the Tibetan diaspora within the terms of Western culture are devoted ultimately towards restoring Tibet as an autonomous homeland.

The enhanced organisational capabilities entailed by improved electronic communication have furthered the cultural dialogue between Tibet and the nominal West. To understand this reciprocal movement of cultural meanings and values, I will argue, is to understand how both Tibetan and Western identity have been reread and reconstructed through an ongoing and increasingly online dialogue. There is a certain ambivalence to these readings: while they have undoubtedly furthered a global awareness of the movement for Tibetan freedom, they remain at least partly a vestige of the historical imaginings of the West's colonial past.

The Internet and new spaces of otherness

For Said (1979), the imaginary of the Orient for the West has historically implied the logic of domination, a conquering of the radical otherness of the East through its creative abstraction as an object of study and discovery. Thus the Orient is the contrivance of a longstanding Western intellectual framework, 'an idea that has a history and a tradition of thought, imagery, and vocabulary that have given it reality and presence in and for the West' (ibid.: 5). 'Orient-alism' is a juxtaposition of colonial power and the psychical construction of self and other. It allowed the colonial subject to overcome the spatial and temporal boundaries of the exotic, both to reaffirm the superiority of the West and to allow the Occidental 'to give shape and meaning to the great Asiatic mystery' (ibid.: 44). Hence the 'textuality' of the Orient for the West, entailing a fictional construction of difference, offering the dual satisfaction of colonial mastery and the ambivalence of desire. By textualising the Orient, '[I]ts foreignness can be translated, its meanings decoded, its hostility tamed; the *generality* assigned to the Orient, the disenchantment that one feels after encountering it, the unre-solved eccentricity it displays, are all redistributed in what is said or written about it' (ibid.: 103).

For Bhabha (1994), the confrontation of cultures offers articulations of identity which transcend the liminality of self and other. The spaces between different cultural meanings 'provide the terrain for elaborating strategies of self-hood . . . that initiate . . . innovative sites of collaboration, and contestation, in the act of defining the idea of society itself' (ibid.: 1–2). Like Said, Bhabha emphasises that the construction of cultural meaning is akin to the narrativity of texts. Unlike Said, however, the relationship between cultures is seen as 'interstitial' and reciprocal, rather than a subjugation of peripheral meanings by a dominant discourse. In contrast, Bhabha's schema is emancipatory, for the creation of new 'knowledges' through cultural dialogue implies new political strategies for liberation, as the 'agonistics' of cultural confrontation re-politicises subjects, opening up the discursive possibilities of otherness (ibid.: 23). I can therefore understand culture as a text, a dynamic writing and rewriting of iden-tity through the mutual confrontation of cultural meanings.

The meaning of Tibetan independence now lies in the 'intervening space' between the 'real' claims of traditional Tibetan culture and the imaginings of the West. But there are still remnants of the old Orientalism in this imaginary, involving the logic of Occidental superiority and a romanticisation of Tibetan culture and spirituality. Hence the ambivalence of this dialogical construction of Tibetan identity: while Western concern for Tibet is in part motivated by a vestigial Orientalism, it has helped to create new discursive spaces that facili-tate political awareness and action.

The idea of new discursive and cultural spaces resonates quite clearly with the reinscription of a political and cultural movement in electronic space. The questions that cyberspace poses in this regard are likewise fundamental to the registration of otherness and the interstitial articulations of culture. How does the virtuality of online community challenge my conceptions of otherness (as a sort of 'cyber-Orientalism'), and how do we begin to interrogate the 'interven-ing spaces' of virtual cultural interaction? This is merely to point out that, in cases like Tibet, it is imperative that we try to understand the translation of material exigences to the textual space of the Internet. As David Harvey (1990) suggests, the mobilisation of spatial resources has traditionally been vital to social movements, in the anamnestic construction of the 'places' of history and culture, but also significantly to the orientalist production of the rightful place of the other in a spatial order that was, like imperialism, essentially a product of Enlightenment rationalism (ibid.: 252). The issue of space becomes even more salient considering the fundamental objective here of the recupera-tion of a homeland, clearly considered by the Tibetan diaspora to be the *raison d'être* of any Tibetan mobilisation. As I will suggest further, in accordance with Bhabha, the textual confrontation of cultures opens up new discursive spaces and new emancipatory possibilities that have likewise hinged in some way on an ineluctably spatial realisation of the other. What becomes important is how a reterritorialisation (and retextualisation) of culture may impact a seemingly global social praxis circumscribed very much by material realities.

The New Age movement and neo-Orientalism

Western interest in the East to the present has often involved a fascination with its 'alternative' spirituality. The creation of 'New Age' spirituality has been theorised as a definitively Orientalist pursuit, dating back in the modern period to the travel records of Western 'seekers' and missionaries of the mid-nineteenth century (Diem and Lewis 1992; Ellwood 1992; Korom 1997). These 'New Age pioneers' were among the first to construct an imaginary of the East as a spiritual utopia, creating for Western audiences an eclectic composite of Eastern symbols and ideas, and Western spiritual philosophies. Tibet specifically epitomised a mystical East and a homogenised Buddhism, a vision of the region which offered a utopian alternative to 'a political, colonial vision of Central Asia'. The common misperception of geographical isolation connoted the exotic spatial otherness of Tibet, offering seekers of alternative spiritual paths the mystery necessary to validate Tibet's imagined claims to a hidden wisdom (Korom 1997: 78, 85). The 'materialistic West/spiritual East' dichotomy was used by Thoreau and Emerson, among others, to found a critique of the superficiality of Western culture (Diem and Lewis 1992: 54–5). Thus Buddhism penetrates the Western 'intellectual landscape', providing a new spiritual perspective upon which a countercultural critique of American society would be founded, and often inspiring pilgrimage by its adherents to the East (Korom 1997: 78).

Here we can observe the importance of geographic space and barriers to the construction of the Oriental other, '[f]or there is no doubt that imaginative geography and history help the mind to intensify its own sense of itself by dramatising the distance and difference between what is close to it and what is far away' (Said 1979: 55). Two competing visions of the Orient coexist in the Western consciousness: the haven of mystical wisdom, and the backward land of primitives, obligating merciful colonial masters to recover the Orient's 'former classical greatness' by thwarting its tendencies towards barbarism (Diem and Lewis 1992: 53). Korom reads in the reports of missionaries in Tibet in the nineteenth century a dual practice of compassion and condescension for the monks, bespeaking the relational power inherent in the Orientalist outlook, and thus assigning to the Occidental a 'flexible *positional* superiority, which puts the Westerner in a whole series of possible relationships with the Orient without ever losing him the upper hand' (Korom 1997: 79). The Westerner can therefore glean what s/he likes from Tibetan spiritual culture: the imaginary trope of a utopian spiritual centre, a counterpoint for a critique of Western society or the rationale for a colonial restoration of an exotic classical culture.

Discussions of the contemporary New Age movement usually locate its renaissance decisively in the 'counterculture' of the sixties, as there is a fundamental continuity between the 'first wave' of New Age thinking and its more current manifestation. More importantly, it is a sense of this 'New Age Orientalism' which helps to inform a Western reading of Tibetan identity and the online movement for Tibetan freedom. For the sixties counterculture,

Tibet embodied a spiritual and cultural richness and an idealised affinity with nature, in comparison to which Western postwar consumer culture offered a dangerous inferiority, especially *vis-à-vis* the ecological hazards of modern industry (Ellwood 1992: 60). Alongside an apocalyptic vision of industrial progress, however, New Age thought holds out the paradoxical anticipation of an age in which harmonic spiritual transcendence will be universally achieved, thus 'veer[ing] . . . between extremes of disaster and paradise in typical apocalyptic fashion' (ibid.: 59; 67).

The persistent appeal of the imaginary of Tibet is captured within these extremes: the now-spoiled utopia which can nevertheless be restored by the collaborative effort of the West, which in turn holds the promise of its own redemption through a return to a richer spiritual path. The opposition between a materialistic, success-oriented Western culture and Tibetan Buddhist wisdom is a central theme in the Western reading of Tibet, as in one American's description of the importance of the Dalai Lama's recent tour of the USA: 'Even in New York City, businessmen, people who work in offices, want to learn about compassion, patience and wisdom, which he teaches'.[9] The mission statement of the Canada Tibet Committee commits to restoring Tibet as a '"zone of peace", an independent state valuing universal responsibility, welcomed into the international community of nations'.[10] The goals of 'cosmic harmony' and ecological responsibility, rooted in the New Age claim of a holistic universal concern, are indeed rhetorically important to the Tibetan movement.

The fabric of this mindset thereby becomes a weave of textuality – the narrative lineage of Orientalism – and proximity, the cohabitation of the diasporic Tibetan subject within the cultural space of the Occident. What online communication can establish is a debatable 'virtual co-presence', a situation in which the propinquity effected is not that of real physical bodies, but perhaps of a more genuine articulation of the orientation of those bodies to their cultural reality. Conversely, the ambivalent desire registered in the psyche of the Western subject is transcribed in electronic communication, and mirrors the spatial ambivalence simultaneously brought on by and realised in the orientalist outlook. As Dave Healy (1997) offers, the Internet provides 'a kind of "middle landscape" that allows individuals to exercise their impulses for both separation and connectedness' (ibid.: 66).

Even as the time-space of culture is disrupted by this paradoxically mediated co-presence effected by the Internet, subjects continue stubbornly to live offline, bringing about a conjunction of these different landscapes. The result is the persistence of the imaginary of the Orient in the Western consciousness – the force of cultural memory kept alive by the actuality of Tibet and the Tibetan diaspora. Simultaneously, however, there is an acculturative invention of ostensibly global cultures which are the product of an increasingly reciprocal (but by no means equitable) flow of cultural influence, facilitated by the 'time-space compression' (Harvey 1990) effected by global media: 'It is, ironically, the disintegrative moment, even movement, of enunciation – that sudden disjunction of the present – that makes possible the rendering of culture's global reach' (Bhabha 1994: 217). New Age belief systems, the partial products of the Orientalist construction of difference, evince this nascent 'cultural globality'. Moreover, they lay the foundation for a juxtaposition of cultural values which allows Tibetan nationalists to maneuver tactically within the Western imaginary of the Orient, and simultaneously to appropriate elements of the Internet's compressed time-space of acculturation to benefit the movement for Tibetan freedom.

Tibetan diaspora, human rights discourse and the ambivalence of collaboration

As Korom cautions, however, the neo-orientalist romanticisation of Tibet can detract from some of the harsh actualities of Tibet, perhaps obviating a general recognition of the agency of 'real Tibetans'(1997: 85). The tactics of the Tibetan diaspora within and beyond these imaginings refutes this claim. Far from passive in the Western construction of Tibetan identity, the Tibetan community-in-exile has worked to mitigate 'cultural imperialist' readings of Tibet. Instead of reading a unilinear cultural domination in the neo-orientalist imaginary of Tibet, we need to address how the claims of the Tibetan diasporic community intervene in the process of 'cultural translation.' To return again to Bhabha:

> The transnational dimension of cultural transformation – migration, diaspora, displacement, transformation – makes the process of cultural translation a complex form of signification . . . The great, though unsettling advantage of this position is that it makes you increasingly aware of the construction of culture and the invention of tradition.
>
> (1994: 172)

The confrontation of cultural meanings between the Tibetan transnational community and the West, fostered and accelerated in part by the use of new media, produces new spaces of cultural translation which allow a global construction of 'community' to emerge.

Western awareness of the recent situation in Tibet is credited mainly to the activity of the Tibetan diaspora, especially the government-in-exile in Dharamsala and the Tibetan community in the United States (Korom 1997; Venturino 1997). With the rescinding of the Asian Exclusion Act in the United States in 1965, Eastern religious leaders were encouraged to pursue 'divine missions to spread their faiths among the Western materialists' (Melton 1992: 20). According to Venturino, the displacement of Tibetans is seen as an opportunity to heighten Western awareness; 'resettled' Tibetans 'are expressly instructed to remember that "as Tibetan ambassadors you are to raise the voice of Tibetan freedom and independence"' (1997: 103). Increasingly, however, the Internet is looked to as a more efficacious means of disseminating information and awareness about the Tibetan situation. Tibet Online, for instance, endeavours to 'leverage the Internet's ability to harness grassroots support for Tibet's survival' as 'the spreading of awareness is one of [the Tibetans'] chief weapons in this fight'.[11]

The status of the Dalai Lama as leader-in-exile gives special importance to the Tibetan diaspora. He acts as unifying agent in what has become of necessity a diverse transnational culture, but one no less devoted to an 'essentialist' claim to a homeland. 'His personal example and Tibetan Buddhism with its profound development of compassion and personal responsibility is a central cultural theme for the Tibetan Canadian community'.[12] His recent popularity and esteem in the international community, the image of the Dalai Lama as 'the enlightened embodiment of compassion', and his willingness to tour extensively to promote awareness, have been crucial to the mobilisation of a global movement. He is determined to promote a dual image of the movement for a free Tibet as a project for both the reclamation of the Tibetan homeland and the universal amelioration of the world's spirituality, offering that we 'need to approach the next millennium more holistically, with more openness and far-sightedness'.[13]

So while the West has constructed its own imaginings of Tibet, the aim of the Tibetan diaspora has been to negotiate this imaginary towards its movement for freedom. The fragmentation of the Tibetan transnational community has remained purposeful − survival amidst displacement is not an end in itself, nor is it a postcolonial hybridisation of cultural meaning. For the transnational Tibetan community, 'the "aggregate" nature of identity is not a conclusion, but a beginning . . . for Tibetans "mobile and processual" identity does not march into opposition to essential identity claims' (Venturino 1997: 108). The call to diasporic Tibetans to maintain a sense of ambassadorial responsibility is an example of how constructions of ethnic identity can be intentionally collaborative, especially in a transnational context, and not simply unilinear or 'imperialist'. In the complexity of globalisation, unilinear readings of transnational cultural influence must yield to understanding the 'dynamic interaction between external cultural influence and local cultural practice' (Tomlinson 1997a: 182). The 'cultural imperialism' thesis, according to Tomlinson, must be rethought in light of evidence of the reciprocity of cultural influence.

Venturino takes Tomlinson to task, however, for his critique of claims to 'cultural authenticity', asserting as above that cultural reconstructions in the diaspora are not ends in themselves, but means towards an essentialist recovery of cultural heritage (Venturino 1997: 109). On the notion of cultural imperialism, Tomlinson opines that 'it is difficult to see how its generalised rhetoric of "cultural authenticity under attack" can possibly account for the lived experience of hybridity − of precisely not belonging to one culture'; further, the collapsing of physical distance obligates the Occident to throw off its own 'myths of identity', rendering it susceptible to a sort of reverse colonialism which effectively belies the traditions, and undermines the coherence of, Western culture − much as Western imperialism had accomplished at the expense of other indigenous populations (ibid.: 184). In my estimation, however, the activities of the Tibetan diaspora demonstrate both the untenability of any singular theory of cultural imperialism, and how identities constructed by diasporic communities can be seen as tactical gestures towards such an essentialist recuperation of homeland. These gestures, furthermore, should not necessarily be seen as an affirmation of the priority of any newly contrived 'hybrid' culture, nor a renunciation of the idea of cultural authenticity. Perhaps more suitably they may be thought of as indices of the ambivalence of social movements; they must often make use of contradictory elements in order to combat some of the effects of those elements or otherwise achieve the aims of the movement (Calabrese 1999: 263–7).

Accordingly, in the endeavours of the Tibetan diaspora exists a tactical awareness not only of the sympathies actualised by the Western imaginary of Tibet, but also of an applicable discourse of Western democratic ethics. The 'universal' attention brought to bear on human rights violations articulated by the United Nations Universal Declaration of Human Rights of 1948 provides a compelling legitimation of Tibetan claims for freedom. The distribution within Tibet of 'contraband' Tibetan-language copies of this Declaration by the government-in-exile is a case in point, showing further the saliency of these ideals for the independence movement (Schwartz 1994: 8). It is not insignificant that the impetus for the Declaration was the atrocities suffered by Jews during the Holocaust, as the Jewish transnational community is seen historically as the archetype of diaspora, inspiring comparisons made by the Dalai Lama himself, in terms of learning to sustain tradition and culture amidst hostile conditions.[14]

The interactions of Tibetans with the world community and the West especially have afforded Tibetans their own imaginings of essentially Western notions of the recourse available to peoples suffering under oppressive regimes. Thus 'Tibetan protest, while drawing its strength from religious passions, remains morally and politically "rational", committed to universalistic values and appealing for human rights and democracy' (ibid.: 223). The extent to which the discourse of universal human rights has been fixed in the minds of Tibetans is illustrated in a letter by a Tibetan 'underground association', issued through 'Western contacts', and addressed to the United Nations Secretary General, the United States President and the Tibetan government-in-exile. This organisation decried the refusal of the United Nations in 1992 to censure China for the oppression in Tibet, objecting that the 'UN liberated Kuwait within 48 days. We have been fighting for 40 years to get free from the rule of the Red Chinese' (cited in ibid.: 224). Although this particular organisation was threatening destructive measures to force the hand of the United Nations, it nevertheless shows the degree to which ideas of universal social justice have informed the cause for Tibetan freedom. Conversely, that this group pointed to the efficacy of terrorist actions in other countries in bringing attention to their plight demonstrates how a dialogue with other cultures, however mediated and destructive, has affected Tibetan cultural identity.

The Tibetan appropriation of the discourse of universal democratic ethics, nevertheless, demonstrates again the ambivalence of the dialogical articulation of the identity of the Tibetan movement. What Martin Shaw calls a 'global culture . . . [of] expectations, values, and goals', which manifest institutionally in organisations like the United Nations and philosophically in the aforementioned Universal Declaration of Human Rights, is still arguably dictated by Western ideals (1997: 33–4). Similarly, Hamelink claims a lingering 'European bias in human rights thinking' derived from the rationalist political philosophy of the Enlightenment, which of course privileges 'rational' claims to legitimacy – as opposed to, for instance, religious or spiritual belief (1997: 97–8). This raises a particular problem for a project of essentialist recuperation validated mainly by spiritual conviction.

Indeed, an element vital to Western imaginings of Tibet – the Orientalist appeal of a mystical spirituality – is compromised for the sake of legitimating Tibetan claims in the arena of 'officially sanctioned' universal ethics. The Dalai Lama has increasingly encouraged a secularised reading of his message, insisting that the fostering of universal sympathy and benevolence 'can be done without necessarily involving religion. One could therefore call this "secular ethics", as it in fact consists of basic human qualities such as kindness, compassion, sincerity and honesty'.[15] More specific to Tibet, he has proposed democratic reforms that would restrict his status to that of spiritual leader, eliminating his traditional political status, in a diplomatic move to further the legitimacy, in 'universal' terms, of Tibetan emancipation. This is part and parcel of a recognition of both the 'inferior currency of religious and cultural identities' in claims for independence. It is predominantly Western powers who determine the conditions of legitimacy, and the boundaries and conventions of human rights discourse (Kolas 1996: 59–61).

There are a number of ways to conceptualise the paradox of the Orientalist appeal of Tibetan spirituality and its 'inferior currency' as validity claim. One is the reading of cultural imperialism, which would point to the exclusion of religious sentiment from a rationalist discourse of ethics as indexical of the power relations that inhere between dominant and peripheral cultures. Second is a 'progressive' reading which would see this exclusion as simply a rearticulation of Tibetan identity in the context of the global community – but, *contra* Tomlinson, one that does not rule out the possibility of a recovery of cultural authenticity or essentialist claims to a homeland. As the Dalai Lama claims, the 'positive result [of exile] is that I and many of my compatriots have had to become citizens of the world' (cited in Kapstein 1998: 150). And this has meant, for better or for worse, the (re)construction of Tibetan identity and the movement for independence within the confrontation between traditional Tibetan culture and global community. As Ronald Schwartz puts it, the 'symbols of Tibetan protest, linking Tibetan nationhood to universalistic values, enable Tibetans to leap over the ideologies of Chinese domination and build a bridge to the modern world' (1994: 223).

Ideally, cyberspace provides the Tibetan diaspora with the constellation of community, 'global citizenship', and egalitarianism seemingly necessary to fuel any movement in a social environment shaped increasingly by the use of new media. The flourishing of CMC has been constructed rhetorically as a parallel to the spread of democracy to countries suffering under authoritarian regimes, as with former USA Vice-President Al Gore's proposed 'global information infrastructure'. As the principles of international community like the United Nations were informed by Enlightenment-based ideals of rational self-determination, fundamental human rights and equality, so too have these values helped to construct the Internet rhetorically as a refuge of freedom, individuality and public dialogue, unfettered by state or economic considerations. According to Jon Stratton, however, the actuality implied by this promise 'is that American ideology, founded on European Enlightenment values, will form the homogenising basis for the Internet community', evolving the medium along a capitalist trajectory, and obviating its more emancipatory potential (1997: 271). He maintains further that the globalisation of culture, through the effect of despatialisation wrought by CMC, works to deprive nation states of self-identity, and therefore peripheral groups with minimal access to the Internet will see CMC as endangering the preservation of national cultures (ibid.: 259–60).

While the threat of cultural homogenisation must be recognised, one would be remiss in assuming the inability of cohesive social formations to maintain stronger convictions that inform their deployment of communications media. The unique situation of the Tibetan government-in-exile exemplifies the circumstances that have compelled the Tibetan diaspora to embrace CMC – much as it has embraced Western institutional notions of human rights and individual freedoms – in a project of essentialist recuperation that must navigate its course with the guidance of a more pragmatic or 'progressivist' reading of its aims. What emerges in this case is an online community motivated in its praxis by a political campaign for the self-determination of an ethnic formation and the redress of historical injustices. But in addition to the movement cohering around a particular ethnic origin, there is a necessary inclusiveness of the movement that transcends ethnicity. The movement for Tibetan freedom depends on appeals and invitations to non-Tibetans to participate in the campaign, to become aware and to circulate that awareness, to urge action on behalf of governments – in short, to experience an expansive and collaborative Tibetan culture, focused as it is on pressing political circumstances. CMC to Tibetans is less likely a singular threat to national culture than a vital means of sustaining a cross-cultural dialogue crucial to Tibet's cultural recovery and survival.

Conclusion

I have attempted to show that the construction of Tibetan identity and the 'meaning' of the movement for an independent Tibet must be read within the interaction of Tibetan culture, both indigenous and diasporic, and the Western 'imaginary' of Tibet. Invoking a reading 'between' Said and Bhabha, I have maintained that this construction is ambivalent: while it contains the remnants of Orientalism, there remains an extent to which legitimate Tibetan cultural claims have negotiated this imaginary in the attempt to foster a transnational awareness of the situation. This has been accomplished mainly through the reaches of the Tibetan diaspora and its strategic appeals to a sympathetic audience in the West, but also more recently through an extensive online community devoted to awareness and political activism. While there is an abundance of literature attempting to deal with new conceptions of identity and collectivity as a result of new media, the Tibetan freedom movement testifies to the multiplicity of identities and communities that can be constructed online and that may elude initial theorisation. Further, there is potentially no limit to the different ways that the landscapes of 'reality' and virtuality may coalesce, providing many new points of cultural construction and possibilities for praxis.

What the radical compression of the time-space of CMC offers therefore are new possibilities for theorising the formation of community. Further research need not only account for the commonalities that define Internet communities along a single axis of ethnic affiliation, for instance, but across a number of dynamically interrelated characteristics, and accounting for a variety of unifying objectives which may dictate the particular development of the group. In Tibet's case, and contrary to Stratton's postulation, CMC lends itself well to a movement which hinges on maintaining a distinct cultural identity through communication across a dispersed population, *and* constructing new communities through a process of cultural exchange and inclusion, to bolster and legitimate its project. What is important to remember about these two disparate senses of community is their essential ambivalence – they must be simultaneously interpenetrating and mutually exclusive. That is, while their interrelation is tactically necessary to the movement, the hybridised and constructed variants of identity and collectivity lionised by the canon of postmodernism cannot be assumed to belie the essentialist objective of independence for Tibet.

Notes

1 The history of Sino-Tibetan conflict is centuries old and, therefore, complex and prone to varying interpretations. My aim here is of course only to provide the background requisite to an understanding of current circumstances.
2 *New York Times*, 'In 13th Visit, Dalai Lama Goes from Obscurity to Celebrity', *New York Times*, 11 August 1999. Online, available at www.tibet.com/NewsRoom/us-visit-1.html.
3 Reuters, 'Dalai Lama not seeking Tibet's Independence from China', 20 November 1999. Online, available at www.tibet.com/NewsRoom/no-independence.html.
4 Tibet Online (2000), *About Tibet Online*. Available at www.tibet.org/tibet.org/.
5 Wisconsin Tibetan Association. (2000) 'Mission Statement'. Online, available at www.geocities.com/Tokyo/3528.
6 Tibet Information Network (2000). Online: www.tibetinfo.net.
7 Tibet Online (2000) *About Tibet Online*. Available at www.tibet.org/tibet.org/.
8 One possible reason for this is that the Tibetan situation had already been addressed quite substantially by the USA government, as detailed at length on the Tibet Online website.

9   *New York Times*, 'Dalai Lama brings message of inner peace to frenetic New York City', 12 August 1999. Available at www.tibet.com/NewsRoom/us-visit-3.html.

10   Canada Tibet Committee (2000) *About the CTC*. Available at www.tibet.ca/about ctc.htm

11   Tibet Online (2000), *About Tibet Online*. Available at www.tibet.org/tibet.org/.

12   Tibetans in Canada (2000), *Canada Tibet Committee*. Available at www.tibet.ca/ tibetans.html.

13   Tibetan Government-in-Exile's Official Website (2000), 'His Holiness the Dalai Lama's New Millennium Message'. Available at www.tibet.com.

14   Reuters 1999, cited in note 3 above.

15   Tibetan Government-in-Exile's Official Website (2000) 'His Holiness the Dalai Lama's New Millennium Message'. Available at www.tibet.com.

15 Ghanaian Seventh Day Adventists on and offline

Problematising the virtual communities discourse

William Ackah and James Newman

According to the dominant discourse of 'virtual community' espoused by, what we term 'cyberoptimistic' theorists such as Rheingold (e.g. 1993b), the affordances of ICTs such as the Internet and the attendant communicative forms they enable should present diasporic communities with significant opportunities. Given the apparent capability of these new communication services such as the World Wide Web, e-mail and Usenet to enable communication and interaction that can overcome the perceived barriers of space and time, the perception is that these communication forms can reorientate our thinking about community and diaspora. This chapter interrogates the virtual community discourse, in particular focusing on three of its more significant claims. First, that ICTs are inherently beneficial, second, that they are ubiquitous and accessible and, third that they pave the way for the realisation of a utopian community where race, gender and other forms of identity are potentially meaningless. The chapter examines the discourse via an analysis of the activities of a contemporary African diasporic community, the Ghanaian Seventh Day Adventists (GSDA) and their on- and offline communication. The chapter calls into question the claims of the 'cyberoptimistic' theories and suggests alternatives in relation to ICTs and their use by diasporic communities.

GSDA community: formation and development

The Seventh Day Adventist church has had a presence in the nation state of Ghana for over a hundred years and now has some 200,000 adherents. The development of the Ghanaian SDA community in the diaspora is a more recent phenomenon and is much smaller in terms of numbers, with between 1,500 and 2,000 attending the three churches in London, New York and Toronto.[1] The formations of the three GSDA churches in London, New York and Toronto have unique histories that cannot be fully outlined here. They all, however, can trace their origins to the migration of Ghanaians to Europe, in particular Britain, in the 1960s, but later to Germany, Holland, the US and Canada from the 1970s to the present (Peil 1995; Akyeampong 2000). This mass migration of Ghanaians to the West and other parts of the world has been due to a range of political and economic factors both internal and external to developments in Ghana in its post-independence period (Hall 1992: 306; Van Hear 1998).

Ghanaian Seventh Day Adventists have been part of the larger exodus of Ghanaians to the West in the postwar period. On arrival many experienced adjustment problems particularly in trying to adhere to the tenets of their faith, while seeking employment and accommodation.[2] Some left the church as a result of these difficulties. A small group of GSDAs in Ghana and in the diaspora recognised what had been happening and decided to utilise their ethnicity to draw their former fellow believers and other Ghanaians back into the religious fold. They established small fellowships that placed emphasis on singing Ghanaian songs and conducting Bible studies in Ghanaian languages. These informal associations, which drew on the desire of Ghanaians in the diaspora to associate and express their identities, proved attractive (Attah-Poku 1996); in the US, Canada and the UK. There were enough people attending such gatherings for the groups to become formally recognised churches under the umbrella of the Seventh Day Adventist church. These churches have proven to be an important mechanism for Ghanaians seeking to settle in the diaspora, with the churches assisting people with employment, accommodation and immigration issues, as well as providing a spiritual home (Ter Haar 1995, 1998; Warner 1998).

The profile of those attending the churches is similar across the diaspora. The GSDAs in the three congregations comprise a small group of professionals, who generally serve as leaders of the churches. A small number of people work within the churches' denominational structure, others work within the health care profession and the majority are engaged in manual work. Students and people in transit are also a feature of the congregations. Most of the congregations are comprised of first-generation migrants and their children, with the majority of people being aged between 30 and 50. But in London the church has more people who are 50 and over, which is consistent with the longer Ghanaian presence in Britain. The London GSDA community also has in its midst more people who were born and raised in the diaspora as a consequence of being in the diaspora longer. On the surface the GSDA appears to be a cohesive community, but it has cleavages around language, generational differences, class and gender. At present these differences are subsumed by the needs of the group to survive and prosper in the diaspora and community cohesion and collective identity are important factors in determining the communication mechanisms that the GSDAs use. ICTs in theory at least could be an important tool for a community like the GSDAs who are separated not only from their mother country but also from fellow believers who are in different parts of the diaspora. However, the positive outlook of the cyberoptimists in regards to ICT use is problematic.

ICTs inherently beneficial for all?

The advent of networked computer communications has given rise to a discourse that at once stresses the centrality of a range of new media technologies (unhelpfully and inaccurately conflated as 'cyberspace', 'virtuality' or 'Internet') in facilitating group interaction and the creation of new virtual social spaces. In an overwhelming majority of cases, the discourse is presented as high technological determinism, imposing top-down fixes to the perceived problems experienced by contemporary 'real world' communities. Simultaneously, the discourse frequently presents these (enabling) technologies as neutral – little more than tools or channels – pipes through which content may flow. It would appear that for cyberoptimists the process of community formation is a simple matter of connecting and communicating.

However, our suggestive findings outlined here, drawn from survey data, interviews and ongoing observation and investigation of the community, reveal that as a community there is considerable non-engagement with ICTs amongst the GSDA. Though individual members, notably some church leaders and some people born in the diaspora, did utilise them, as a diasporic community it was evident that ICTs were not the vehicle whereby Ghanaian SDA identity was being transmitted. Where use as a diasporic community was identifiable (see discussion www.firstghanasda below) it did not appear to be paving the way for a communication-derived utopian community.

Technological development and innovation are an inescapable feature of modern societies, but our analysis of the GSDA suggests that the presence of technology in and of itself does not guarantee anything and that cyberoptimists have overdetermined the impact of ICTs on community formation. As Webster (1995) has asserted, there is a tendency in the cyberoptimistic literature (e.g. Rheingold 1993b; Featherstone and Burrows 1995) towards an unrepresentative overstressing of the palpable presence of technology. The degree to which high technology is portrayed as a central, prevalent and persistent element of contemporary life has been overstated. Even the prevalence and integratedness of technologies as 'mundane' and 'commonplace' as the Internet has been overplayed. The GSDA community, even though stemming from a wider religious tradition that makes major use of satellite technology, the Internet and other communication media to spread its message (Lawson 1995; Knight 1999), has not as yet displayed a desire to make ICTs the central means by which it communicates among itself or in the wider society. Rather, its communication mechanisms appear to be much more basic by comparison, with a focus on group identity and cohesion in a diasporic environment.

Much of the communication takes place at church meetings. Ghanaian Adventists for the most part meet at church once or twice a week. As expressed in interviews church provided an opportunity for individuals to truly express their Ghanaian identity. In an environment dominated by first-generation migrants, Ghanaians can converse in their languages and wear traditional Ghanaian clothing without reference or deference to a wider societal gaze. Church was where Ghanaians could express themselves, where their communication represented who they were, in a way that was not possible in secular work environments or in church contexts where English was the predominant language spoken. That enjoyment of being part of a fellowship is also seen in the time that Ghanaian SDAs spend in their churches. Saturday or Sabbath for Adventists is a day of rest and GSDAs traditionally spend all day at church, starting at 9.30 am and ending at 6.30–7.00 pm. Ghanaian food is brought to church and during breaks in the services people spend time catching up on news about home and everyday life in the diaspora.

Music as a means of communication also plays an important role in the life of Ghanaian fellowships. Spaces in programmes always seemed to be filled with singing of one form or another. The joy of singing in one's own language was expressed as a key feature as to why people attended the GSDA church. Speaking, singing, eating and dressing seem to encapsulate the Ghanaian SDA experience. These communication forms implicitly place emphasis on a sense of immediacy, of appealing to the senses in a very direct and emotional way. In order to get the taste of Ghana communicated to you, you need to be there in the moment, sharing and spending time with your brothers and sisters in order to make it an authentic Ghanaian church experience. This is not something that can be readily recaptured via new media and may in part account for the seeming lack of engagement with ICTs in this particular group.

In analysing the communication that takes place within and across the Ghanaian SDA community, it is evident that the dominant forms of communication within the churches' environment are those that readily facilitate a literal transmission of Ghanaian identity in a diasporic context. These findings echo the work of Loader *et al.* (2000) who argue that for most people ICTs are not particularly beneficial, neither do they hold much interest. More importantly, the apathy associated with them is due to the fact that they are not compatible with the needs and desires of groups like the GSDAs.

ICTs readily available, readily accessible?

An important yet easily overlooked consideration as to why a group like the GSDAs are not more fully engaging with ICTs is the issue of access. Cyberoptimists appear to have glossed over the fact that for many people ICTs are expensive, complicated to operate and beyond the reach of many people (Shields 1996; Porter 1997; Mitchell 1999). In the case of the GSDA community, use of ICTs among ordinary members to maintain a dialogue with 'homeland' Ghana was extremely low. Less than 1 per cent of respondents in a survey conducted in the London GSDA community in 2000 stated that they used ICTs to contact friends and family in Ghana. One of the key reasons cited was the fact that people did not have access to ICTs in Ghana and so this was not a viable communication mechanism even for those few GSDAs that had access to and used the equipment in the diaspora. Recent statistical data (NUA Internet Surveys) corresponds to our findings noting that in Ghana at present only 0.1 per cent of the population has access to the Internet, or some 20,000 people.

The members of the GSDA both in London and in North America utilised more 'traditional' forms of communication to stay in contact with Ghana.

These took the form of regular visits 'home', the telephone, letters and cassette tapes (Manuh 2000). The use of cassette tapes and in more recent times video-tape as a means of maintaining connections between the diaspora and the homeland highlights another aspect of access in relation to ICTs which goes beyond the idea of just being able to obtain the hardware. Conversing in the mother tongues of Ghana is a crucial element as to why first-generation Ghanaian migrants to Europe and North America joined the GSDA. Most adherents are able to speak but not read or write in their mother tongue. ICTs are primarily text-based media and the dominant language that exists on the various communication forms (the Web, Usenet, e-mail and so on) is English, effectively denying full access to a group like the GSDAs on its own terms. The issue of access involves a more fundamental reorientation of approach that looks at the environment in which ICTs are going to operate and whether the use of technologies in such environments is going to be both viable and benefi-cial for the communities concerned. The assumption that ICTS inherently will be beneficial certainly cannot be taken for granted.

The intrinsic homogeneity of the structure of Internet sociality, whether Web or Usenet based, is essentially in conflict with the dominant discourse of virtual community that stresses the online realm's powers to encourage diver-sity and difference. The homogeneity that is the inevitable result of an environment in which groups are organised around common (and, as we will see, increasingly narrow) interests is compounded by the fact that Internet use remains 'unknown and irrelevant to daily life in the world-at-large' (Lockard 1997: 228). Healy (1997) notes the lack of demonstrable commitment required by the virtual community. While the ease with which people can join the com-munity is cited as one of its strengths, this mobility becomes one of its most serious weaknesses. Virtual community members, or 'participants' as Baym (1998) perhaps less charitably terms them, can leave the community with a single click of their mouse; online communities 'do not oblige their partici-pants to deal with diversity' (Healy 1997: 63). These are communities chosen rather than given and if they choose not to engage there is in fact little that can be done to engender a sense of community and this would appear to be the case with the Ghanaian SDAs' foray into the online realm.

www.firstghanasda.org

This site is the most visible representation of an online GSDA presence that has been encountered in our research. The site relates to the activities of the GSDAs in New York and is significant in that it was evidence of a GSDA community presence online. An initial foray into the site revealed it to be a site of primarily religious motifs and symbols all conveyed in the English lan-guage. www.firstghanasda.org appeared not to have a clearly defined *raison d'être* or to have clearly identified and demarcated its audience. More signifi-cantly, firstghanasda's 'online-ness' is minimally expressed, save for the obvious fact that it exists as a series of pages on the open Web. Firstghanasda exists in

something of a hypertextual vacuum and effectively functions as a virtual
dead-end by underexploiting the functional potentialities of its medium, particularly in terms of interaction. These characteristics are by no means exclusive
to firstghanasda, yet suggest a dual uncertainty as to the role and function of
the online forums, and the target audience/participants.

At the time of writing (mid-2001), the firstghanasda website is presently
under construction (illustrated by animated construction icons in the form of
mechanical diggers on many pages). Notably, the site has presented itself in
this state of (in)completion for at least 18 months. Again, while by no means a
unique state of affairs on the open Web, the notion of websites being 'under
construction' is revealing. Notably, it implies that the site may, at some indeterminate point, reach completion. At least part of the Web's purchase is to be
found in its dynamism and fluidity. As Nielsen (2000) has observed, websites
are always under construction. They are, by nature, works in progress. The
conception of websites as 'completable' is indicative of what may be termed
an 'old media' approach, namely one in which, as is the case with printed
matter or more established forms of broadcasting such as radio and television,
a tangible product is 'published', fixed and effectively released into the world
of the consuming audience. It cannot represent too great a surprise to find
that the products of this approach amount to what is effectively an online
newspaper.

Examining the site reveals an apparent reluctance to engage further with
and embrace more fully the attendant machinery of online communication.
For example, firstghanasda's 'contacts' page[3] lists no e-mail addresses (though
a generic site-wide address is indicated elsewhere on the site). Instead, names,
postal addresses and telephone numbers are listed. Moreover, while a semiotic
reading of the site is beyond the scope of this study, it is notable that firstghanasda's 'History' page explaining 'How we got here'[4] includes three
photographs of both Seth and Dora Boamah (part of the original group that
established the church), pictured individually and together in what one takes
to be their home. Interestingly, they are seated beside a small table upon
which sits a very large and very prominent telephone. Viewing the page, particularly in light of the apparent reluctance to communicate online (e.g. no
site-wide e-mail address), it is difficult not to picture the Boamahs as eagerly
awaiting your call and thus reinforcing the notion that the 'online-ness' of
firstghanasda is, at present, rather minimal.

Similarly, while usability concerns abound regarding the problems associated with download times and rich multimedia, animated or even highly visual
material, firstghanasda presents a rather static series of pages that not only
potentially confound the expectations of Web users keen to experience the
interactive dynamism of the medium, but also convey little of the vibrancy
and dynamism of the group themselves. While evident in the URL and
through references within the body of its text panels, firstghanasda does little
to create a sense of Ghanaian-ness online. In this regard, perhaps the single
most important characteristic of the site is that it is presented entirely in

(American) English and that the language and message of the site focuses solely on religion with the community's ethnic dimension not being in evidence aside from the name.

The lack of a clear definition between a Web presence and other 'traditional' media forms, evidences itself further in the provision of opportunities for collaborative involvement and engagement with the site construction process. While firstghanasda offers a feedback page, it appears to have been derived from a standard template. Users are invited to 'please tell us what you think about our website, company, products, or services'.[5] Similarly, the page includes a pull-down menu from which the user selects one of two options in order to indicate whether the feedback concerns the 'Web' or the 'company'. The use of non-project-specific templates is widespread on the Web and again is not a specific failing of firstghanasda. However, that the page appears generic and not specifically tailored to the group it represents forwards an image of a group if not unconcerned with its Web presence then perhaps not entirely in control of it.

Ultimately, and perhaps most significantly, firstghanasda appears to exist in a hypertextual vacuum. The site does little to create a sense of connection with wider communities (used here in its loosest sense) of Ghanaians, SDAs or even, more broadly, online religious or theological discussion groups. The provision of links to other sites from within firstghanasda would go at least part of the way to generating a greater sense of integration and connnectedness (most commonly, sites will provide a discrete page or set of pages concerned with links to related external sites of relevance or interest. Some may even incorporate such links into the 'body' of the site as addenda to individual pages, or even embedded within the content of pages). At present the GSDA site is a place of isolated seclusion, rather than being an integrated and inclusive communication device. Stripped of these complex sets of hyperlinked interrelationships between sites, the very notion of 'Web' unravels and utopian visions of community remain unfulfilled.

Shifting identities, shifting communications

Theorists such as Rheingold (1993b) and Turkle (1995) have enthused that the coming of cyberspace has brought a fluidity to identity and a situation in which the 'virtual' is as real as the 'real'. One of the most extreme expressions of this cyberoptimism can be found in the online writing of John Perry Barlow. His declarations of the independence of cyberspace and assertions as to the inherent utopianism of the online realm has influenced and echoes a good deal of scholarly and popular writing on the subject of cyberspace and community online: '[cyberspace is] a world that all may enter without privilege or prejudice accorded by race, economic power, military force, or station of birth'.[6]

Offering a vision akin to Eden online, for Barlow, cyberspace offers:

the promise of a new social space, global and antisovereign, within which anybody, anywhere can express to the rest of humanity whatever he or she believes without fear. There is in these new media a foreshadowing of the intellectual and economic liberty that might undo all the authoritarian powers on earth.[7]

At the heart of the online community discourse has been the idea that fundamentally different types of social arrangement occur as a direct consequence of the processes of online interaction (see Reid 1999; Wellman and Gulia 1999).

The discourse also reduces the notion of community down to the idea of communication, with this communication being nothing more than the exchange of informational content. Our analysis of the GSDA suggests that the relationship between community and communication is more complex and that the mere act of connectivity does not necessarily equate with community (Baker 2000; Mitchell 1999).

The New York church's website certainly lacks a sense of being part of a wider online community. This, allied to the fact that it is the only one of the three congregations to even have a 'public' Web presence at the time of writing, is also illustrative of the limitations of the theorising surrounding the 'wonders' of the technology. Looking at the GSDAs Web presence and its other mechanisms for connecting with the world outside itself, it would appear that connectivity actually stifles creativity and community vibrancy rather than enhancing it. A look at the opening page of the Ghanaian website and some of the promotional literature of the churches in London and Toronto adds to that sense of communication without connectivity:

> The London Ghana SDA church sees its mission as proclaiming the ever-lasting gospel of Christ as outlined in Revelation 14: 6–12 in the context of acceptable Ghanaian culture, appealing to all who can identify with this approach to serve God.[8]

Online and in print in English the perception of the GSDA community is manifestly different from the experience of being in the congregation on a church day. The dynamism and vibrancy that gives the community impetus and meaning is missing online; particularly important is the fact that the promotional literature and the online presence are not in Ghanaian languages. In removing them, the Ghana in Ghanaian Seventh Day Adventist seems to disappear and what remains is just Seventh Day Adventist and a rather anodyne version of it. The sense of it being Ghanaian and conveying the identity of the community to the world outside itself is not there online.

This can account for the seeming lack of engagement of the GSDA as a community in utilising ICTs. Inherent in their unfolding identity is an uncertainty in regard to how to project themselves to the world that exists outside their ethnic particularity. The claims that the message of the GSDA is for everyone, rather like the claims of virtual community discourse, are perhaps over-inflated. On the surface the message is for everyone, but this analysis of the communication methods used by the GSDAs reveals that their communication, if not their message, is ostensibly for first-generation Ghanaian migrants who can directly relate to their homeland Ghana. The churches' other attempts at communicating with a broader constituency appear cumbersome and ineffectual by contrast (a website with no links and which is difficult to access).

The Ghanaian Adventist community perhaps has no need to seriously consider engagement with broader communication media based on technology at this stage in its development in the diaspora. After all, the groups are growing and have an internal logic and ways of communicating that meet their needs as diasporas seeking cohesion and unity in a very fragmented environment (Ter Haar 1998; Owusu 2000). The technology as it is presently being utilised appears to be stifling their vibrancy and not enabling their ethnic identity to emerge from under a religious identity. The GSDAs' lacklustre use of ICTs suggests that on one level that they are uncertain as to what the technology is for; it also suggests that as a community they are uncertain how to engage with a world that is not Ghanaian and Christian. These are issues that they will need to come to terms with as a community, as it is evident that GSDAs will not remain a predominantly first-generation migrant group forever.

If the young people within the GSDA community show signs of change in their attitude towards their ethnic particularity, then it must be assumed that the wider Ghanaian community from which the church derives its membership is also subject to these changes and possibly at a faster rate (Ifekwunigwe 2000). If this is indeed the case then it must be posited that the speech, music and other forms of communication that undergird the identity of the GSDA in the diaspora at present may not generate the same loyalties and feelings of association in people to whom these cues are much less familiar. Thus if the church is not to stagnate and follow the way of many European ethnic identity faiths in the diaspora (Lawson 1998) then it requires its internal vibrancy to find new external modes of expression and an identity that can reach across generations and shifting cultural tides. It is open to question at this stage whether computer-based communication technologies actually assist groups like the Ghanaian Seventh Day community in the diaspora to come to terms with these changes or whether they compound the uncertainty. It is clear, however, from this analysis of the GSDAs, that the cyberoptimist view that ICTs are inherently beneficial and widely accessible and that they offer a new form of community free from the problems associated with identities in the so-called 'real world' is wide of the mark.

Community informatics: enabling diasporic communities locally

The top-down theorising of Rheingold, Barlow, Negroponte *et al.* can in no way be seen to have disappeared from the popular or academic agenda. And while the conceptualisations derived from their studies continue to provide the framework within which a good deal of contemporary academic study is operationalised (for example, the various contributions to Smith and Kollock 1999), it is interesting to note that recent perspectives in the field of Community Informatics (CI) signal something of a sea change in the perceived role and function of ICTs in the social sphere. As a consequence perhaps of its greater emphasis on providing operationalisable strategies for implementation, and its empirical grounding in observations of the actual use of social ICTs in specific community settings, much work in the field of CI fundamentally questions the schismatic relationship between the 'real' and the 'virtual' espoused in more traditional online community work (Burkhalter 1999; O'Brien 1999; see also Webster 1995 on problems regarding the overstated palpable presence of technology).

Thus, while many of the 'traditionally' positive expositions of online community networking have positioned the enabling technologies as providing forums within which new communities, interactions and social relationships may be fostered, a number of more recent projects (inspired, perhaps, by Schuler's (1996) seminal *New Community Networks: Wired for Change*) position technology as a means of supporting and facilitating pre-existing, often geographically proximate communities. This shift away from the locationlessness and other-worldliness of 'cyberspace' to support systems for geographically bounded communities is significant and signals a shift away from the use of ICTs as a tool or forum for community formation. For Loader *et al.* (2000), ICTs are no less empowering than the 'community of interest' theorists have suggested, but their ability to empower pre-existing, 'locally spaced' communities is a function that has been overlooked.

The CI approach with its stress on enabling pre-existing communities provides a more meaningful environment within which to discuss a group like the GSDAs. This study has shown that the GSDAs are a vibrant community, but they have difficulty seemingly transmitting that vibrancy and Ghanaian identity outside the specific church environment. Although ICTs at present do not appear to be meeting their requirements, it cannot be presumed that the group are the equivalent of twenty-first century Luddites and that they will never engage with ICTs, or that ICTs cannot be developed in such a way as to deliver in part means by which Ghanaian SDA identity can be transmitted in a way that is both meaningful and relevant to a changing diasporic community. The CI approach with its emphasis on working with and for the community perhaps offers a means by which identity and community formation offline can be reflected in online form. To a degree the technology in the form of video conferencing and other non-text-based modes of communication may be moving in that direction and could provide GSDAs with a mechanism whereby they can capture some of the face-to-face communication that gives the GSDAs their vibrancy, while at the same time reaching out to the second and third generation of the Ghanaian diaspora, who may want new ways in which to affirm or explore their identity (see Bastian 1999 for a discussion of Nigerian diaspora online).

It is important to note that at the heart of the project of CI proponents and investigators, such as Loader *et al.*, is an apparent desire to bridge the conceptual gap between on- and offline community and communication. The implications of such a shift are profound. Most notably, it demands a reorientation of the relationship between technology and users away from the often brutal determinism of the technological fix:

> [A CI perspective] is an approach which emphasises the need for the new technologies to be shaped by the human aspirations and desires emanating from existing community social structures rather than the expectation of new modes of social intercourse required to meet the technical, commercial and political designs of 'outsiders' . . . it is an approach which stresses that technologies should be embedded within existing cultural and social relations.
>
> (Loader *et al.* 2000: 82)

Fundamentally, a CI approach demands a more pragmatic approach to the deployment of ICTs. It is critical that technology is released from the restrictive position of intrinsic provider of solutions. The positioning of ICTs as black-box panacea leads merely to a situation in which their limitations are imposed and, more significantly, elevated to the position of constraints. By offering primacy or at least being sensitive to existing social structures and attempting to identify ways in which ICTs may be integrated so as to facilitate and enhance these patterns of activity and behaviour, CI approaches acknowledge and accommodate the existence of activity critical to maintaining the cohesion and coherence of community that ICTs cannot (presently, at least) either support or facilitate. In this way, online communication does not constitute community or seek to replace the 'real world' with a new community form and forum. Rather, ICT systems can be harnessed alongside other technologically dependent/independent activity.

Conclusion

This case study of the GSDAs on- and offline has highlighted some the limitations of the cyberoptimistic approach to ICTs. It has also shown that online forms of communication are misunderstood and their potentiality and uniqueness largely underexploited or ignored wholesale. This should be unsurprising given the comparative infancy of the Web as a popular medium. This does not simply mean downsizing expectations for ICTs. At least part of the key to understanding any new medium is not merely to explore its strengths but also to identify its weaknesses. And as we have illustrated here, the weaknesses of ICTs are many. What is somewhat unfortunate, especially for diasporic communities such as the Ghanaian SDAs, is that the virtual community discourse stresses the inherent ability of global networked ICTs to effectively eradicate the notion of diaspora in terms of geographic dislocation. This notion was founded largely upon a misunderstanding of the importance of these weaknesses and limitations of the technical capability of ICTs and a misunderstanding of the constituents of community cohesion and sustenance of identity.

If ICTs are to make a useful contribution to the empowerment of community (see Schuler 1996 and the various contributors to Gurstein 2000), a bottom-up approach that sensitively considers, accommodates and supports extant social activity in an attempt to reconnect the local will be necessary. Importantly, the notion of 'virtual community' is replaced by 'community informatics' stressing the shift from communities as solely or predominantly online entities where 'cyberspace' constitutes the place of that community and dictates the means by which it interacts, to a situation in which ICTs support community activity and the 'real' and 'online' realms are not constituted in opposition.

As the GSDAs develop in the diaspora it is conceivable that their engagement with ICTs will increase, particularly if access improves and the technology develops in line with the current and changing needs of this particular diasporic community. By placing the emphasis on putting the technology at the disposal of the community, and stressing the centrality of community over technology, it is hoped that both the diasporic community and the technology that it uses can mature and flourish together. The result being a Ghanaian SDA identity emerging and unfolding that is assured and able to sustain its vibrancy and dynamism both on- and offline.

Notes

1 The GSDA movement is a subset of the broader Seventh Day Adventist Church founded in 1863. It started by Ghanaians migrating to the diaspora. London, New York and Toronto form the basis of this study, but there are GSDA congregations in Holland, Germany and numerous US cities and GSDA fellowships also in Israel and Japan.
2 Seventh Day Adventists are required to abstain from working from sunset on Friday to sunset on Saturday. They also follow certain dietary laws and do not drink tea, coffee or alcohol or eat pork. Migrants, particularly those working at the low end of the employment market, rarely have freedom of choice in relation to the hours that they work.
3 www.firstghanasda.org/church contacts.htm.
4 www.firstghanasda.org/history.htm.
5 www.firstghanasda.org/feedback.htm.
6 John Perry Barlow, 'Declaration of the Independence of Cyberspace' *Cyber-Rights Electronic List*, 8 February 1996.
7 John Perry Barlow, 'Thinking Locally, Acting Globally' *Cyber-Rights Electronic List*, 15 January 1996.
8 London Ghana SDA church bulletin, 2000.

Bibliography

Abramson, B.D. (2001), 'The Spectre of Diaspora: Transnational Citizenship and International Cinema', *Journal of Communication Inquiry*, 25(2): 94–113.

Ackah, William (1999), *Pan Africanism: Exploring the Contradictions: Politics, Identity, and Development in Africa and the African Diaspora*, Aldershot: Ashgate.

Ackah, William (2000), 'Diasporas of Faith: Exploring Ethnic and Religious Identity in the Ghanian Seventh Day Adventist Community in Britain', paper presented at the New African Diasporas Colloquium, University of London.

Adam, A. and Green, E. (1998), 'Gender, Agency, Location and the New Information Society', in Brian Loader (ed.), *Cyberspace Divide: Equality, Agency and Policy in the Information Society*, London: Routledge.

Ahmed, Sara (1999), 'Home and Away: Narratives of Migration and Estrangement', *International Journal of Cultural Studies*, 2(3): 329–47.

Akhtar, Shabir (1990), *A Faith for All Seasons: Islam and Western Modernity*, London: Bellew.

Akin, Salih (1995), 'Désignation du peuple, du territoire et de la langue kurde dans le discours scientifique et politique turc', thèse, Doctorat en Sciences du Langage, École doctorale de Lettres, Université de Rouen, France.

Aksoy, Asu and Robins, Kevin (1997), 'Peripheral Vision: Cultural Industries and Cultural Identities in Turkey', *Paragraph*, 20(1): 75–99.

Aksoy, Asu and Robins, Kevin (2000), 'Thinking across Spaces: Transnational Television from Turkey', *European Journal of Cultural Studies*, 3(3): 345–67.

Akyeampong, E. (2000), 'Africans in the Diaspora: The Diaspora and Africa', *African Affairs*, 99: 183–215.

Alia, V. (1999), *Un/covering the North: News, Media, and Aboriginal People*, Vancouver: UBC Press.

Alvarado, M. (ed.) (1988), *Video World-Wide: An International Study*, UNESCO, London: John Libbey.

Anderson, Benedict (1983), *Imagined Communities: Reflections on the Origin and Spread of Nationalism*, London: Verso.

Anderson, Benedict (1991), *Imagined Communities: Reflections on the Origin and Spread of Nationalism*, revised edition, London: Verso.

Anderson, Jon (1995), '"Cybarites," Knowledge Workers, and New Creoles on the Superhighway', *Anthropology Today*, 11(4): 13–15.

Anderson, Jon (1996), 'Islam and the Globalization of Politics', paper presented to the Council on Foreign Relations Muslim Politics Study Group, New York City.

Anderson, Jon (1997), 'Cybernauts of the Arab Diaspora: Electronic Mediation in Transnational Cultural Identities', paper presented at the Couch-Stone Symposium on 'Postmodern Culture, Global Capitalism and Democratic Action', University of Maryland.

Ang, Ien (1990), 'The Nature of the Audience', in J. Downing, A. Mohammadi and A. Sreberny-Mohammadi (eds), *Questioning the Media*, London: Sage Publications.

Ang, Ien (1996), *Living Room Wars: Rethinking Media Audiences for a Postmodern World*, London: Routledge.

Anon. (1956), *Indian Talkie: 1936–56*, Bombay: Film Federation of India.

Appadurai, Arjun (1996), *Modernity at Large: Cultural Dimensions of Globalization*, Minneapolis, MN: University of Minnesota Press.

Appadurai, Arjun (March 1998), 'The Politics of Repetition: Notes on the Reception of Indian hit films', Workshop on Media and Mediation in the Politics of Culture, Centre for Studies in Social Sciences, International Globalization Network, Calcutta.

Atiyeh, George N. (ed.) (1995), *The Book in the Islamic World: The Written Word and Communication in the Middle East*, Albany, NY: SUNY Press.

Attah-Poku, Aggemang (1996), 'Asanteman Immigrant Ethnic Association: An Effective Tool for Immigrant Survival and Adjustment Problem Solution in New York City', *Journal of Black Studies*, 27(1): 56–76.

Babb, Lawrence A. and Wadley, Susan (eds) (1995), *Media and The Transformation of Religion in South Asia*, Philadelphia, PA: University of Pennsylvania Press.

Baker, Paul (2000), 'The Role of Community Information in the Virtual Metropolis: The Coexistence of Virtual and Proximate Terrains', in M. Gurstein (ed.), *Community Informatics: Enabling Communities With Information and Communications Technologies*, Hershey, PA: Idea Group Publishing, 104–35.

Bakhtin, Mikhail (1981), *The Dialogic Imagination*, Austin, TX: University of Texas Press.

Barber, Benjamin (1995), *Jihad vs. McWorld*, New York: Times Books/Random House.

Bar-Haim, Gabriel (1992), 'Revista Mea: Keeping Alive the Romanian Community in Israel', in Stephen Harold Riggins (ed.), *Ethnic Minority Media: An International Perspective*. Newbury Park, CA: Sage, 196–216.

Barkatulla, Abdul Kadir (1992), 'Information Technology and Islamic Studies', unpublished MPhil thesis, University of Wales at Lampeter.

Barker, C. (1999), *Television, Globalization and Cultural Identities*, Buckingham and Philadelphia, PA: Open University Press.

Bastian, Misty (1999), 'Nationalism in a Virtual Space: Immigrant Nigerians on the Internet' *West Africa Review*, 1(1): 1–14.

Baym, N. (1995), 'The Emergence of Community in Computer-mediated Communication', in Steven Jones (ed.), *CyberSociety: Computer-Mediated Communication and Community*, Thousand Oaks, CA: Sage, 138–63.

Baym, N. (1998), 'The Emergence of On-line Community', in Steve Jones (ed.), *Cybersociety 2.0: Revisiting Computer Mediated Communication and Community*, Thousand Oaks, CA and London: Sage, 35–68.

Beach, D. (1986), *War and Politics in Zimbabwe 1840–1900*, Gwero: Mambo Press.

Becker, Jörg (2001), 'Zwischen Abgrenzung und Integration: Anmerkungen zur Ethnisierung der türkischen Medienkultur', in Jörg Becker and Reinhard Behnisch (eds), *Zwischen Abgrenzung und Integration: Türkische Medienkultur in Deutschland*, Rehburg-Loccum: Evangelische Akademie, 9–25.

Bednall, David H.B. (1988), 'Television Use by Melbourne's Greek Community', *Media Information Australia*, 47(February): 44–9.

Bednall, David (1993), 'What the Media Has Contributed to Ethnic Communities in Australia', *Migration Action*, 15(3): 7–10.

Belden, Elionne L.W. (1997), *Claiming Chinese Identity*, New York and London: Garland.

Bell, Philip (1993), *Multicultural Australia in the Media*, Canberra: Office of Multicultural Affairs.

Bell, Philip, Heilpern, Sandra, McKenzie, M. and Vipond, J. (1991), *Different Agenda: Economic and Social Aspects of the Ethnic Press in Australia*, Working Papers on Multiculturalism no. 8, Centre for Multicultural Studies: University of Wollongong for Office of Multicultural Affairs.

Benedikt, Michael (ed.) (1991), *Cyberspace: First Steps*, Cambridge, MA: MIT Press.

Berger, Arthur Asa (1995), *Essentials of Mass Communication Theory*, Thousand Oaks, CA: Sage.

Berger, John (1980), *About Looking*, New York: Pantheon Books.

Berko, Lili (1989), 'Video: in Search of a Discourse', *Quarterly Review of Film Studies*, 10(4): 289–307.

Bhabha, Homi K. (1990a), 'DissemiNation: Time, Narrative, and the Margins of the Modern Nation', in H. Bhabha (ed.), *Nation and Narration*, London: Routledge, 291–322.

Bhabha, Homi K. (1990b), 'Introduction: Narrating the Nation', in H. Bhabha (ed.), *Nation and Narration*, London: Routledge, 1–7.

Bhabha, Homi K. (1994), *The Location of Culture*, New York: Routledge.

Blaut, J.M. (1993), *The Colonizer's Model of the World: Geographical Diffusionism and Eurocentric History*, New York: Guilford.

Bonus, Rick (1997), 'Homelands Memories and Media: Filipino Images and Imaginations in America', in Maria P.P. Root (ed.), *Filipino Americans: Transformation and Identity*, Thousand Oaks, CA: Sage, 208–18.

Bottomley, Gillian (1992), *From Another Place: Migration and the Politics of Culture*, Cambridge: Cambridge University Press.

Bourdieu, Pierre (1980), 'The Aristocracy of Culture', *Media, Culture, and Society*, 2(3): 225–54.

Bourdieu, Pierre (1984), *Distinction: A Social Critique of the Judgement of Taste*, tr. R. Nice, Cambridge, MA: Harvard University Press.

Bozorgmehr, Mehdi, Der-Martirosian, Claudia and Sabagh, Georges (1996), 'Middle Easterners: A New Kind of Immigrant', in Roger Waldinger and Mehdi Bozorghmer (eds), *Ethnic Los Angeles*, New York: Russell Sage Foundation Press, 345–78.

Brah, A. (1996), *Cartographies of Diaspora*, London: Routledge.

Brecher, J., Costello, T. and Smith, B. (2000), *Globalization from Below: The Power of Solidarity*, Cambridge, MA: South End Press.

Brody, H. (2001), *The Other Side of Eden: Hunter-Gatherers, Farmers and the Shaping of the World*, London: Faber and Faber.

Brown, Robin (1995), 'Globalization and the End of the National Project', in John MacMillan and Andrew Linklater (eds), *Boundaries in Question: New Directions in International Relations*, London: Pinter Publishers, 55–68.

Brune, François (1993), *'Les Médias pensent comme moi!': Fragments du discours anonyme*, Paris: Harmattan.

Buchignani, Norman (1980), 'The Social and Self-identities of Fijian Indians in Vancouver', *Urban Anthropology*, 9(1): 75–97

Bunt, G. (1999), 'Islam@britain.net: "British Muslim" identities in cyberspace', *Islam and Christian–Muslim Relations*, 10: 353–63.

Bunt, G. (2000), *Virtually Islamic: Computer Mediated Communication and Cyber Islamic Environment*, Cardiff: University of Wales Lampeter Press.

Burkhalter, Byron (1999), 'Reading Race Online: Discovering Racial Identity in Usenet Discussions', in Marc Smith and Peter Kollock (eds), *Communities in Cyberspace* London: Routledge, 60–75.

Calabrese, Andrew (1999), 'The Welfare State, The Information Society, and the Ambivalence of Social Movements', in Andrew Calabrese and Jean-Claude Burgelman (eds), *Communication, Citizenship, and Social Policy*, New York: Rowan and Littlefield, 259–78.

Campbell, Persia Crawford (1969), *Chinese Coolie Emigration to Countries within the British Empire*, New York: Negro University Press.

Canadian Radio-television and Telecommunications Commission (CRTC) (1980), *The 1980s: A Decade of Diversity: Broadcasting, Satellites, and Pay-TV. Report of the Committee on Extension of Service to Northern and Remote Communities*. Hull, Quebec: Supply and Services Canada.

Canadian Radio-television and Telecommunications Commission (September 1998), 'Audience viewing habits and audiences with respect to programming and Canadian content'. Ottawa: CRTC.

Canclini, N.G. (1995), *Hybrid Cultures: Strategies for Entering and Leaving Modernity*, tr. C.L. Chiappari and S.L. López, Minnesota, MN: University of Minnesota Press.

Canetti, Elias (1991), *The Secret Heart of the Clock*, London: André Deutsch.

Carey, James (1989), *Communication as Culture*. Boston, MA: Unwin and Hyman.

Carruthers, Ashley (2001), 'National Identity, Diasporic Anxiety and Music Video Culture in Vietnam', in Yao Souchou (ed.), *House of Glass: Culture, Modernity and the State in Southeast Asia*, Singapore: ISEAS, 119–49.

Castells, Manuel (1989), *The Informational City: Information Technology, Economic Restructuring, and the Urban-Regional Process*, Oxford: Blackwell.

Chakravarty, Sutima S. (1993), *National Identity in Indian Popular Cinema: 1947–1987*, Austin, TX: University of Texas Press.

Chambers, Iain (1996), *Migrancy, Culture, Identity*, London and New York: Routledge.

Chan, Joseph Man (1996), 'Television in Greater China: Structure, Exports and Market Formation', in John Sinclair, Elizabeth Jacka and Stuart Cunningham (eds), *New Patterns in Global Television: Peripheral Vision*, Oxford and New York: Oxford University Press, 126–60.

Chatterjee, Partha (1993), *The Nation and Its Fragments: Colonial and Postcolonial Histories*, Princeton, NJ: Princeton University Press.

Chatterjee, Partha (1995), 'Religious Minorities and the Secular State – Reflections on an Indian Impasse', *Public Culture*, 8(1): 11–39.

Chen, Kuan-Hsing (1996), 'The Formation of a Diasporic Intellectual: An Interview with Stuart Hall', in David Morley and Kuan-Hsing Chen (eds), *Stuart Hall: Critical Dialogues in Cultural Studies*, London and New York: Routledge, 484–503.

Chennells, A. (1982), 'Settlers, Myths and the Southern Rhodesian Novel', DPhil thesis, University of Zimbabwe.

Chow, Rey (1993), *Writing Diaspora: Tactics of Intervention in Contemporary Cultural Studies*, Bloomington, IN: Indiana University Press.

Chyet, Michael (1995), 'Sabri, the Teacher', *Kurdistan Report*, 21: 57–9.

Clark, Brian (1992), 'Arab-Americans on the Air', *Aramco World*: 12–15.

Clifford, J. (1989), 'Notes on Travel and Theory', *Inscriptions*, 5: 177–88.

Clifford, J. (1992), 'Traveling Cultures', in L. Grossberg, C. Nelson and P. Treichler (eds), *Cultural Studies*, London and New York: Routledge, 96–116.

Clifford, J. (1994), 'Diasporas', *Cultural Anthropology*, 9(3): 302–38.

Clifford, J. (1997), *Routes: Travel and Translation in the Late Twentieth Century*, Cambridge, MA: Harvard University Press.

Cohen, Anthony P. (1994), *Self Consciousness: An Alternative Anthropology of Identity*, London, Routledge.

Cohen, Robin (1997), *Global Diasporas: An Introduction*, London: UCL Press/Routledge.

Colley, Linda (1992), *Britons: The Forging of a Nation*, New Haven, CT: Yale University Press.

Collins, Richard (1990), *Television: Policy and Culture*, London: Unwin Hyman.

Collins, Richard (1994), 'Trading in Culture: The Role of Language', *Canadian Journal of Communication*, 19: 123–35.

Cottle, S. (ed.) (2000), *Ethnic Minorities and the Media*, Buckingham and Philadelphia, PA: Open University Press.

Coupe, Bronwyn and Jakubowicz, Andrew with Randall, Lois (1993), *Nextdoor Neighbours: A Report for the Office of Multicultural Affairs on Ethnic Group Discussions of the Australian Media*, Canberra: Office of Multicultural Affairs, Department of the Prime Minister and Cabinet, Commonwealth of Australia.

Courrier international (1999), 'Kurdes: Les Impasses sanglantes', *Courrier international*, 434, du 25 février au 3 mars 1999.

Crow Dog, M. and Erdoes, R. (1991), *Lakota Woman*, New York: Grove Press.

Cubitt, Sean (1991), *Timeshift: On Video Culture*, London: Routledge.

Cunningham, Stuart and Jacka, Elizabeth (1996), *Australian Television and International Mediascapes*, Melbourne: Cambridge University Press.

Cunningham, Stuart and Sinclair, John (eds) (2001), *Floating Lives: The Media and Asian Diasporas*, Lanham, MD: Rowman and Littlefield.

Danforth, Loring M. (1997), *The Macedonian Conflict: Ethnic Nationalism in a Transnational World*, Princeton, NJ: Princeton University Press.

Dassetto, Felice (1993), 'Islam and Europe', paper presented at the International Conference on Muslim Minorities in Post-Bipolar Europe: Skopje, Macedonia.

Davies, John (2000), 'On the Sources of Interethnic Conflict in Fiji', *Peace Initiatives*, 1: 1–3.

Dávila, A. (2001), *Latinos Inc.: The Marketing and Making of a People*, Berkeley, CA: University of California Press.

Dayan, Daniel (1998), 'Particularistic media and diasporic communication', in Tabar Liebes and James Curran (eds), *Media, Ritual and Identity*, London: Routledge: 103–13.

Dean, Michelle (1996), 'Foucault, Government and the Enfolding of Authority', in Andrew Barry, Thomas Osborne and Nikolas Rose (eds), *Foucault and Political Reason: Liberalism, Neo-Liberalism and Rationalities of Government*, Chicago: University of Chicago Press, 209–29.

Deleuze, Gilles and Guattari, Félix (1987) *A Thousand Plateaus: Capitalism and Schizophrenia*, Minneapolis, MN: University of Minnesota.

Denny, Fred M. (1991), 'The Legacy of Fazlur Rahman', in Yvonne Yazbeck Haddad (ed.), *The Muslims of America*, Oxford: Oxford University Press, 96–109.

Dernersesian, A.C. (1994), '"Chicana! Rican? no, Chicana-Riqueña!": Refashioning the Transnational Connection', in D. Goldberg (ed.), *Multiculturalism: A Critical Reader*, Cambridge, MA: Basil Blackwell, 269–95.

DeSipio, Louis (1998), 'Talking Back to Television: Latinos discuss how television portrays them and the quality of programming options', Claremont, CA: Tomas Rivera Policy Institute.

DeSipio, Louis (1999), 'Engaging Television in English y en Espanol', Claremont, CA: Tomas Rivera Policy Institute.

Diem, Andrea Grace and Lewis, James R. (1992), 'Imagining India: the influence of Hinduism on the new age movement', in James R. Lewis and J. Gordon Melton (eds), *Perspectives on the New Age* Albany NY: State University of New York Press, 48–58.

Eaton, W.G. (1996), *A Chronicle of Modern Sunlight*, Rohnert Park, CA: Innovision.

Ebben, M. and Kramarae, Ch. (1993), 'Women and Information Technologies: Creating a Cyberspace of our Own', in H.J. Taylor, Ch. Kramarae and M. Ebben (eds), *Women, Information Technology, and Scholarship*, Urbana, IL: Centre for Advanced Study Economic Restructuring and the Urban-Regional Process, Oxford: Blackwell, 15–27.

Edwards, J. A. (1978), 'Southern Rhodesia 1935–39: The Response to Adversity', PhD Thesis, University of London.

Egerer, Claudia (2001), 'Ambivalent Geographies: The Exotic as Domesticated Other', *Third Text*, 55: 15–28.

Eickelman, Dale F. (1982), 'The Study of Islam in Local Contexts', *Contributions to Asian Studies*, 17: 1–16.

Eickelman, Dale F. (1989), 'National Identity and Religious Discourse in Contemporary Islam', *International Journal of Islamic and Arabic Studies*, 6(1): 1–20.

Eickelman, Dale F. and Piscatori, James (1996), *Muslim Politics*, Princeton, NJ: Princeton University Press.

Ellwood, Robert (1992), 'How new is the new age?', in James R. Lewis and J. Gordon Melton (eds), *Perspectives on the New Age*, Albany, NY: State University of New York Press, 59–67.

Elsaesser, Thomas (July 1994), 'European Television and National Identity, or "What's there to Touch when the Dust has Settled"', paper presented to the conference on Turbulent Europe: Conflict, Identity and Culture, London.

Embree, Ainslie (ed.) (1988), *Sources of Indian Tradition*, vol. 1, Harmondsworth: Penguin.

Esman, Milton (1986), 'The Chinese Diaspora in Southeast Asia', in Gabriel Sheffer (ed.), *Modern Diasporas and International Politics*, London and Sydney: Croom Helm, 130–63.

Falk, R. (1993), 'The making of global citizenship', in J. Brecher, J. Childs and J. Cutler (eds), *Global Visions: Beyond the New World Order* Boston, MA: South End Press, 39–50.

Farmer, Gary (1998), 'Letter from the Editor: Time in a Computer Chip', *Aboriginal Voices*, July–August, 6.

Featherstone, M. and Burrows, R. (1995), *Cyberspace/Cyberbodies/Cyberpunk: Cultures of Technological Embodiment*, London: Sage.

Featherstone, Mike (1995), *Undoing Culture: Globalization, Postmodernism and Identity*, London: Sage.

Fernback, J. (1997), 'The Individual within the Collective: Virtual Ideology and the Realization of Collective Principles', in Steven Jones (ed.), *Virtual Culture: Identity and Communication in Cybersociety*, London: Sage, 36–54.

Fernback, J. and Thompson, B. (1995), 'Computer-mediated Communication and the American Collectivity: The Dimensions of Community Within Cyberspace', paper presented at the annual convention of the International Communication Association, Albuquerque, New Mexico, May 1995. See also 'Virtual Communities: Abort, Retry, Failure?' Online at www.well.com/user/hlr/texts/Vccivil.html.

Fienup-Riordan, Ann (1995), *Freeze Frame: Alaska Eskimos in the Movies*, Seattle: University of Washington.

First Nations Film and Video World Alliance (1993), 'Organizational plan by working group', unpublished paper.

Fiske, John (1987), *Television Culture*, London: Methuen.

Foucault, Michel (1986), 'Of Other Spaces', *Diacritics*, 16(1): 22–7.

Gandhi, Leela (1998), *Postcolonial Theory: A Critical Introduction*, Sydney: Allen and Unwin.

Ganguly, Keya (1992), 'Migrants' Identities: Personal Memory and the Construction of Selfhood', *Cultural Studies*, 6(1): 27–50.

Garcia Canclini, Nestor (1995), *Hybrid Cultures: Strategies for Entering and Leaving Modernity*, Minneapolis, MN: University of Minnesota Press.

Gaski, H. (1997), 'Voice in the Margin: A Suitable Place for a Minority Literature?', in H. Gaski (ed.), *Sámi Culture in a New Era: The Norwegian Sámi Experience*, Karasjok, Norway: Davvi Girji OS, 199–220.

George, J. (2001), 'All Nunavik communities will soon get access to the Internet', *Nunatsiaq News*, March 9, 25, 31.

Geschiere, Peter and Meyer, Birgit (1998), 'Globalization and Identity: Dialectics of Flow and Closure', *Development and Change*, 29: 601–15.

Giddens, Anthony (1990), *The Consequences of Modernity*, Stanford, CA: Stanford University.

Gillespie, Marie (1989), 'Technology and Tradition: Audio-visual Culture among South Asian Families in West London', *Cultural Studies*, 3(2): 226–39.

Gillespie, Marie (1993), 'Soap Viewing, Gossip and Rumour Amongst Punjabi Youth in Southall', in P. Drummond, R. Paterson and J. Willis (eds), *National Identity and Europe: The Television Revolution*, London: British Film Institute, 25–42.

Gillespie, Marie (1995), *Television, Ethnicity and Cultural Change*, London and New York: Routledge.

Gilroy, Paul (1993), *The Black Atlantic: Modernity and Double Consciousness*, Cambridge, MA and London: Harvard University Press/Verso.

Gitlin, Todd (1998), 'Public Sphere or Public Sphericules?', in Tamar Liebes and James Curran (eds), *Media, Ritual and Identity*, London: Routledge, 168–74.

Goldstein, Melvyn C. (1998), 'Introduction', in Melvyn C. Goldstein and Matthew T. Kapstein (eds), *Buddhism in Contemporary Tibet: Religious Revival and Cultural Identity*, Berkeley, CA: University of California Press, 1–14.

Gómez-Peña, Guillermo (1996), *The New World Border*, New York: City Lights.

Gripsrud, Jostein (ed.) (1999), *Television and Common Knowledge*, London: Routledge.

Grossberg, Lawrence (1996), 'The Space of Culture, the Power of Space', in Iain Chambers and Lidia Curti (eds), *The Post-Colonial Question: Common Skies, Divided Horizons*, London: Routledge, 169–88.

Gunew, Sneja (1993), *Framing Marginality: Multicultural Literary Studies*, Melbourne: Melbourne University Press.

Gupta, Akhil and Ferguson, James (eds) (1997), *Culture, Power, Place: Explorations in Critical Anthropology*, Durham, NC and London: Duke University Press.

Gürbey, Gülistan (1996), 'The Kurdish Nationalist Movement in Turkey since the 1980s', in Robert Olson, *The Kurdish Nationalist Movement in the 1990s: Its Impact on Turkey and the Middle East*, Lexington, KY: University Press of Kentucky, 9–37.

Gurstein, M. (ed.) (2000), *Community Informatics: Enabling Communities with Information and Communications Technologies*, Hershey, PA: Idea Group Publishing.

Habermas, Jürgen (1990), *Moral Consciousness and Communicative Action*, Cambridge: Polity Press.

Habermas, Jürgen (1992), *The Structural Transformation of the Public Sphere: An Inquiry into a Category of Bourgeois Society*, Cambridge: Polity Press.

Ha-il, Kim (1992), 'Minority Media Access: Examination of Policies, Technologies, and Multi-Ethnic Television and a Proposal for an Alternative Approach to Media Access', unpublished PhD dissertation, University of California, Los Angeles.

Hall, S. (1980), 'Race, Articulation and Societies Structured in Dominance', in *Sociological Theories: Race and Colonialism*, Paris: UNESCO, 305–45.

Hall, S. (1992), 'The Question of Cultural Identity', in S. Hall, D. Held and A. McGrew (eds), *Modernity and its Futures*, Cambridge: Polity Press, 274–316.

Hall, S. (1993), 'Culture, Community, Nation', *Cultural Studies*, 7(3): 349–63.

Hall, S. (1997a), 'Cultural Identity and Diaspora', in L. McDowell (ed.), *Undoing Place? A Geographical Reader*, London: Arnold, 231–42.

Hall, S. (1997b), 'The Local and the Global: Globalization and Ethnicity', in Anne McClintock, Aamir Mufti and Ella Shohat (eds), *Dangerous Liaisons: Gender, Nation, and Postcolonial Perspectives*, Minneapolis, MN: University of Minnesota, 173–87.

Hall, S. (2000), 'Cultural Identity and Diaspora', in Nicholas Mirzoeff (ed.), *Diaspora and Visual Culture: Representing Africans and Jews*, London: Routledge, 21–33.

Hamelink, Cees J. (1997), 'International Communication: Global Market and Morality', in Ali Mohammadi (ed.), *International Communication and Globalization*, London: Sage Publications, 92–118.

Hamilton, A. (1993), 'Video Crackdown: Censorship and Cultural Consequences in Thailand', *Public Culture*, 5(3): 515–31.

Hannerz, Ulf (1990), 'Cosmopolitans and Locals in World Culture', in Mike Featherstone (ed.), *Global Culture: Nationalsm, Globalization and Modernity*, London: Sage, 237–51.

Hannerz, Ulf (1996), *Transnational Connections: Culture, People, Places*, London: Routledge.

Hannerz, Ulf (1997), 'Notes on the Global Ecumene', in A. Sreberny-Mohammadi, D. Winseck, J. McKenna and O. Boyd-Barrett (eds), *Media in a Global Context*, London: Arnold, 11–18.

Haq, Rupa (1997), 'Asian Kool? Bhangra and beyond', in Sanjav Sharma and John Hutnyk (eds), *Disorienting Rythms: The Politics of the New South Asian Dance Music*, London: Zed Books, 61–80.

Hargreaves, A.G. and McKinney, M. (eds) (1997), *Post-Colonial Cultures in France*, London: Routledge.

Hargreaves, Alec G. and Mahdjoub, Dalila (1997), 'Satellite Television Viewing among Ethnic Minorities in France', *European Journal of Communication*, 12(4): 459–77.

Harvey, David (1990), *The Condition of Postmodernity: An Enquiry into the Origins of Cultural Change*, Cambridge, MA: Blackwell.

Hasan, R. (2000), '*Da-Sein* in the Diaspora: Some Thoughts on British Telephone Cards', *Third Text*, 52 (Summer): 79–82.

Hassanpour, Amir (1997), 'AMed-TV, Großbritannien und der Türkische Staat: Die Suche einer Staatenlosen Nation nach Souveränität im Äther', in Carsten Borck, Eva Savelsberg and Siamend Hajo (eds), *Ethnizität, Nationalismus, Religion und Politik in Kurdistan*, Münster: LIT Verlag, 239–78.

Hassanpour, Amir (1998), 'Satellite Footprints as National Borders: MED-TV and the Extraterritoriality of State Sovereignty, *Journal of Muslim Minority Affairs*, 18(1): 53–72.

Hassanpour, Amir (1999), 'Language Rights in the Emerging World Linguistic Order: The State, the Market, and Communication Technologies', in Miklos Kontra, Robert Phillipson, Tove Skutnabb-Kangas and Tibor Varady (eds), *Language: A Right and a Resource: Approaching Linguistic Human Rights*, Budapest: Central European University Press: 223–41.

Healy, Dave (1997), 'Cyberspace and Place: The Internet as Middle Landscape on the Electronic Frontier', in David Porter (ed.), *Internet Culture*, New York: Routledge, 55–68.

Helsinki Watch (1988), *Destroying Ethnic Identity: The Kurds of Turkey*, New York: Helsinki Watch.

Herring, Suzan (1994), 'Politeness in Computer Culture: Why Women Thank and Men Flame', in M. Bucholtz, A. Liang and L. Sutton (eds), *Communicating In, Through, and Across Cultures: Proceedings of the Third Berkeley Women and Language Conference*, Berkeley, CA: Berkeley Women and Language Group, 96–125.

Herring, Suzan (1996), 'Posting in a Different Voice: Gender and Ethics in CMC', in Charles Ess (ed.), *Philosophical Perspectives on Computer-Mediated Communication*, Albany NY: State University of New York Press, 115–46.

Hill, Peter (1989), *The Macedonians in Australia*, Carlisle, WA: Hesperian Press.

Hill, Steven (1988), *The Tragedy of Technology: Human Liberation Versus Domination in the Late Twentieth Century*, London: Pluto Press.

Hirst, Paul (1996), 'Democracy and Civil Society', in Paul Hirst and Sunil Khilnani (eds), *Reinventing Democracy*, Oxford: Blackwell Publishers, 97–116.

Hoffman, Eva (1991), *Lost in Translation: Life in a New Language*, London: Minerva.

Hoskins, Colin, McFayden, Stuart and Finn, Adam (1991), 'The USA Competitive Advantage in the Global Television Market: Is It Sustainable in the New Broadcasting Environment?', *Canadian Journal of Communication*, 20(3): 207–24.

Hoskins, Colin, McFayden, Stuart and Finn, Adam (1994), 'The Environment in which Cultural Industries Operate and Some Implications', in S. McFayden, C. Hoskins, A. Finn and R. Lorimer (eds), *Cultural Development in an Open Economy*, Burnaby, British Columbia: *Canadian Journal of Communication*, 99–122

Husband, C. (ed.) (1994), *A Richer Vision: The Development of Ethnic Minority Media in Western Democracies*, Paris: UNESCO/London: John Libbey.

Ifekwunigwe, Jayne (2000), 'Writing Home: Reconfiguring the African Diaspora', in Owusu, Kwesi (ed.), *Black British Culture and Society*, London: Routledge, 489–98.

Jameson, Fredric (1984), 'Postmodernism, or the Cultural Logic of Late Capitalism', *New Left Review*, 146: 53–93.

Jankélévitch, Vladimir (1974), *L'Irréversible et la nostalgie*, Paris: Flammarion.

JanMohamed, A. (1992), 'Worldliness-without-world, Homelessness-as-home: Toward a Definition of the Specular Border Intellectual', in M. Sprinkler (ed.), *Edward Said: A Critical Reader*, Oxford: Basil Blackwell, 96–120.

Jayawardena, Chandra (1980), 'Culture and Ethnicity in Guyana and Fiji', *Man*, 26: 430–50.

Jocks, C. (1996), 'Talk of the Town: Radio Talk Shows', in Valerie Alia, Brian Brennan and Barry Hoffmaster (eds), *Deadlines and Diversity: Journalism Ethics in a Changing World*, Halifax: Fernwood, 173–85.

Jones, Steven G. (1995), 'Understanding Community in the Information Age', in Steven G. Jones (ed.), *CyberSociety: Computer-Mediated Communication and Community*, Thousand Oaks, CA: Sage, 10–35.

Jones, Steven G. (1997), 'The Internet and its Social Landscape', in Steven Jones (ed.), *Virtual Culture: Identity and Communication in Cybersociety*, London: Sage, 7–35.

Kapstein, Matthew T. (1998), 'Concluding Reflections', in Melvyn C. Goldstein and Matthew T. Kapstein (eds), *Buddhism in Contemporary Tibet: Religious Revival and Cultural Identity*, Berkeley, CA: University of California Press, 139–50.

Karim, K.H. (1998), 'From Ethnic Media to Global Media: Transnational Communication Networks among Diasporic Communities', Transnational Communities Programme, Working Papers Series, Oxford: University of Oxford. Available online at www.transcomm.ox.ac.uk/working%20papers/karim.pdf.

Karim, K.H. (2002a), 'Globalization, Communication and Diaspora', in P. Attallah and L.R. Shade (eds), *Mediascapes: New Patterns in Canadian Communication*, Toronto: Nelson Canada, 272–94.

Karim, K.H. (2002b), 'Public Sphere and Public Sphericules: Civic Discourse in Ethnic Media', in S. Ferguson and L.R. Shade (eds), *Civic Discourse and Cultural Politics in Canada*, Ablex/Jai, Westport, CT: Ablex, 230–42.

Kelly, John Dunham (1991), *A Politics of Virtue: Hinduism, Sexuality, and Countercolonial Discourse in Fiji*, Chicago: University of Chicago Press.

Kelly, John Dunham (1998), 'Time and the Global: Against the Homogeneous, Empty Communities in Contemporary Social Theory', *Development and Change*, 29: 839–71.

King, A. (1996), 'Guarding the Democratic Shrine: Rhodesian Debates on the Franchise, 1898–1960', paper presented at the Historical Dimensions of Democracy and Human Rights in Zimbabwe Conference, University of Zimbabwe, Harare, September 1996.

Kirpitchenko, Liudmila and De Santis, Heather (1999), 'Social Cohesion and Cultural Practices: Beyond the Mainstream', monograph, SRA Reports, Hull, Quebec: Department of Canadian Heritage.

Knight, George (1999), *A Brief History Of Seventh Day Adventists*, Hagerstown Review and Herald.

Kolar-Panov, Dona (1997), *Video, War and the Diasporic Imagination*, London and New York: Routledge.

Kolas, Ashild (1996), 'Tibetan Nationalism: The Politics of Religion', *Journal of Peace Research*, February: 51–66.

Korom, Frank J. (1997), 'Old Age Tibet in New Age America', in Frank J. Korom (ed.), *Constructing Tibetan Culture: Contemporary Perspectives*, St-Hyacinthe: World Heritage Press, 73–97.

Kotkin, J. (1992), *Tribes: How Race, Religion, and Identity Determine Success in the New Global Economy*, New York: Random House.

Kutschera, Chris (1995), 'Kurdistan: Parliament or Propaganda Ploy?', *The Middle East*, June: 11–12.

Lal, Brij (1983), *Girmitiyas: The Origins of the Fiji Indians*, Journal of Pacific History Monograph, Canberra: Australian National University.

Lal, Brij (1992), *Broken Waves: A History of the Fiji Islands in the Twentieth Century*, Pacific Island Monograph Series, no. 11, School of Hawaiian, Asian and Pacific Studies, Honolulu: University of Hawaii Press.

Lal, Brij (2001), 'Fiji: A Damaged Democracy', in Brij Lal (ed.), *Coup: Reflections on the Political Crisis in Fiji*, Canberra: Pandanus Books, 11–13.

Landman, Nico (1997), 'The Islamic Broadcasting Foundation in the Netherlands: Platform or Arena?', in Steven Vertovec and Ceri Peach (eds), *Islam in Europe: The Politics of Religion and Community*, London: Macmillan, 224–43.

Larkin, Brian (1999), 'Theatres of the Profane: Cinema and Colonial Urbanism', *Visual Anthropology Review*, 14(2): 46–62.

Lawson, Ronald (1995), 'Sect–State Relations: Accounting for the Differing Trajectories of Seventh Day Adventists and Jehovah's Witnesses', *Sociology of Religion*, 56(4): 351–7.

Lawson, Ronald (1998), 'From American Church to Immigrant Church: The Changing Face of Seventh Day Adventism in Metropolitan New York', *Sociology of Religion*, 59(4): 329–51.

Levene, Mark (1998), 'Creating a Modern Zone of Genocide: The Impact of Nation- and State-Formation on Eastern Anatolia, 1878–1923', *Holocaust and Genocide Studies*, 12(3): 393–433.

Levene, Mark (1999), 'A Moving Target, the Usual Suspects and (Maybe), a Smoking Gun: The Problem of Pinning Blame in Modern Genocide', *Patterns of Prejudice*, 33(4): 3–24.

Lewis, Pete (1994), *Islamic Britain: Religion, Politics and Identity among British Muslims*, London: I. B. Tauris.

Liu, Xin (1997), 'Space, Mobility, and Flexibility: Chinese Villagers and Scholars Negotiate Power at Home and Abroad', in Aihwa Ong and Donald M. Nonini (eds), *Ungrounded Empires: The Cultural Politics of Modern Chinese Transnationalism*, New York: Routledge, 91–114.

Loader, Brian, Hague, B. and Eagle, D. (2000), 'Embedding the Net: Community Empowerment in the Age of Information', in M. Gurstein (ed.), *Community Informatics: Enabling Communities with Information and Communications Technologies*, Hershey, PA: Idea Group Publishing, 81–102.

Lockard, Joseph (1997), ' Progressive Politics, Electronic Individualism and the Myth of the Virtual Community', in D. Porter (ed.), *Internet Culture*, New York and London: Routledge, 219–31.

Lotman, Jurij M. (1990), *Universe of the Mind: A Semiotic Theory of Culture*, tr. A. Shukman, Bloomington, IN: Indiana University Press.

Luke, Timothy (1997), 'Reconsidering Nationality and Sovereignty in the New World Order', *Political Crossroads*, 5(1 and 2): 3–17.

Lull, James (1995), *Media, Communication, Culture: A Global Approach*, New York: Columbia.

MacKinnon, Richard C. (1995), 'Searching for the Leviathan in Usenet', in Steven Jones (ed.), *CyberSociety: Computer-Mediated Communication and Community*, Thousand Oaks, CA: Sage, 112–37.

McLaughlin, Margaret L., Osborne, Kerry K. and Smith, Christine B. (1995), 'Standards of Conduct on Usenet', in Steven Jones (ed.), *CyberSociety: Computer-mediated Communication and Community*, Thousand Oaks, CA: Sage, 90–111.

McLuhan, Marshall (1965), *Understanding Media*, London: Routledge.

Mandaville, Peter (2001), *Transnational Muslim Politics: Reimagining the Umma*, London: Routledge.

Manuh, Takyiwaa (2000), 'Efie or the Meanings of Home among Female and Male Ghanaian Migrants in Toronto', paper presented at the New African Diasporas Colloquium, University of London.

Marden, Peter (1997), 'Geographies of Dissent: Globalization, Identity and the Nation', *Political Geography*, 16(1): 37–64.

Mardin, Serif (1989), *Religion and Social Change in Modern Turkey: The Case of Bediüzzaman Said Nursi*, Albany, NY: State University of New York Press.

Marques de Melo, Jose (1995), 'Development of the Audiovisual Industry in Brazil from Importer to Exporter of Television Programming', *Canadian Journal of Communication*, 20(3): 312–28.

Marshall, Stuart (1979), 'Video: Technology and Practice', *Screen*, 5: 109–19.

Massey, Doreen (1994), *Space, Place, and Gender*, Minneapolis, MN: University of Minnesota.

Maxwell, R. (1996), 'Technologies of National Desire', in M.J. Shapiro and H.R. Alker (eds), *Challenging Boundaries: Global Flows, Territorial Identities*, Minneapolis, MN: Univeristy of Minnesota Press, 143–69.

Med-TV (1995), *Kurdish Satellite Television*, London: Med-TV.

Melton, J. Gordon (1992), 'New Thought and the New Age', in James R. Lewis and J. Gordon Melton (eds), *Perspectives on the New Age*, Albany, NY: State University of New York Press: 15–29.

Messick, Brinkley (1993), *The Calligraphic State: Textual Domination and History in a Muslim Society*, Berkeley, CA: University of California Press.

Metcalf, Barbara D. (1996), 'Introduction: Sacred Words, Sanctioned Practice, New Communities', in Barbara Daly Metcalf (ed.), *Making Muslim Space in North America and Europe*, Berkeley, CA: University of California Press, 1–27.

Meyrowitz, Joshua and Maguire, John (1993), 'Media, Place and Multiculturalism', *Society*, 30(5): 41–8.

Milikowski, Marisca (2000), 'Exploring a Model of De-ethnicisation: The Case of Turkish Television in the Netherlands', *European Journal of Communication*, 15(4): 443–68.

Minde, H. (1996), 'The Making of an International Movement of Indigenous Peoples', in Frank Horn (ed.), *Minorities and their Rights of Politial Participation*, Rovaniemi: University of Lapland, 90–128.

Mishra, Vijay (ed.) (1979), *Rama's Banishment: A Centenary Tribune to the Fiji Indians 1879–1979*, London: Heinemann Educational Books.

Mishra, Vijay (1985), 'Towards a Theoretical Critique of Bombay Cinema', *Screen*, 26(3/4), May–August, 133–46.

Mishra, Vijay (1992), 'Decentring History: Some Versions of Bombay Cinema', *East-West Film Journal*, 6(1): 111–55.

Mitchell, Don (2000), *Cultural Geography: A Critical Introduction*, Oxford: Blackwell.

Mitchell, William (1999), 'Equitable Access to the Online World', in Donald Schon, Bish Sanyal and William Mitchell, *High Technology and Low Income Communities: Prospects for the Positive Use of Advanced Information Technology*, Cambridge, MA, London: MIT Press, 151–62.

Mitra, Ananda (1997), 'Virtual Commonality: Looking for India on the Internet', in Steven G. Jones (ed.), *Virtual Culture, Identity and Communication in Cybersociety*, London: Sage, 55–79.

Mirzoeff, N. (ed.) (2000), *Diaspora and Visual Culture: Representing Africans and Jews*, London: Routledge.

Morley, David (2000), *Home Territories: Media, Mobility and Identity*, London: Routledge.

Morley, D. and Robins, K. (1995), *Spaces of Identity: Global Media, Electronic Landscapes and Cultural Boundaries*, London: Routledge.

Mortimer, Edward (1996), 'An Identity Crisis', *The Financial Times*, 3 January, reprinted in Med-TV, *The International Impact of MED-TV (March 1995–March 1996)*, London: Med-TV.

Muller, Mark (1996), 'Nationalism and the Rule of Law in Turkey: The Elimination of Kurdish Representation during the 1990s', in Robert Olson (ed.), *The Kurdish Nationalist Movement in the 1990s: Its Impact on Turkey and the Middle East*, Lexington, KY: The University Press of Kentucky, 173–99.

Nadwi, Abdul Hasan A. (1993), *Muslims in the West: The Message and Mission*, Leicester: The Islamic Foundation.

Naficy, Hamid (1993), *The Making of Exile Cultures: Iranian Television in Los Angeles*, Minneapolis, MN: University of Minnesota Press.

Naficy, Hamid (2001), *An Accented Cinema: Exilic and Diasporic Filmmaking*, Princeton, NJ: Princeton University Press.

Nairn, Tom (1981), *The Break-up of Britain*, London: Verso.

Nazeri, H. (1996) 'Imagined Cyber Communities: Iranians and the Internet' *MESA Bulletin*, vol. 30.

Newman, James (1998), 'Videogames, Space and Experience: Critically Examining a Player's Perspective', PhD Thesis (unpublished), Lancaster University.

Nielsen, Jakob (2000), *Designing Web Usability: The Practice of Simplicity*, Indianapolis, IN: New Riders.

Nielsen, Jørgen (1995), *Muslims in Western Europe*, 2nd edition, Edinburgh: Edinburgh University Press.

NUA Internet Surveys. Homepage. Online: www.nua.ie/surveys/.

O'Brien, Jodi (1999), 'Writing in the Body: Gender (Re)Production in Cyber Inter-actions', in Marc Smith and Peter Kollok (eds), *Communities in Cyberspace*, London: Routledge, 76–106.

Öcalan, Abdullah (1999), *Declaration on the Democratic Solution of the Kurdish Question*, London: Mesopotamian Publishers.

Olson, Robert (1999), 'The Kurdish Question and Turkey's Foreign Policy toward Syria, Iran, Russia and Iraq since the Gulf War', in Robert Olson (ed.), *The Kurdish Nationalist Movement in the 1990s: Its Impact on Turkey and the Middle East*, Lexington, KY: The University Press of Kentucky, 84–113.

Ong, Walter J. (1982), *Orality and Literacy: The Technologizing of the Word*, London: Methuen.

Oppenheim, L. (1955), *International Law*, vol. 1, 8th edition, London: Longman.

O'Regan, Tom (1993), *Australian Television Culture*, St Leonards: Allen and Unwin.

O'Regan, Tom and Kolar-Panov, Dona (1993a), 'SBS-TV: Symbolic Politics and Multicultural Policy in Television Provision', in T. O'Regan (ed.) *Australian Television Culture*, St Leonards: Allen and Unwin, 121–42.

O'Regan, Tom and Kolar-Panov, Dona (1993b), 'SBS-TV: A television service', in T. O'Regan *Australian Television Culture*, St Leonards: Allen and Unwin, 143–68.

Owusu, Thomas (2000), 'The Role of Ghanaian Immigrant Associations in Toronto, Canada', *International Migration Review*, 34(4): 1155–81.

Panov, Anton (1938/1983), *Pecalbari (The Migrant Workers)*, Skopje: Kultura.

Paredes, M.C. (2001), 'The Reorganization of Spanish-Language Media Marketing in the United States', in V. Mosco and D. Schiller (eds), *Continental Order? Integrating North America for Cybercapitalism*, Oxford: Rowman and Littlefield, 120–35.

Paxman, A. and Saragoza, A.E (2001), 'Globalization and Latin Media Powers: The Case of Mexico's Televisa', in V. Mosco and D. Schiller (eds), *Continental Order? Integrating North America for Cybercapitalism*, Oxford: Rowman and Littlefield, 64–85.

Peil, Margaret (1995), 'Ghanians Abroad', *African Affairs*, 94: 346–64.

Perrot, M. (1993), 'L'Etat des médias en Tchoukotka', in Boris Chichlo (ed.) *Sibérie III: Questions sibériennes*, Paris: Université de Paris, 149–57.

Pham, Duy (1973), *Musics of Vietnam*, Carbondale, IL and London: Southern Illinios University Press and Feffer and Simons.

Phimister, Ian (1986), 'Discourse and the Discipline of Historical Context: Conserva-tionism and Ideas about Development in Southern Rhodesia 1930–1950', *Journal of Southern African Studies*, 12(2): 263–75.

Pierse, Katherine (1997), *Cultural and Language Rights for the Kurds*, London: Medico International and Kurdish Human Rights Project.

Piscatori, James (1990), 'The Rushdie Affair and the Politics of Ambiguity', *International Affairs*, 66(4): 767–89.

Porter, David (ed.) (1997), *Internet Culture*, New York, London: Routledge.

Portes, Alejandro, Guarnizo, Luis E. and Landolt, Patricia (1999), 'The Study of Transnationalism: Pitfalls and Promise of an Emergent Research Field', *Ethnic and Racial Studies*, 22(2): 217–37.

Prasad, Madhav (1998), *Ideology of the Hindi Film: A Historical Construction*, Delhi: Oxford University Press.

Preis, Ann-Belinda Steen (1997), 'Seeking Place: Capsized Identities and Contracted Belonging among Sri Lankan Refugees', in K.F. Olwig and K. Hastrup (eds), *Siting Culture: The Shifting Anthropological Object*, London and New York: Routledge, 86–100.

Rahman, Fazlur (1982), *Islam and Modernity: Transformation of an Intellectual Tradition*, Chicago: University of Chicago Press.

Rajadhyaksha, Ashish and Wildman, Paul (1994), 'Introduction', *Encyclopedia of Indian Cinema*, London: British Film Institute.

Rambo, A. Terry (1987), 'Black Flight Suits and White Ao-dais: Borrowing and Adaptation of Symbols of Vietnamese Cultural Identity', in Truong Buu Lam (ed.), *Borrowings and Adaptations in Vietnamese Culture*, South East Asia Paper No. 25, Centre for South East Asian Studies, School of Hawaiian, Asian and Pacific Studies, University of Hawaii at Manoa, 115–23.

Ranger, T.O. (1967), *Revolt in Southern Rhodesia*, London: Heinemann.

Reddick, Randy and King, Elliot (1997), *The Online Journalist: Using the Internet and Other Electronic Resources*, 2nd edition, Orlando, FL: Harcourt Brace.

Reid, Elizabeth (1996), 'Informed Consent in the Study of the On-Line Communities: A Reflection on the Effects of Computer-Mediated Social Research', *The Information Society*, 12(2): 169–74.

Reid, Elizabeth (1999) 'Hierarchy and Power: Social Control in Cyberspace', in M.A. Smith and P. Kollok (eds), *Communities in Cyberspace*, London: Routledge, 107–33.

Republic of Turkey (1995), 'An Act Amending the Preamble and Some Articles of the Constitution of the Republic of Turkey No. 2709 of 7.11.1982', in Ömer Faruk Gençkaya (ed.), *Republic of Turkey Supplement*, in Gisbert H. Flanz (ed.), *Constitutions of the Countries of the World. Turkey.* Dobbs Ferry, New York: Oceana Publications, Inc.: 1–8.

Rheingold, Howard (1993a), 'A Slice of Life in My Virtual Community', in L.M. Harasim (ed.), *Global Networks: Computers and International Communication*, Cambridge, MA: MIT Press, 57–80.

Rheingold, Howard (1993b), *The Virtual Community: Homesteading on the Electronic Frontier*, Reading, MA: Addison-Wesley Publishing.

Rheingold, Howard (1994), *The Virtual Community: Finding Connections in a Computerized World*, London: Secker and Warburg.

Riggins, Stephen Harold (ed.) (1992), *Ethnic Minority Media: An International Perspective*, Newbury Park, CA: Sage.

Robina-Bustos, Soedad (1995), 'The Hemispheric Village: the Case of Televisa, *Mexican Journal of Communication*, 2. Accessed 3 February 1999 at www.cem.itesm.mx/dacs/buendia/ingles/mjc.html.

Robins, Kevin and Aksoy, Asu (2001a), 'Abschied von Phantomen: kulturelle Identitäten im Zeitalter der Globalisierung', in Brigitta Busch, Brigitte Hipfl and Kevin Robins (eds), *Bewegte Identitäten: Medien in Transkulturellen Kontexten*, Klagenfurt: Drava, 71–110.

Robins, Kevin and Aksoy, Asu (2001b), 'From Spaces of Identity to Mental Spaces:

Lessons from Turkish-Cypriot Cultural Experience in Britain', *Journal of Ethnic and Migration Studies*, 27(4): 683–713.

Robinson, Francis (1993), 'Islam and the Impact of Print', *Modern Asian Studies*, 27(1): 229–51.

Rodriguez, América (1997), 'Cultural Agendas: The Case of Latino-oriented USA Media', in Maxwell McCombs, Donald L. Shaw and David Weaver (eds), *Communication and Democracy*, Mahwah, NJ: Lawrence Erlbaum, 183–94.

Rogers, E.M. (1983), *Diffusion of Innovations*, New York: Free Press.

Root, Maria P. (1997), *Filipino Americans: Transformation and Identity*, Thousand Oaks, CA: Sage.

Roper, Geoffrey (1995), 'Faris al-Shidyaq and the Transition from Scribal to Print Culture in the Middle East', in George N. Atiyeh (ed.), *The Book in the Islamic World: The Written Word and Communication in the Middle East*, Albany, NY: SUNY Press, 209–33.

Rose, Gillian (1997), 'Spatialities of "Community", Power and Change: The Imagined Geographies of Community Arts Projects', *Cultural Studies*, 11(1): 1–16.

Rose, Nikolas (1996), 'The Death of the Social? Re-figuring the Territory of Government', *Economy and Society*, 25(3): 327–56.

Roth, L. (2000), 'Bypassing of Borders and Building of Bridges: Steps in the Construction of the Aboriginal Peoples Television Network in Canada', *Gazette*, 62(3–4): 251–69.

Rouse, Roger (1991), 'Mexican Migration and the Social Space of Postmodernism', *Diaspora*, 1(1): 8–23.

Rouse, Roger (1995), 'Questions of Identity: Personhood and Collectivity in Transnational Migration to the United States', *Critique of Anthropology*, 15(4): 351–80.

Roy, Olivier (1994), *The Failure of Political Islam*, London: I.B. Tauris.

Safran, W. (1991), 'Diasporas in Modern Societies: Myths of Homeland and Return', *Diaspora*, 1(1): 83–99.

Said, Edward W. (1979), *Orientalism*, New York: Vintage Books.

Sánchez-Ruiz, Enrique (1999), 'Globalizacíon, industrial cultural y libre comercio. Hacia un ànalysis comparartivo de políticas de comunicación: México, Canadá y la Unión Europea', paper presented at the II Colloquium on Communications and Cultural Identities in NAFTA and MERCOSUR, Austin, Texas.

Sardar, Ziauddin (1993), 'Paper, Printing and Compact Disks: The Making and Unmaking of Islamic Culture', *Media, Culture and Society*, 15(1): 43–59.

Sassen, S. (1996), *Losing Control? Sovereignty in an Age of Globalization*, New York: Columbia University Press.

Sazdov, Tome (1987), *Macedonian Folk Literature*, tr. S. Keesan, Skopje: Macedonian Review Editions.

Scannell, Paddy (1996), *Radio, Television and Modern Life*, Oxford, Blackwell.

Scannell, Paddy (2000), 'For-Anyone-As-Someone Structures', *Media, Culture and Society*, 22(1): 5–24.

Scholte, Jan Aart (1996), 'The Geography of Collective Identities in a Globalizing World' *Review of International Political Economy*, 3(4): 565–607.

Schön, Donald, Sanyal, Bish and Mitchell, W. (1999), *High Technology and Low Income Communities: Prospects for the Positive Use of Advanced Information Technology*, Cambridge, MA, London: MIT Press.

Schuler, Douglas (1996), *New Community Networks: Wired for Change*, New York, Reading, MA: ACM, Addison-Wesley.

Schwartz, Ronald D. (1994), *Circle of Protest: Political Ritual in the Tibetan Uprising*, New York: Columbia University Press.

Seagrave, S. (1995), *Lords of the Rim*, New York: G.P. Putnam.

Şengün, Seda (2001), 'Migration as a Transitional Space and Group Analysis', *Group Analysis*, 34(1): 65–78.

Shaw, Martin (1997), 'The Theoretical Challenge of Global Society', in A. Sreberny-Mohammadi, D. Winseck, J. McKenna and O. Boyd-Barrett (eds), *Media in Global Context: A Reader*, New York: St Martin's Press, 27–36.

Shields, Rob (ed.) (1996), *Cultures of Internet: Virtual Spaces, Real Histories, Living Bodies*, London: Sage.

Shohat, Ella (1991), 'Ethnicities-in-Relations: Toward a Multicultural Reading of American Cinema', in Lester D. Friedman (ed.), *Unspeakable Images: Ethnicity and the American Cinema*, Urbana, IL: University of Illinois Press.

Shohat, Ella and Stam, Robert (1994), *Unthinking Eurocentrism: Multiculturalism and the Media*, London: Routledge.

Sinclair, James and Cunningham, Stuart (2000), 'Diasporas and the Media', in S. Cunningham, and J. Sinclair, *Floating Lives: The Media and Asian Diasporas*, Australia: University of Queensland Press, 1–34.

Sinclair, John (1997), 'The Decentring of Cultural Imperialism: Televisa-tion and Globo-ization in the Latin World', in Kenneth Thompson (ed.), *Media and Cultural Regulation*, London: Sage.

Skutnabb-Kangas, Tove (1981), *Bilingualism or Not: The Education of Minorities*, tr. L. Malberg and D. Crane, London: Multilingual Matters Ltd.

Smith, Anthony D. (1988), *The Ethnic Origins of Nations*, New York: Basil Blackwell Inc.

Smith, Bruce L. and Cornette, M.I. (1998), 'Electronic Smoke Signals: Native American Radio in the United States', *Cultural Survival Quarterly*, summer: 28–31.

Smith, James P. and Edmonston, Barry (1997), *The New Americans: Economic, Demographic and Fiscal Effects of Immigration*, Washington: National Academy Press.

Smith, Mark and Kollock, Peter (eds) (1999), *Communities in Cyberspace*, London: Routledge.

Solbakk, J.T. (1997), 'Sámi Mass Media – Their Role in a Minority Society', in H. Gaski (ed.), *Sámi Culture in a New Era*, Karaskjok, Norway: Davvi Girji OS, 172–98.

Soruco, Gonzalo R. (1996), *Cubans and the Mass Media in South Florida*, Gainesville, FL: University Press of Florida.

Sowell, T. (1996), *Migrations and Cultures: A World View*, New York: Basic Books.

Spickard, Paul R. (1996), *Japanese Americans: The Formation and Transformation of an Ethnic Group*, New York, NY: Twayne.

Stardelov, Georg, Grozdanov, Cvetan and Ristovski, Blaze (eds) (1993), *Macedonia and its Relations with Greece*, Skopje: Macedonian Academy of Sciences and Arts.

Statistics Canada (1996), *1996 Census*, Ottawa: Public Works and Government Services.

Stratton, Jon (1997), 'Cyberspace and the Globalization of Culture', in David Porter (ed.), *Internet Culture*, New York: Routledge, 253–75.

Stratton, Jon and Ang, I. (1996), 'On the Impossibility of a Global Cultural Studies: "British" Cultural Studies in an "International" Frame', in D. Morley and K.-H. Chen (eds), *Stuart Hall: Critical Dialogues in Cultural Studies* London: Routledge, 361–91.

Straubhaar, Joseph D. (1991), 'Beyond Media Imperialism: Assymetrical Interdependence and Cultural Proximity', *Critical Studies in Mass Communication*, 8(1): 39–59.

Straubhaar, Joseph D. (1997), 'Distinguishing The Global, Regional and National Levels of World Television', in A. Sreberny-Mohammadi, D. Winseck, J. McKenna and O. Boyd-Barrett (eds), *Media in a Global Context: A Reader*, London: Arnold, 284–98.

Teaiwa, Teresia (2000), 'An Analysis of the Current Political Crisis in Fiji.' Online at www.fijilive.com.

Ter Haar, Gerrie (1995), 'Strangers in the Promised Land: African Christians in Europe', *Exchange*, 24(1): 1–33.

Ter Haar, Gerrie (1998), *Halfway to Paradise: African Christians in Europe*, Cardiff: Cardiff Academic.

Thomas, L. (1992), 'Communicating Across the Arctic', *CAJ Bulletin* (Spring): 14, 20.

Tölöyan, K. (1996), 'Rethinking Diaspora(s): Stateless Power in the Transnational Moment', *Diaspora*, 5(1): 3–86.

Tomás Rivera Institute (2000) 'Research Areas: Latino Projected Population Growth'. Accessed 4 March 2000: www.trpi.org/facts2.html.

Tomlinson, John (1991), *Cultural Imperialism*, Baltimore, MD: Johns Hopkins University.

Tomlinson, John (1997a), 'Cultural Globalization and Cultural Imperialism', in Ali Mohammadi (ed.), *International Communication and Globalization*. London: Sage Publications, 170–90.

Tomlinson, John (1997b), 'Internationalism, Globalization and Cultural Imperialism', in Kenneth Thompson (ed.), *Media and Cultural Regulation*, London: Sage, 117–62.

Toussaint, Florence (1999), 'TLC's (NAFTA's), Impact on the Mexican Audiovisual Industry', paper presented at the II Colloquium on Communication and Cultural Identities in NAFTA and MERCOSUR, Austin, Texas.

Tracey, Michael and Redal, Wendy W. (1995), 'The New Parochialism: The Triumph of the Populist Flow of International Television', *Canadian Journal of Communication*, 20(3): 343–66.

Turkle, Sherry (1995), *Life on the Screen: Identity in the Age of the Internet*, New York: Simon and Schuster.

Turner, Graeme (1994), *Making it National: Nationalism and Australian Popular Culture*, St Leonards: Allen and Unwin.

Valaskakis, G. (1995), 'Sakajawea and Her Sisters', in Marilyn Burgess and Gail G. Valaskakis, *Indian Princesses and Cowgirls: Stereotypes from the Frontier*, Montreal: OBORO.

Van Hear, Nicholas (1998), *New Diasporas: The Mass Exodus, Dispersal and Regrouping of Migrant Communities*, London: UCL.

Varis, Tapio (1984), 'The International Flow of Television Programs', *Journal of Communication*, 34(1): 143–52.

Varis, Tapio and Nordenstreng, Kaarle (1973), *Television Traffic: A One-Way Street?* Paris: UNESCO.

Venturino, Steven (1997), 'Reading Negotiations in the Tibetan Diaspora', in Frank J. Korom (ed.), *Constructing Tibetan Culture: Contemporary Perspectives*, St-Hyacinthe: World Heritage Press: 98–121.

Vertovec, Steven and Peach, Ceri (1997), 'Introduction: Islam in Europe and the Politics of Religion and Community', in Steve Vertovec and Ceri Peach (eds), *Islam in Europe: The Politics of Religion and Community*, Basingstoke: Macmillan, 3–47.

Wang, Zidong (1998), 'To Become Cross-Century Elite, To Make More Contributions to the Revitalization of China', *Cuiyuan*, no. 2. Online at www.shef.ac.uk/uni/inion/susoc/cssa/cuiyuan.html.

Warner, Stephen and Wittner, Judith (eds) (1998), *Gatherings in the Diaspora: Religious Communities and The New Immigration*, Philadelphia, PA: Temple.

Watson, Nessim (1997), 'Why We Argue About Virtual Community: A Case Study of the Phish.Net Fan Community', in Steven G. Jones (ed.), *Virtual Culture: Identity and Communication in Cybersociety*, London: Sage, 102–32.

Wax, Emily (1999), 'The Mufti in the Chat Room', *The Washington Post*, 31 July: 31.

Webster, Frank (1995), *Theories of the Information Society*, New York: Routledge.

Wellman, Barry and Gulia, Milena (1999), 'Virtual Communities as Communities: Net Surfers Don't Ride Alone', in Marc Smith and Peter Kollok (eds), *Communities in Cyberspace*, London: Routledge, 167–94.

Weyland, Petra (1997), 'Gendered Lives in Global Spaces', in A. Öncü and P. Weyland (eds), *Space, Culture and Power: New Identities in Globalizing Cities*, London: Zed, 82–97.

Wildman, Stephen S. and Siwek, Stephen E. (1988), *International Trade in Films and Television Programs*, Cambridge, MA: American Enterprise Institute for Public Policy Research.

Wise, J. Macgregor (2000), 'Home: Territory and Identity', *Cultural Studies*, 14(2): 295–310.

Wong, Bernard (1988), *Patronage, Brokerage, Entrepreneurship and the Chinese Community of New York*, New York: AMS Press.

Yang, Xiaosheng (1998), 'China's Brain Drain', *Beijing Literature*, 2: 4–28.

Young, R.J.C. (1995), *Colonial Desire: Hybridity in Theory, Culture and Race*, London: Routledge.

Zizek, Slavoj (1997), 'Multiculturalism, or the Cultural Logic of Multinational Capitalism', *New Left Review*, 225 (September/October): 28–51.

Zou, Yali and Trueba, Enrique T. (1998), *Ethnic Identity and Power: Cultural Contexts of Political Action in School and Society*, Albany, NY: State University of New York Press.

Index

Lightning Source UK Ltd.
Milton Keynes UK
UKOW052226050313

207192UK00006B/117/A

9 780415 279307